Praise for *Raising the Bottom*

"Boucher's (*Revelation*) latest challenges women to ask themselves if they're drinking too much. Following up this question with her own story of recovery, as well as other women's experiences, the author demonstrates that alcoholism is a disease that doesn't discriminate by income level, education, or gender. Throughout the narratives, Boucher weaves in facts about drug and alcohol abuse as well as the day-to-day or challenges of early sobriety. Contrary to the thinking that women have to lose it all before making changes, she hopes that, by reading her book, women can recognize and deal with their potential alcoholism early on. VERDICT Boucher offers recognition, empathy, and hope for family and friends and all women who have struggled with addiction. Highly recommended."

—***Library Journal Review***

"*Raising the Bottom* is an excellent resource for anyone who suspects they or a loved one has a problem with alcohol. It doesn't just focus on the problem of alcoholism, it emphasizes the solution and demonstrates that alcoholics can live wonderful, productive lives through sobriety. This is a book of hope."

—**Leslie R. Dye, MD**, President, Medical Toxicology Foundation

"As a physician I applaud Boucher for her insightful discussion of addiction and the difficult road to recovery. *Raising the Bottom* brings to the forefront a very necessary and under-discussed subject. Our health-care system is currently ill-equipped to deal with the complicated problem of alcohol and drug dependence. Now more than ever, it is imperative that physicians receive better training on recognizing, understanding and treating addiction. Onl[illegible] we be truly effective at assisting our patients in their recove[illegible]

[illegible]rnal Medicine

"Spoken from the heart. *Raising the Bottom* is a refreshing take on the issues women have as caretakers and enablers. Boucher writes in a straightforward manner that both the long-time worker in our industry and those new to recovery can comprehend. The stories are relevant to the trials that all women share. Entertaining as well as educational!"

—**Stanley Stone**, President, Resources for Recovery

"Extremely helpful to women (and men) who have been in the grip of alcohol and drugs, *Raising the Bottom* will help alcoholics understand why they do what they do, and provide hope and courage for them to take the steps to overcome. I can especially relate to the stories in the book as they are so similar to my own victory over addiction. Boucher outlines the steps and principles that help so many to rise above the hopelessness of addiction and take back control of their lives."

—**Norbert H. Kox**, visionary artist

"*Raising The Bottom* provides a vivid glimpse of a family in crisis, but you're left with a feeling of hope and an understanding that addiction is a disease. One cannot simply have the willpower to overcome addiction; it's a battle that can be won through God's grace."

—**Jill Kingston**, Executive Director, Brigid's Path

"*Raising the Bottom* reveals the truth about alcohol in a bold and personal way. Boucher shares the warning signs to help women before it's too late. It gets to the heart of the problem, but offers hope for recovery and a life after alcohol."

—**Barbara Daniel**, Publisher/Editor, *The Cleveland Women's Journal*

Raising the Bottom

Raising the Bottom

Making Mindful Choices in a Drinking Culture

Lisa Boucher

She Writes Press

Published 2017
Printed in the United States of America
ISBN: 978-1-63152-214-7 pbk
ISBN: 978-1-63152-215-4 ebk
Library of Congress Control Number: 2017932149

For information, address:
She Writes Press
1563 Solano Ave #546
Berkeley, CA 94707

She Writes Press is a division of SparkPoint Studio, LLC.

The names and identifying details of some characters in this book have been changed.

Mom, this one is for you. You were a beacon of light to so many. The lives that you touched, the souls that you helped awaken, and your fervent dedication to helping others comprise a glowing example of a life well lived.

My mother, Janet, 1933–2011

"Sharing our past is the only way we can effectively help others to change their future."

—L. B.

Contents

Introduction

THE WOMEN IN MY FAMILY bled all over each other; when we weren't hemorrhaging fear, we spent our time looking for an out. None of us knew how to feel and deal. Our one thought was escape, and the answer to every triumph or sorrow was: Drink this. Swallow that.

I realized there was no way I could outrun alcoholism. Everywhere I turned, there it was, and that's when I knew I had to write about it. It was getting harder and harder to say nothing after I realized that so many wonderful women and families were affected and no one had the insight or the guts to call it what it is—alcoholism.

Transformative experiences come on the heels of crises. My transformative experience occurred three years after my mother's death. She died with thirty good years of sobriety, and for a chunk of those years she proposed I write about alcoholism. "So many women are in trouble," she'd say. Mom knew better than most about the sneaky way alcoholism grabs a hold, and the many outfits it wears.

Though my mother's imprint is all over this book, it takes time for a message to ripen; it took twenty-five years for me to sort it all out—from my childhood to what it was that I learned, and what I needed to share. During Mom's last months of life I had asked her when she got to heaven to ask God what was with this writing business. I wanted to know why I kept going back to write book after book; I always felt there was a higher purpose, but what was it? Maybe it was just a hobby, or maybe fiction wasn't the genre where I was supposed to land.

Early or potential alcoholism manifests in ways that, unless you understand the disease, no one labels as alcoholism: multiple marriages, anxiety, health problems, weight problems, lives plagued by resentment, and chaotic relationships with family and friends.

I've been immersed in alcoholism since my first breath of life. Like others who were once immersed in the mayhem of the disease and now are recovering, I've become an expert at recognizing alcoholism and all of the subtle signs that leak out long before others notice that someone has a problem.

I have become an expert on a disease that I hate: I hate what it does to women, their families, and especially their children, who have little say-so in the matter. We are conditioned to believe that alcohol is synonymous with fun, yet for so many families, alcohol bites back in the form of dysfunctional or broken homes, domestic violence, health problems, fractured relationships, and devastating mishaps.

From afar, I recognize the disease swirling around families, yet they remain oblivious to the looming heartaches on the horizon, all because they lack knowledge and don't understand the many faces of alcoholism. My hope is that this book will shed new light on an old subject, challenge worn thought patterns, and provide insight. To do so I've included stories from women who in the earlier stages of their drinking, one could most certainly argue, were just fine and didn't have a problem with alcohol. They were too smart. Too rich. Too kind. Too together. Too much fun. Pick one.

Through reading their stories, as well as anecdotes from other women, you'll come to learn the truth of the statement found in the Big Book of *Alcoholics Anonymous* that female drinkers experience condemned futures far sooner than males. No one wants to be the downer at the party, but for a lot of women, alcohol is a problem—yet they go to the party anyway. Talk of saturated lives and jaundice elicits nary a blink.

Women tell me they drink because they have problems, when the truth is that they have problems because they drink. The solution stares us in the face, but we don't like the option, so we move on to something else: antidepressants, therapy, self-help books, yoga, holistic healers—the list goes on . . . *my God, just don't tell me to quit drinking*. The real question that needs to be asked is this: how can you live a joyous, fulfilling life when alcohol—a depressant—gets invited along on every occasion?

For many, it was only when they put the cork in the bottle that they came to understand that the overall feeling of discontentment that they harbored had a direct correlation to their party lifestyles and preoccupation with alcohol. Few want to believe that alcohol can become the proverbial spoiler—the single thing a woman may never dare want to axe from her life; yet if she gets honest, she'll realize that alcohol is the one agent present in all the discord.

Most women can identify something about their life that they'd like to see changed, but few are willing to do the necessary work to institute any real transformation—unless of course the pain grows greater than the problem. *Raising the Bottom* challenges you to open your mind and consider the *maybe*.

I quit drinking in my late twenties, and that decision mostly had to do with my then-sober mother, who pointed out that my drinking started to look shady. I chose to listen to her concerns, and because I listened, I saved myself from years of self-manufactured hell. With one healthy decision, the whole trajectory of my life changed.

For twenty-three years I've been a registered nurse; I have seen and heard it all. I've worked in emergency rooms and psych wards, and both departments are magnets for dysfunctional drinkers and alcoholics. Lives implode all over the place, and much of the time the blame is placed on everything but the drinking or the prescription- or street-drug use. Furthermore, most doctors know nothing about alcoholism or addiction—they can barely spot a real alcoholic, let alone a budding alcoholic. There, I said it. Health care needs a complete overhaul in this area, so yes, we'll talk about that too.

Raising the Bottom is for intelligent, open-minded women who can appreciate a collective three centuries of experience, as opposed to statistical data and theoretical explanations from people with certificates and degrees who spout theory but have no practical or firsthand knowledge or exposure.

I've lived with an active alcoholic in one form or another my entire life—and, well, it takes one to know one. Chaos and crises become a way of life that seems normal. Often women recognize they have a problem, but plenty of them are okay with that knowledge and party on until the bottom falls out.

I've worked with hundreds of women over the years, and the common thread is that most all the women dubbed themselves *social* drinkers, myself included, until we learned that there was nothing social about the way we drank. In addition, most alcoholics are functional and hold jobs—people don't realize that either.

As for the mothers whose stories are in this book, all said their biggest regret was that they were not present for their children, mentally and/or emotionally. They all agreed they got caught up in their selfishness, depression, and self-centeredness, and that they turned inward, failing to recognize that right under their noses their children were in jeopardy. It's crucial we hear what our kids say, so I will give them a voice. I've devoted an entire chapter to what they say about you and your drinking.

Children have little respect for the woman whose focus is the mommy party, and who laughs about her need for wine and Ativan in order to parent—so why does social media support, congratulate, and even glamorize women who whine that they need wine? What are we doing? Does anyone know?

Some women continue to look outside of themselves for the secret to raising good kids, but here's the truth: maladaptive women will likely raise maladaptive children. The secret is *you*.

The women you will meet range from the über bright—a board-certified surgeon who holds a PhD in neurophysiology (she admits she learned nothing and knew nothing about alcoholism despite all her education and medical training)—to a former Washington DC socialite, to a teacher, nurses, a massage therapist turned jewelry maker, and another physician who admits she used to pass out while breastfeeding her fourth child.

Most of the women had no idea their problems were caused by alcohol. None felt they fit the stereotypical mold of what they thought a problem drinker or alcoholic looked like. All of them, like me, were baffled by their behavior, confused by serial marriages, broken by an unexplained emptiness, and devastated by a loneliness and spiritual bankruptcy that only an alcoholic or addict can understand.

Through all the misery, anyone peering at our lives from the outside in might see suburban normalcy, privilege, or even wealth. I purposely sought out women who were like me when they quit drinking—women who looked like they could not have a problem with alcohol. For most of us, it was inner turmoil that precipitated our higher bottoms.

Families often contribute to the problem. It takes courage to stand up to the family members whose only idea of fun includes copious amounts of drinks, even when you insist that you want a better quality of life than cocktails, bars, and getting blotto on the beach.

The biggest testimony that I made a great decision in 1989 to quit drinking is that I'm not the same person I used to be. By God's grace, my twins have only known a sober mother. I have changed in a big way—and all of the positive modifications allowed me to complete my education, hold a job, stay married to the same man for thirty-plus years, and raise my sons, both of whom went on to become Division I athletes, graduate college, and secure jobs. Not bad for what *certainly* would have been a very different outcome had I not quit drinking.

You have nothing to lose and everything to gain. Please join me as we travel on a journey that is all about changing and saving lives. It's all about *Raising the Bottom*.

~ 1 ~

Crazy Is Normal, Right?

HER FOOT NEVER TOUCHED THE BRAKE. Even seconds before the imminent impact, my mother looked serene: one hand draped over the steering wheel, her glazed stare fixed on the road, rubbery lips puffing on a Salem menthol like she had all the time in the world to consider the options. She never flinched—not once—in spite of our howls. The brown Chrysler barreled toward the crowded intersection at forty miles per hour. The outcome was inevitable.

My mother stumbled out of the car mumbling something about low blood sugar. My brother and I tossed about inside, him in the backseat and me up front in the passenger seat. My brain registered shock: the entire front end of the car was gone.

Intoxicated driving was her specialty. Mother swiped endless mailboxes, jumped countless curbs, plowed through walls and closed garage doors, and drove herself and her four children into numerous ditches.

I share this story because I want to give you a picture of what happened to my mother and what it was like for me as her child. It would be impossible to appreciate Mom's miraculous recovery without understanding how deeply she sank and how her disease of alcoholism affected our entire family. Alcoholism may isolate the drinker, but it's impossible to isolate the disease.

My mother's descent into addiction started innocently enough. A physician—perhaps the family doctor—prescribed her Equanil, a mild tranquilizer, to calm her frazzled nerves. She had four kids and a crazy Italian husband who was still locked in childhood himself. My dad's mother died when he was five, and to this day I think he hates women: he never forgave his mother for dying on him. Of course Mom needed help coping.

One winter morning back in the sixties, Mom loaded her four small children into the black-and-white Pontiac for a quick run to the drugstore. On any given day, never mind the sleet, snow, or blizzard conditions that were common in northeastern Ohio, she did what she had to do. My two sisters, six and eight, sat in the backseat and held onto the bungee-like cord stretched across the rear of the front seat. I was four, and I sat unbelted in the front seat holding my brother, who at the time was an infant. Like a toboggan pointed downhill, the Pontiac sped down Chestnut Ridge, slipping and sliding, and without much more fanfare than a loud whoosh, my mother drove us right into a deep ditch. My brother bounced out of my arms and hit the floorboard like a loose gourd. Mother, after the sudden jolt, regained a modicum of composure and crawled out of the car, seemingly unfazed by the biting wind, the poor visibility, or the fact that one side of the car lay snuggled into the ditch.

She puffed on the Salem clamped between pink lips, blue eyes bleary, yet again. In spite of the winter weather, she crawled out of the car dressed in short shorts; her sandals and pink painted toenails spoke volumes about her state of mind. I can still clearly see her scantily clad feet stepping into the mid-calf-high drift of fresh powder. She muttered about what in the hell she was supposed to do now as she exhaled a cloud of white smoke.

Some man driving along stopped to help—it seemed someone always showed up. And so it went, for years, one escapade after another. She drove high on Equanil or Valium and eventually lit up on alcohol and pills. Often, she was too drunk to stand, but that never stopped her from getting behind the wheel.

As a child, if I had to pick one prevalent emotion, it would be fear. I had frequent recurring night terrors. I wet the bed until I was seven. I remember sheer horror the one time I witnessed my father smack my mother in the hall as she cried and packed a suitcase. I stood in my bedroom, frozen in place, watching the spectacle unfold. The idea of her leaving was unthinkable.

When coherent, my mother was beautiful, fun, and just plain wonderful. She didn't have a mean bone in her body, and there was never a doubt that she loved us. Most of my childhood was a blur, except a few sharp memories, or traumas—however you want to couch them. But there were years when Mom controlled her pill use and rarely drank, except for the occasional time at card club or when she and Dad had dinner with friends. We picked berries, shopped, helped Mom can produce from the large garden my father and grandfather tended in the backyard, scoured county fairs, and spent weeks at a cottage on the lake with throngs of friends in tow.

There were good times, especially during the years I had a horse. From the age of five I was nuts about horses. I rode my bike a mile down the road to the dairy farm that also boarded horses, and they had a Shetland pony that I couldn't get enough of. I learned to ride on that Shetland, and my love affair with horses began.

Of course I wanted a horse of my own, and after much pleading and many rosaries later, my parents bought me a palomino quarter horse. I named him Sham. Sham had been abused by men and kicked out to pasture. It was love at first sight: he was beautiful, solid, but much too wild for a twelve-year-old girl. He was terrified of people, and terrified of the saddle I wanted to rest on his back. A snapping branch was all it took for him to haul ass to the other side of the pasture. He had zero trust in anyone. Though he was still young, the horse people had written him off as ruined.

My mother had carted me around to look at and ride at least a dozen other quarter horses, all of them wise choices for a twelve-year-old, but my heart was set on the wild palomino, and of course my mother said yes.

With help, I broke that horse and developed the first solid relationship I ever had. We were a perfect match. We both had trust issues. I understand now why equine therapy is effective: those times when I could escape the madness, the emptiness, the dark gloom that saturated our home, turned out to be pure bliss. I spent most days, all day, in the barn. I'd saddle up and ride wherever I wanted. I loved that horse fiercely, and I loved the freedom of being on his back. It helped that I had an idyllic setting in which to ride: miles of trails, meadows, and orchards. Looking back, I think if I didn't have that wholesome reprieve, I may have fallen harder, faster, and deeper into my own addiction at a much younger age.

My father, good-looking in an Elvis Presley sort of way, had his own demons. He knew nothing about soothing reassurance or how to broker peace—both concepts were foreign ideas to him. He incited fear and dread when he walked in the door, barking orders or hollering about something we did or didn't do from the moment his foot hit the threshold. His presence alone was an accelerant, the turpentine that set our fragile nerves on fire. We all loved it when he traveled out of town on business.

When I was young, pretty much everyone in my family was out of control in his or her own way; we used whatever coping skills we could cleave on to in order to deal with the violence and predictable unpredictability. My oldest sister babysat a lot for the neighbors; my middle sister, full of her own rage, spent a lot of time elsewhere. It's hard to find your gift or live up to your potential when, in order to survive, you're always looking to escape. We later learned she started down the path of her addiction at eleven years old.

My little brother was a terror. He ran around the house with a pair of scissors and whacked the hair off of our dolls, chopped up our party dresses to make rags to grease his bicycle, and pretty much destroyed whatever property was in his way. He and his friends built dangerously high ramps in the driveway, then hurled themselves and their bicycles right off of the edge of them, just like we were all doing in real life.

I'm sure in today's world his behavior would warrant a diagnosis of ADD or ADHD—something of that nature—but I tend to think his unsettled countenance was nothing more than the result of poor parenting. Regardless, my parents were oblivious to his pain, to my pain, to my sisters' pain. I remember when, at five years old, my brother swiped his chubby arms across end tables and coffee tables, sending crystal lamps and the beautiful gold mermaid planter that my mother kept on the coffee table crashing to the floor. Looking back, I think my brother just wanted attention. I think we all wanted some attention, or perhaps calm order. I remember my older sister called my mother's parents, who lived about a mile down the road, to tell them we needed some help up here.

I started drinking beer and smoking an occasional joint at twelve years old. Not often, just here and there on the weekends. Innocent enough, right? I had two older sisters who were experimenting, and that's what kids do, or so I thought.

My father stayed angry and desperate to dictate and control everything, including my mother's drinking, which was a losing proposition. He marked the liquor bottles or filled them with water—as if those attempts could in any way deter an alcoholic. My father was a social drinker. He had one small cabinet in our house where he kept maybe three or four bottles of liquor. He cleared out the bottles to keep her from drinking—another lame gesture, like plugging a sinkhole in the highway with Play-Doh. Alcoholics will not, and cannot, be deterred. It's not that they want to keep drinking and screwing up their lives and the lives of everyone else around them—it's just that it gets to a point, like it did with my mother, that they have no other choice but to drink.

Bewilderment and confusion is how I would categorize my mother's early addiction. She could function, but she was never fully present, as if she'd encased herself in a cocoon, or as though she'd erected a screen between herself and reality and then sifted through and allowed only the particles that she could handle to seep in.

By the time we were teenagers, my mother's judgment was so skewed that, had other mothers been aware of her incompetence, they perhaps would have kept their kids from visiting our home—although back in the sixties and seventies, parents didn't micromanage their children like they do nowadays.

When my father traveled on business, we all exhaled and ran amok. Between my mother, one of my sisters, and me, the car wrecks continued. My father arranged for rentals, and we wrecked those vehicles too. Our house was full of teenagers, all camped out around the kitchen table, smoking and laughing or crying our asses off, depending on whatever happened to be going on with any specific friend or sister at that particular time.

Looking back, the progressive nature of my mother's alcoholism was already evident, but no one knew what early alcoholism looked like. No one, including the medical professionals, understood or recognized that irrational thinking and the inability to see problems that were mushrooming right in front of you were a big part of the disease. For instance, we went from Queenie Mae, a kind and loving woman whom Mom hired to do the ironing, to wacky Irene.

Queenie Mae doted on us kids. She was reliable, honest, and a darn-near perfect person. She wore her hair arranged in such a manner on top of her head that it looked like a bird's nest. We'd put trinkets—like wrapped peppermints, jacks, broken crayons, and miniature baby dolls—in the nest, and then, standing next to the ironing board, she'd lean over so we could examine all the surprises hiding in her hair.

She even put up with my Sicilian grandpa, who lived with us until I was sixteen, when he died. We all loved grandpa and his old-world charm. He'd do things like, well . . . lie. He'd tell Queenie Mae that we were locked out of the house, but what he wanted was for her to sit at the picnic table under the maple tree in the backyard and help peel apples. Grandpa liked my mom's homemade applesauce, and as long as the apples were peeled, Mom would make it for him. If Grandpa wasn't peeling apples or shelling peas, he could be found under the tree reading a Western. When my mother worked, he was the resident chauffeur for us kids. At night he'd dart off to some club to play poker with his friends. He was the bright spot in all of our lives.

As for Queenie Mae, I don't know whatever happened to her or why she quit coming around, but I could guess. Queenie Mae was gone, and here came Irene, a scraggly Russian woman who had the same proclivity for vodka as my mother. Mom supposedly hired Irene to help clean the house, but what she really hired was a self-proclaimed psychic who fancied gathering around the kitchen table to read tea leaves and have a cocktail, rather than doing any actual work.

Every week, Mom fetched Irene at the bus stop and brought her to our home. She might do a little cleaning, or at least hold a dust rag and a spray can of Pledge, but not too long after settling in, she'd beeline over to my dad's meager stash of booze, nip on that, and take a break to chat with Mom, who was already in the kitchen brewing Turkish tea so Irene could read the leaves. Without fail, the kitchen would end up a mess and we'd find Irene passed out on the sofa. We kids would huddle together, whispering about what to do while Mom stood there wringing her hands—I guess hoping Irene would come to so she could take her to the bus stop before our father came home.

This was a perfect display of the insanity in an alcoholic's mind. My mother knew Irene would drink, pass out, and not do any work, but every week, Mom fetched her at the bus stop and brought her home to clean the house. How crazy was that?

People in the throes of their disease lack the ability or insight to see the insanity of their thinking. They continue on, act abnormally, and when called out on their behavior, they twist it back on you, or, as some say, "flip the tortilla." That's one of the most heartbreaking riddles of alcoholism. Alcoholics do not see what they don't want to see. They'll dig down into that trench of denial, furnish the space, and hang curtains. They'll convince themselves that their thinking and their ways, regardless how fucked-up they may be, are logical and without reason for reproach. They will manipulate. (*I need Irene to help me.* Translation: *I want someone to drink with.*) They will accuse others of doing and saying things they never said, just to get the focus off of their drinking. (Translation: *you guys don't like Irene because you can't understand her Russian accent.*) Alcoholics will lie, and you'd better believe they will lie without so much as flinching a muscle or twitching an eye.

My parents fought constantly. My mother never said no to us kids about anything. My father never wanted to say yes. It was important to Mom that we had fun; it was important to Dad that we worked. Looking back, I think Mom always said yes because it was her way to assuage any guilt for not being the mother I know she wanted to be. Physically, she was present, but mentally and emotionally, she was absent—and clueless.

Mom worked in hospitals as a nurse, and she could brilliantly diagnose better than most of the doctors, with only a fraction of the information. For years, she worked for an equally brilliant and gregarious orthopedic surgeon. As her drinking and Valium use increased, I believe she was fired from her job.

Over a period of a few short years, she got to where she was almost unemployable. She could barely function. Her thinking was nowhere near normal—which was evident the day she toted home from work one of the residents from a nursing home.

My mother walked through the door with a big black woman (remember this is back in the '60s) in tow—think of a person the size of Tyler Perry's "Madea"—and the second they arrived, it was clear that something was amiss. The woman had bulging eyes and a clumsy gait, and she invaded our personal space. She'd latch on to an arm, then go about patting or touching whatever body part was within reach. She also appeared to have the mental capacity of an eight-year-old.

The boom fell well after midnight, when the lady fled the bed my mother had made for her on the living room couch and tried to crawl in bed with my parents. My father was apoplectic. His voice thundered throughout the house, rousing us all out of our slumber. Every light in the house blazed. My dad stood there in his underwear, his face purple with rage. He demanded that my mother haul the crazy-ass woman the hell out of his house, right now! Dad's tirade scared the senseless woman. She screamed and ran around the house like a toddler with a sugar buzz. The four of us kids and my grandpa crowded around our respective bedroom doors, all practically in shock. My mother, as usual, stood there wringing her hands and looking bewildered, like she might want to understand, but like she couldn't quite figure out what all the ruckus was about this time, either.

And so it went.

While writing this book, I called my dear friend Kim. I've known Kim since middle school. She used to spend a lot of time at our house, especially around the holidays. Back in the day, Kim loved all the Christmas decorations, especially the tree. I remember her wishing that her mom would forgo the traditional menorah in favor of a decorated Hanukah bush.

I wanted Kim's perspective, to see if she could recollect a bit more than I could, or fill in any blanks. Her memory was as fuzzy as mine, but she did remember my mother's frequent exploits with the car. She also remembered Mom mixing grasshoppers and some pink alcohol concoction at Christmas, and, of course, she remembered the Ramada Inn.

Mom was too busy to have a lot of friends, so when she wanted to go out for a martini, she enlisted me, one of my sisters, or whoever happened to be available to accompany her to the smoky lounge. Kim remembered tagging along on more than one occasion.

Years later, my mother and I would laugh about her horrible judgment. Eventually, she got to where she could joke about some of her behavior, but I could always tell by the way she fidgeted and lowered her gaze that she felt uncomfortable reminiscing about the past. She would later confide that her shame regarding her choices and shoddy judgment ran deep.

At fifteen, I stole my older sister's driver's license. Then, allegedly, I was eighteen. I had unlimited access to Tony's Bar, a seedy dive that attracted college students and underage drinkers, armed with fake IDs, like myself. This was back in the time of 3.2 beer. I drank freely at that bar. I began to practice and solidify my modus operandi: fake names, fake IDs, and being anybody but who I was, because I had no clue who I was.

There were nights I didn't go home, and one time, on a whim, I left the country. I had four close friends, two of them sisters, and we decided it was time for a road trip to Mattawa, Ontario. The sisters had family and boyfriends up north that they wanted the rest of us to meet. We enlisted the help of a few car-savvy guy friends to give us a hand. They disconnected the odometer. Mattawa was a good five hundred miles away. How could we have explained logging a thousand miles on my friend's mom's car in only a few days? It was in Mattawa that I discovered spicy Bloody Marys, the fine art of playing pool, and the word *eh*: "You want a drink, eh?"

I was gone a couple of days, and the only thing my dad thought to say when I got home that Sunday morning was, "You look like a whore." He couldn't have been more wrong. I guess he didn't know that I was never boy-crazy and relationships were not my thing anyway. When he called me a whore, something inside of me shifted, shut down, and hardened up. I was a crumpled mess—not from drinking, but because I'd been asleep for the last five hours in the backseat of my friend's car.

My mother had no comment about my two-day absence. I explained that I wasn't MIA, that I had, in fact, called and told her that

I'd be staying at a friend's house for a few days. It wasn't my problem that she couldn't remember shit. Got that? Not my fault.

Aha. I saw how this lying-and-manipulating thing worked. Mom nodded and agreed: "Yes, of course, Lisa called me. She stayed with her friend last night, and the night before . . ." Of course Mom had no clue where I was, and of course she wasn't going to admit that she didn't know, because then the focus would ricochet right back on her and her drinking. What could Dad say? He was out doing his thing too, so he sure didn't have a clue. The dysfunction wasn't all with my mother.

I was a good student, but by the time my senior year rolled around, things at home continued to unravel. I still smoked a little pot, and I added snoozing in class to my repertoire. Here again, nothing about my behavior—my alcohol use or my pot smoking—concerned me in the least. I convinced myself I was nothing like my mother. I wasn't doing anything that half, if not all, of the other teenagers weren't doing as well. Rationalize. Rationalize. Rationalize.

My sisters were away at college. My father mentioned once or twice that I should go to college too, but I wasn't feeling that option. I wasn't feeling much of anything those days. I was numb, fearful, lost, confused. Most of my close friends had graduated high school and moved on. My whole senior year, I was miserable.

Mom's outrageous behavior usurped all the attention. My brother and I flew under the radar, doing the best we could to live our lives. All I could think about was graduating high school so I could break free of the chaos.

Regularly, I came home drunk and slept with one foot on the floor to stop the spinning. When I had to puke, which I did a lot, I stripped the pillowcase from my pillow, vomited in it, and then stashed the whole soggy mess under my bed. When I woke the next morning, I hiked to the rear of our acre lot and threw the stinking pillowcase over the barbed-wire fence into the woods that lined the perimeter of our backyard. My mother never questioned all the disappearing linen.

Mom and I lived in parallel universes. I didn't recognize that I drank more than I used to, and she surely wasn't cognizant of my behavior. I argued frequently with my dad and started mouthing back. I was sick to death of his verbal abuse, and my mouthing off just enraged him more. He smacked me around, and I still didn't shut up.

Then one day, I figured out what I wanted to do with my life! The vision was so clear. I planned to become a famous makeup artist. Of course, the *famous* part was a good indication I was already leaning toward grandiose thinking, but my mother didn't think so. In fact, she applauded this idea and said, "Marvelous! Yes, go for it."

She loved beauty of any kind. She was the kind of woman who in her later years wasn't shy about getting a few nips and tucks. She wore brown curls till the day she died, and she instructed my sisters and me to not even think about letting our hair go gray. She hated Florida in the winter for that very reason: she used to say, "All you see is gray and white, gray and white. Bunch of old people. No, thank you."

With minimal research, I learned that in order to be a makeup artist, first I needed a cosmetology license. So during my senior year of high school I enrolled in beauty school. It was a nine-month program; easy enough, right? Well, I had a problem with showing up. On the way to beauty school, I passed by the house where two of my best friends lived. My plan was to drop by to say hello, then be on my way. More often than not, I never made it to school. Nine months passed and the administrator informed me that I needed to reenroll and pay for a second year. I was nowhere close to having the fifteen hundred hours needed to sit for my managing cosmetology license.

At this point, my mother's drinking was beyond out of control. My brother and I never knew what to expect. We toggled between worrying about her, feeling it was our responsibility to keep her safe (mostly from herself), and wanting to run as far away from home as possible. The whole environment was just too crazy and depressing. And what was really strange was that, as drunk as Mom got every day, none of us witnessed her drinking. We found empty bottles stashed in the laundry bin, in cupboards, and under the seats in her car; several times, we found baggies full of white pills buried down in the dirt of the various potted plants scattered about the house, but we never witnessed her drinking the booze or taking the pills.

Dad was in full-blown crazy mode. He couldn't control her addiction. But like a possessed maniac, he tried anyway. One day, stalker-style, he followed her. They ended up—where else?—at a drug store. He later told me that from the shampoo aisle he had a clear view of the pharmacist. He watched the pharmacist hand my mother a small brown lunch bag that looked lumpy and full.

I remember my father regaling us with the tale: "After I saw that asshole hand over that bag, I told the son of a bitch I was going to mop the goddamn floor with his head if he gave her one more pill! The pharmacist threatened to call the police. I told him, 'Go ahead, call. While you're on the phone, tell them about the bag of pills you just gave my wife. Go ahead—call them. I don't give a rat's ass if you lose your license.'"

That pharmacist, a.k.a. educated drug dealer, had kept my mother illegally stocked with whatever poison she was taking at the time. Those lunch bags filled with white pills, called either *714s* or *Quaaludes*, were no doubt responsible for making her loopier than she already was most days. After my father's brazen appearance at the drug store, the pharmacist must have had a change of heart. Perhaps he decided not to peddle any more drugs to *that* nurse with the crazy Italian husband. We never found another Quaalude buried in a houseplant; instead, Mom's drinking picked up.

Addicts and alcoholics do this sort of thing all the time—that is, switch addictions. When one addiction gets too out of control or the supply runs out, they just make the shift to something else. People do it with food, sugar, sex, gambling—anything that is addicting. If you take away a substance or an activity that an addict is attached to, chances are the addict personality will find a substitute. Any vice will do, and the disease marches on.

My father's desperate attempts to control my mother's addiction were futile. Just because he eliminated one problem—the Quaaludes—didn't mean he found a solution, a cure, or the cause of my mother's addiction.

I drove my little brother around as much as possible. My mother's drinking was at the critical stage where she could barely even get herself together to get into the car. My father's solution, when at fourteen my brother complained to him about Mom's drunk driving, was to instruct: "If she comes to get you and she's drunk, tell her to move over." My brother drove frequently when he was only fourteen.

Most days when I came home from school in my senior year, Mom was passed out either in the garden, in the kitchen, or on the dining room floor. Almost always, she was in various stages of undress, and she'd stagger around the kitchen, slurring her words to where you couldn't understand her.

My father was who knows where—out of town working, or perhaps trying to escape, too. I remember feeling so callous that, when it got to the point that I'd find Mom passed out on the floor yet again, I'd step over her, call 911, and go off to cosmetology school or my waitress job. Perhaps having to detach or dissociate from the constant drama and chaos reinforced my ability and my need to compartmentalize my feelings. I can't say that I ever felt much of anything. The first time I found her like that, yes, fear welled up inside of me. My heart pounded, I couldn't breathe, and the whole anxiety package showed up. As the pattern continued over and over, though, I learned that she'd go to the hospital for a few days, or maybe she'd be gone a week or two, but eventually she'd come home . . . until the next time.

With all the passing out she did, it was a miracle she didn't burn down the house. By this time, my mother was guzzling a fifth of vodka a day. Her goal: oblivion.

One afternoon, my brother and I realized the house was filling with smoke while my mother snoozed on the dining room floor. I tried to wake her to get her out, but she was dead weight. My brother and I couldn't lift her. In the kitchen, like a chugging smokestack, the oven billowed out black, acrid smoke. When we realized where the smoke was coming from, we figured we could handle things. Mom was in the prone position, and she murmured something about cooking dinner. The dinner part turned out to be true: we opened the oven, and, bless her heart, she'd plopped an entire package of frozen chicken right onto the rack—she didn't even bother with a pan—and the yellow Styrofoam tray and clear plastic wrap was responsible for the acrid black smoke.

I don't remember my drinking getting worse or better around this time. I tried to survive the black hole of having a mom but not having a mom. I know my mother had to be in her own hell. She'd gotten to the point where I don't think she even tried to control her drinking anymore. She was dying: physically, mentally, and spiritually.

Physically: Well, her skin was yellow and she looked eight months pregnant. She was sloppy, out-of-her-mind drunk every day. Mentally: she couldn't make good decisions or function as an adult. Spiritually: I could only guess. No one can ever know the inner workings of someone else's mind. Yet with all the obvious outward signs, I can say with certainty that she was in a dark place.

This picture I've painted of my mother is just one of the many faces of alcoholism. Everyone has a different bottom: The disease exists on a bell curve of sorts. What is rock bottom for one may be the starting point where another alcoholic is just revving up. My mother hit one of the lowest bottoms I have ever seen, and I have worked with and seen a lot of alcoholics in various stages of their disease. To this day, she represents the *ne plus ultra* of alcoholism.

Countless times, we asked about her drinking: "Mom, are you drunk again? You can't even stand. What's the matter with you?" Of course she denied drinking. Never mind that she smelled like she'd spritzed herself with vodka and her eyes were perpetually glazed. Where's the glass?

Mom enlisted the help of my brother and me to dispose of her growing stack of empty bottles. She instructed us to clear them out of her car, the laundry baskets, the bathroom closet, and wherever else we could round them up. She had us take the arsenal of empties to one of the many fields or wooded lots surrounding our house so we could properly dispose of them. Can you say *codependents in the making*?

She saw one psychiatrist after another. She visited one counselor after another. No one diagnosed her as an alcoholic. Instead, they said things like she was having a nervous breakdown, or she was depressed, or maybe she was a manic-depressive.

Bullshit. We were the ones having a nervous breakdown. She was in her own world, sleeping or passed out almost all of the time. She spent multiple stints in the psych ward, and she came out pretty much the same as when she went in—flat affect, dead eyes, bewildered and confused. I remember visiting her in the hospital: the doctors had her so medicated on Thorazine or Lithium and God only knew what else that she sat there and stared, an empty shell of her former self, helpless and hopeless.

Alcoholics always think they're in control. The other lie they tell themselves is that no one knows about their drinking. Maybe for a while that's true, but as the disease progresses, everyone knows the alcoholic is a lush—everyone, that is, except for the alcoholic. It's a disease of denial. The sickest alcoholic will hold on to the belief that he or she is fine. Later, I would chuckle at the twelve-step definition of *FINE*: Fucked-up, Insecure, Neurotic, and Emotional.

Alcoholism/drug addiction is also the only disease I know of that is self-diagnosed. You have to believe you are an alcoholic/addict, or at least be willing to consider that option, for any treatment center, twelve-step support group, vitamin therapy, cleanse, Naltrexone, church, or finding God—whatever solution du jour is out there—to work, to cure the malady.

As mentioned, alcoholism is also a threefold disease. It affects a person physically, mentally, and spiritually. In order to recover, all three aspects need to be treated. To make the disease even more difficult to treat, most alcoholics are noncompliant. They refuse to stay away from alcohol, or if they agree to forego alcohol, they will start smoking pot. (Those of us in recovery call that the "marijuana maintenance program.") Others can't be treated because of their deep denial, evidenced by the millions of people who try and fail to stay sober, the millions who need to get sober but won't even consider that option, the repeat offenders who pretend they want sobriety when they really want to get people or the judge off of their backs, and others who have any number of ulterior motives. There are those, too, who use treatment centers, hospital emergency rooms, and psych wards like their own personal bed-and-breakfast or respite stop.

Despite the madness swirling about, I attempted to grasp a bit of normalcy, and going on a date seemed like a fair idea, even though I wasn't a fan of dating. One night, though, I thought I'd give it a try. I was seventeen; he was nineteen. There was something about the two-year age difference that set my dad on fire. He forbade me to go out with this person, yet ironically, the young man had far more sense than all of my family members put together. I was looking forward to the date because any escape from the drama at home was a solid option. Mom was all for it because she thought I seemed depressed. She told me I'd been moping.

Dad flipped out. He blamed his over-the-top reaction on the two-year age difference, but I wasn't buying that reason. I think my father was so inflamed by my mother's alcoholism that he pounced on the one thing he thought he could still control, and that was me. Like a poltergeist, he physically attacked me in the kitchen. I argued and fought back, which enraged him even more. At one point he had me pressed against the kitchen counter with his hands around my neck. He kept squeezing. I couldn't breathe, and I kept thinking, *Maybe the last thing I'll see will be his red face with those map-like veins bulging at his temples.*

I do believe my father was enraged over his powerlessness over his wife's disease. He couldn't fix my mother, he couldn't build relationships with his children, and he couldn't control anything, including himself.

This was the first time in years that I'd seen my mother rally. She pounded her fists on his back and screamed for him to stop. It must've been her voice that snapped him back to reality and out of a blind rage. Had Mom stayed silent, I believe we all would have made for a tragic blurb in the next morning's newspaper.

The good news was that my mother's instinctual reaction proved that the woman I knew and loved was still alive somewhere in that body, even if her essence was drowning in all that booze. I needed to leave because I couldn't deal with my father anymore, and I couldn't stand to watch my mom commit slow suicide.

Two days after high school graduation, I packed up and moved to Columbus. I found another cosmetology school and an apartment where I acquired two roommates—a new life had begun.

I liked my roommates well enough, and this time, I actually showed up at beauty school. We saved our partying for the weekends, along with the thousands of other students who lived on or near The Ohio State University (OSU) campus. I was eighteen years old, and I never considered there was anything abnormal about my current lifestyle. So I had a few drinks on the weekends. Big deal.

Over the years, I've heard other recovering alcoholics talk about how they drank alcoholically from the get-go. For most of us, that was not, and is not, the case. For the vast majority of alcoholics, alcoholism tiptoes up on us. It starts with weekend drinking, and then maybe along the way, over a period of years, beers or drinks on Thursdays creep into the picture. Then maybe Thursday *and* Friday nights enter. Maybe we go on vacation and feel that daily drinking is perfectly fine: after all, we tell ourselves, we work hard and deserve to relax. This sort of thinking can be an early warning sign. Why is alcohol the only way you know to reward yourself? Why is drinking the only way you know to relax? Have you whittled your life down to one narrow hallway where the only fun things you can think to do revolve around alcohol?

Of course, we like that warmth, the mellow glow, that soothing release of tense emotions that melt away after the first sips of wine, beer, or a cocktail. Suddenly, all feels right with the world. But as we've seen, for the alcoholic, or even the potential alcoholic or problem drinker, one innocent drink can lead to a lifetime of misery.

The book *Alcoholics Anonymous*, first written back in 1939, issued a dire warning that, in my mother's case, turned out to be all too true: "Potential female alcoholics often turn into the real thing and are gone beyond recall in a few years."[1] Why is this warning not shouted from rooftops and through bullhorns? The topic of women and alcohol is just now starting to be dissected and discussed more openly.

Sure, Mom's pill addiction started years before her alcoholism, but she didn't drink alcoholically her whole life. Yes, she drank socially, as most people like to believe they do, but her most destructive drinking happened during a short span of five years.

Columbus was a blast. One of my roommates liked to drink like me. We jibbed and jabbed our way up and down High Street. In various campus bars, we'd instigate fights that turned into brawls. We fell down the steps at Kitty's Bar, listened to McGuffey Lane—the American country rock band that started its journey in Columbus—and partied our asses off, all in the name of fun. And yes, it was fun. Never mind that we dwelled in a roach-infested apartment on Lane Avenue; the location was superb! We lived across the street from the stadium and right next door to the Varsity Club, a campus bar. Talk about convenient.

My roommate and I branched out to classier places, like restaurant lounges that had a Ramada Inn–type feel. I wore wide-brimmed hats, carried a rhinestone cigarette holder, and doled out fake names like a blackjack dealer deals cards. I liked the name Brook, but I used Alexis a lot too. I love that name. At these upscale lounges, if you'd ask to buy me a drink, I'd tell you to order me a Glenlivet Scotch, Drambuie, or Jim Beam and water. If the drink was on my dime, Coors Light would do, thank you very much.

I rubbed elbows with outliers, people like Evel Knievel, who back in the 1970s was considered the American daredevil, and Eddie Arcaro, the Hall of Fame jockey, who landed perched on my lap inside a crowded limo, hunched over in a ball much like he'd be when on top of a Thoroughbred. I had no idea why so many people were piled into that limo, or where we went. What I can assume, though, is that most all of the people in the limo probably didn't know I was only eighteen and well on my way to becoming a professional bullshit artist.

I finished beauty school, took and passed the test for my managing cosmetologist license, and immediately realized I had made a colossal mistake. I wasn't at all interested in hair—not your hair, not my hair—and I sucked at styling. As for the makeup-artist plan: ridiculous! I liked makeup okay, but not enough to paint faces all day. A life of dipping brushes and cotton swabs into blush and eye shadow pots . . . this was not for me. Seriously, what was I thinking?

I needed to go to college, a real college. So instead of walking across the street to enroll at The Ohio State University, I drove downtown and enrolled in the community college. I can't say why I chose that option, other than, I suppose, that the community-college route looked like the easier, softer way. I could easily have enrolled at OSU. Keep in mind: this was back in the day when if you had a pulse, you were admitted. Plus, I was familiar with the OSU campus, my friend Kim lived in one of the dorms, and, lest we forget, I already lived on campus. It made no sense, but nothing I did back then made sense.

At the community college, I took all sorts of math—binary math, algebra, more algebra—and told myself I needed to learn how to do something with computers. It was the wave of the future, you know? But was my dyslexia getting worse or what? *Was that number forty-two or twenty-four? Oh, hell, forget these numbers!*

It didn't take long for me to realize I hated working with figures. The numbers had a life of their own—they transposed themselves all the time and all over the place, or maybe I was just lazy and didn't want to work that hard. Homework interfered with my social life, so perhaps, I thought, I needed to take a quarter off and think about my options, maybe switch my major and take business classes. Yes, I looked handsome in suits and scarves. I would be a businesswoman.

I pursued this new businesswoman plan for just a while, and then I called my mother. I relayed to her how hard I was working and asked her what she thought about me taking a vacation. Through slurred speech, Mom, as usual, agreed. "Yes, my God—go, have fun!"

I failed to mention to her that I'd already arranged financing and had booked the cruise. The student loan I secured—not for classes, but for my hiatus—was small. I rationalized this foolhardy plan by telling myself I'd pay back the loan in no time. I wanted to go to Mexico, and I'd heard the snorkeling in Grand Cayman was awesome.

An early manifestation of my alcoholism was rationalizing poor decisions. My mind was like a ticker tape: fast-moving messages reeled on through, and every once in a while I'd pluck one of those messages off the imagined scroll and run with it, like the idea to take a cruise. I had no clue where that idea originated, or why I thought to cruise at nineteen years old, all by myself.

I got back from my adventure, and my fun-loving roommate splashed me with a dose of reality: she informed me she was moving out to get married. I was stunned. We were too young for marriage. *Now what do I do?* I sure as hell didn't want to move back home. I didn't make enough money to support myself without a roommate. I needed to figure something out before she skated off to wedded bliss.

Not long after she dropped the marriage bomb, it came to my attention that someone had rented the space above our apartment. I heard muffled voices, and the phone upstairs never stopped ringing. I learned, through peeking in the windows, that the new tenants had turned the ratty upstairs apartment into a makeshift office. One day, I walked out to my car and found it blocked in by a big blue Cadillac. I climbed the rickety stairs, and, through the open screen door, I commanded the tall blonde guy to move his goddamn car. Two months later we were married.

I was nineteen, and the blonde guy, Gary, was twenty-nine. He was witty, charming, and about as unstable as they came. I liked him. Shortly after we met, he inundated me with red roses and trips to Atlantic City. On our way to Atlantic City one particular night, he told me we needed to swing by his friend's house to get money. Gary explained that he didn't trust banks. Hmmm. Well, wasn't that interesting? Of course something about that statement bothered me, but I brushed off any discomfort.

I wondered where he lived because I never saw his apartment. Later, I realized he didn't have one! Couch hopping and blankets in the backseat of his car kept him warm and dry. The topic of living together cropped up because I did need a roommate, but my father, two hundred miles away, still wielded influence. He blew a gasket and told me that living with Gary wasn't an option for a Catholic girl like me. But there was always Plan B: Fine. We'll get married.

Gary and I attended Catholic premarital classes. The results of the compatibility tests and whatnot were disastrous. Actually, we were so incompatible that everyone at the church vigorously shook their heads and frowned. They advised us to wait a while, get to know each other—what's the big hurry?

Gary lied and told the priest he'd never been married. I didn't know it then, but I later learned that I was wife number three. I had a tough decision: Move home? Shyster? Move home? Shyster? I chose the shyster.

As my dad walked me down the aisle, he whispered, "I'll call this off right now." I kept walking. We had the ceremony, and a week later the officiating priest died. An auspicious sign, indeed.

After the I do's, I learned Gary had a nine-year-old son. Now I knew for certain he was a worthless daddy, too. My father ran a Dun & Bradstreet on Gary's so-called company and mailed me the proof that he was a big fat liar.

I was waiting tables and going to school. Gary was doing God knows what. Either he'd come home with wads of cash or he stayed broke. He drank more than my mother—was that even possible? He liked to cook and had a great sense of humor, but he had a disappearing problem. For days at a time, he'd go missing. Then he'd come back and accuse me of cheating. He'd get all possessive and jealous if a stranger glanced my way. Bookies called the house, constantly. He carried around a small amber vial filled with cocaine, complete with a tiny glass spoon. He became proficient at the Pac-Man game and darts at the local watering hole.

I dealt with him by saying fuck you and took flying lessons—the lessons no doubt indicative of my subconscious desire to fly away for real. I got to where I could land the Cessna—well, sort of land, and then I ran out of money and moved on to something else.

In between the fighting and dysfunction, Gary and I drank—and he shared his cocaine. We did lots of both, together.

We lived in an apartment only marginally better than the roach-infested pad on Lane Avenue. One afternoon, I looked out the kitchen window; we had a splendid view of the street and the parking lot. Imagine my astonishment when a tow truck pulled up and attached the blue Cadillac—and away it went.

Now, I know my upbringing was screwed-up in a lot of ways, but this total lack of financial resources and instability was a whole other kind of race. I asked Gary about the car, and he blamed someone else. He became verbally aggressive after he'd been drinking. One night he came home in a blackout and was violent. I'd had to run out of the apartment a few times before, but on this occasion, I was terrified. He threw a portable TV at my head, missing by millimeters.

I snapped. I mustered every bit of strength, all one hundred and twenty-five pounds, and rammed his sorry ass into a cupboard in the hall. One of the knobs punctured his head at the base of his skull. When he reached back to inspect the spot, blood trickled down his hand. I believe the sight of blood jarred him out of his blackout. He stood there inspecting the blood on his hand, then slunk off to bed. I think we were both lucky that I didn't have a baseball bat.

I barricaded myself in the spare bedroom and called my sister. She, in turn, unbeknownst to me, called my dad. My sister relayed to me that she called Dad to inform him that my loser husband was beating on me. My father, always ready for confrontation, left his house at 3:00 a.m., and at 6:00 a.m. he arrived at my door in Columbus, with my mother in tow.

My father stormed into the bedroom, grabbed Gary by the ankles, and dragged him out of bed. Gary begged to be allowed to shower first. My father relented, so the three of us waited, huddled around the kitchen table. My mom looked haggard and bemused. True to form, she doled out Valium like Pez candy while she smoked and sighed.

The Valium kicked in. I felt much calmer. I didn't realize that a significant thirty minutes or more had passed. The shower kept running. Dad finally asked me to go see what the hell was going on in the bathroom, so I nudged the door and peeked in, and that's when I saw the opened window—the shower curtain fluttering in the breeze.

My father went berserk. He insisted on a manhunt. I didn't have the energy to participate, but he was hell-bent on scouring the city: by God, we would find that son of a bitch! Dad had no clue that locating Gary was akin to discovering the one student at OSU who, come game day, would not root for the Buckeyes. Nonsense! It wasn't going to happen. We visited about a dozen bars. Mom nodded off in the passenger seat, and, frankly, I was mentally and emotionally beaten. I couldn't care less if I ever saw Gary again.

My first foray into recovery rooms happened during that brief marriage. A respectable gentleman, the kind of guy with clean clothes, a job, his own teeth, and a real bank account, tried to twelve-step Gary. I went with them to the meeting, but I couldn't relate at all. The speaker talked about injecting drugs into his eyes because he'd blown out all his other veins. Those people were seriously messed up and sick.

At the time, no one in my extended Catholic family had ever been divorced, but when I told my mom I was done with the marriage, she said, "I think that's a good idea." Even then, before I learned what playing the tape forward meant, I couldn't envision a future with Gary. He was a disaster, and I was sick to death of alcoholics. Do you hear me? No more alcoholics. I was twenty-one years old. Already, I was done with alcoholics' chaos and their never-ending drama.

Crazy is normal, right? At least in my world, it was the norm. We repeat the same patterns over and over unless we change. For things to change, I had to change, but I didn't know that then. I didn't realize that if I wasn't the problem, there was no solution.

After the bathroom escape, I never saw Gary again. I divorced that whack-a-doodle through a little-known process called Notification by Publication. At least, it was little-known to me at the time. (I was so naive that I thought I could get an annulment without first getting divorced. I thought the annulment *was* the divorce). With this process, the courts publish, in some obscure newspaper that no one reads, intentions for divorce. If there is no response within ninety days, then all one has to do is stand before a judge with a witness to collaborate the given statement, and that's the end of the show.

Months after the divorce, Gary called. He acted nonchalant, like we'd only parted ways a few hours ago. He asked how I was doing. I told him better, now that we were divorced. He couldn't believe I was so heartless. He said, "Lisa, why'd you go and do that? You didn't give me a chance. I'm gonna get it together. Come to Texas. You'll love it here."

Click.

~

My divorce happened about the same time that my father called and told me he was done with my mother. I couldn't say I blamed him, but I didn't think now was the time to part ways, since she couldn't function and she was a danger to herself and others. And what would she do?

A few days later, in the morning, I was on the phone with Mom.

Even at such an early hour, her speech was slurred. A long lull in the conversation preceded a thud and a crash. I yelled into the receiver, "Mom! Mom!" Silence.

I couldn't hang up the phone since it was a landline, so I ran across the courtyard to my neighbor's. I called my grandmother—my mother's mother—and told her that I'd been on the phone with Mom, had heard all sorts of noises, and then the line went dead. I asked: could she go check on her?

~ 2 ~
Blessed Break

Mom. Sobriety date: January 4, 1982

FOR YEARS, MY MOTHER HAD ASKED ME to write a recovery book. It just wasn't time. Instead, I wrote novels—four, to be exact. My mother died in 2011, and at the end of 2014, I made a radical change. I quit my job of twelve years, which I had come to hate. Actually, that job was sucking the life and the creativity right out of me. Within weeks of my newfound freedom, the idea for Raising the Bottom *emerged.*

I felt my mother around me, and I knew she'd be pleased. She was a grand lady. After she got sober, she became selfless and made a vocation of helping other alcoholic women. Women came to her funeral in droves—a human parade of testimony to Mom's tireless efforts. For four solid hours, throngs of women from all walks of life trudged to the casket, and between sobs, sniffles, and condolences, they said things like, "Your mom never gave up on me." "I've been sober three years now because of her." "I loved her so much. She saved my life." "She was so wise. I would be dead if it weren't for your mother." "The twelve steps saved my life; your mother saved my spirit." It went on and on and on. It was a tribute to a life well lived, and a tribute to how God can, and will, use any experience, no matter how virtuous or debauched, to help others find their way.

Also, around the time I started this book, one of my sisters, who had been unable to stay sober, completed a year's stint in a recovery house.

She found a sponsor who knew my mother well and was familiar with Mom's powerful story, having heard her lead in places like Cleveland, Akron, and other cities in and around Ohio and Pennsylvania.

As my sister relayed to me, one cold Saturday morning, her sponsor was adamant they make the hour's drive to attend a women's recovery workshop. My sister hemmed and hawed, but the sponsor insisted, so off they went. Later in the day, my sister met someone at that workshop who knew my mother, and this woman just happened to have three of my mother's lead tapes in her car!

Now, you tell me: is that odd, or is that God? I find it remarkable that my mother sobered up in 1982 and that in all those years, because we lived in different cities and different parts of the state, I'd only heard her lead once, about twenty-plus years before, while still early in my own recovery.

Mom was fervent about recovery. Now that I have those tapes, she can continue to pass on her message of hope and recovery to those who still suffer. I transcribed the tapes, so here we have her message, in her words, and I will let her tell you what happened the day the phone went dead.

Mom, Speaking to a Group in Clarion, Pennsylvania, in 2009

I am overwhelmed by God's grace that I am even here today. I was born to be here; I believe that. I function well here, my family functions well here, and I love what this fellowship has done for me, my family, and my daughter, who is in this fellowship. And we'll just keep praying for the ones who need to be here but haven't found their way yet.

A few stats: I am married—to the same husband, and that's a blessing. I need to tell you that when I got here he was sicker than I was. I have four children. I have a sponsor, and she has a sponsor—it's God. I got sober when I was forty-eight. My sobriety date is January 4, 1982.

Here we go. Yale or jail, Park Avenue or park bench, it doesn't matter. I grew up poor, with an outhouse. I remember my mother: we never got along. Like I said, we had this outhouse, and I used to dry corn silk on the cistern, wrap the corn silk in newspaper, and smoke in the outhouse. I caught the outhouse on fire, multiple times. My mother scolded me, and I became indignant. Disease of entitlement: I never saw wrong in anything I did. Ever.

My parents were from the old country—Depression-era people. They were full of fear about everything. I grew up Catholic. The God my parents knew was the God you needed to fear. One way or the other, He was going to get you.

Alcohol was no stranger in our home. My father made wine. Everyone drank, probably to medicate themselves, because life was hard. I remember, during WWII, wearing paper shoes. The first time I went on a date, the boy asked me if I planned to wear shoes; I went barefoot most of the time.

I don't remember any drunkenness in our home, but like I said, people drank. I never saw my mom or dad drunk, yet I became a falling-down drunk—a mother. A mother.

I was bound by all that nothingness: I never felt like I measured up. I never felt okay. I always felt inferior . . . or I'm better than you, but never on the same page, never just one of God's kids.

I believe today that my parents would like who I am. I went up to the cemetery for Easter and said to my parents, "I think you'd love the person I am today." I had a nice morning with my husband. He was getting ready for golf. When he left the house he didn't have to say, "Are you going to stay off the sauce today?" He used to say things like that all the time. "When are you going to get off the sauce?" But he didn't have to say that today. Isn't that nice?

A friend reminded me the other day that for the first five years of my sobriety, I bitched about my husband. The good thing is, you guys took it instead of him. That's a blessing. Today, I love him, and he loves me. It took a long time to get there.

If having it all makes you alcoholic, well, I qualified. My mother didn't raise me to be an alcoholic. I had a good life. When I was young I had goals, dreams. I always wanted to be a nurse, and I did become a nurse. But behind any accomplishment was fear. Fear of failure, fear of rejection, fear of being found out. God, I hated that fear—glad I don't have that anymore.

I had a great job with a doctor who I liked. I didn't even have to look for that job: he came to me. My father bought me a car, and I lived with my parents. I never paid a dime. My mother ironed and starched all my uniforms. What strikes me now is that I never knew the word *gratitude*. Until I came into this fellowship, gratitude was a foreign concept. I never said thank you for any of it. I took everything for granted, like having everything I wanted was my right. I spent all my money. I didn't save a dime.

I met my husband, but he scared me. I'll tell you why: he worked in his aunt's bar. I remember him telling me that he had to throw some drunk woman into a taxi. He said she looked ugly—makeup streaked down her face, slobbering all over herself. He made a point of saying he hated a woman who got drunk. Little did he know . . . Back then, we didn't have money to drink; we went to the hamburger place.

I didn't know resentments can kill an alcoholic. My first resentment was toward my husband for going to college after we got married. I thought he should've done that before we got married. I let that resentment poison me. When he graduated, I didn't bother to go to the ceremony. Resentments. I believe it's true what they say: for the alcoholic, resentments are the number one offender.

A few examples of how resentments can kill: I had a cousin who got a divorce and was out on the street with two little children. She'd gone to a Catholic charity to get help, but they didn't help her. For twenty-five years, until the day she died, she sat on the porch, drinking her beer, ruminating about the Catholic charity that didn't help her. She died from complications of alcoholism. Resentments.

Another lady I know kept drinking because her husband refinanced a loan to help his son from a previous marriage. I met her in treatment. I'd give her a call now and then to see how she was doing, and she'd say, "Oh, well, I'm okay. I'm doing it," but she wasn't doing it. She was hiding her bottles in the flower shop she owned. Died when the esophageal varices in her throat burst. Resentments. She couldn't let it go that her husband loaned his son money. She just couldn't let it go.

My alcoholism was, and still is, powerful and patient. Back then, Catholics didn't use birth control. They'd tell us: "Use the rhythm method." Forget that: it didn't work. I went to a doctor, whining about my life: I lived in the country, I had these four kids hanging on me, and I couldn't take it. He gave me a tranquilizer, Equanil. I swear that prescription read, "Take five pills every hour." That's a lead in itself. It says a lot about my personality: I did a lot of whining. Self-pity. I had a beautiful home in the country, there were people around, but I felt completely alone.

They say women go down faster than men. I absolutely believe that. I was bound in nothingness. When I was in Italy, one of the tour guides talked about people wanting to know how Michelangelo managed to get David out of that block of marble. Michelangelo said he just chipped and chipped until he released the prisoner inside. Alcoholics get that—we become prisoners, locked inside our bodies. Locked inside our minds.

I was an isolator. Lonely. Ended up drinking at home, a fifth a day. As you get older you get back problems, foot problems. Then I started thinking about it . . . my current aches and pains, no doubt, have something to do with all that falling down I did.

I had a hell of a time with honesty. I made up stories. I believed those stories. I remember being so drunk, and my husband accused me of drinking again. I stood in front of the bathroom mirror, crying, wailing, carrying on that I'm not drunk and how can he accuse me?

How I loved those vodka martinis! After one sip—no, who am I kidding, I didn't sip anything. After one gulp—it was just all okay. The doctor I worked for, we had mutual respect for each other, but after fifteen years I lost that respect, and he fired me. I got to the point where I didn't care. I drank a few vodka martinis at lunch, and I came back to the office completely out of it. I just didn't care. The doctor asked me to write out a script for a patient. After that martini lunch, I'd forget what he wanted me to do, and think, *The heck with it, that patient didn't need that script anyway.* Eventually things like that get back to the doctor.

I wish I knew if he was still alive so I could tell him what was going on with me. That's an amends I never got to make. I may never get to make. I went from that job with the doctor to a lesser job, to a lesser job, to a lesser job, to a lesser job, to no job.

I could tell you one sad story after another that happens with an alcoholic like me, but you've all heard drunk-a-logs. I'll tell you this one story, though, so you can get an idea of how crazy I was.

My husband had one bottle of Scotch. I swear that bottle talked, and it wanted me to open it. I steamed off the paper that goes around the top of the bottle and drank that whole bottle. After it was gone I realized what I'd done, and now I'm worried and need to cover my tracks. I hiked out to the rear yard, threw the bottle over the barbed-wire fence, went back inside the house, and then thought maybe that wasn't such a good idea. What if my husband decided he wanted a nip of that Scotch when he got home? I hiked back out in the woods, through the barbed-wire fence, found the empty bottle, brought it back in the house—but now I was all cut up from wading through the barbed wire and blackberry bushes. I drove to the grocery store and bought a cheap bottle of Scotch. I planned to pour the cheap stuff into the expensive empty bottle, but before I could execute that part of the plan, I drank the cheap bottle of Scotch, too. That's the kind of alcoholic I was, and still am: I'm powerless. Powerless over alcohol.

My husband grabbed me one night and said, "I hate you, I hate you! I don't know what to do with you." Most times he told me, "Just go to bed."

I banged into doors, bounced off of walls, you name it. I had all these bruises and told my husband I needed to go to the hospital. I thought I had leukemia. I wore a ratty robe with burn holes, smoked those cigarettes. I had this liver sticking out like I was nine months pregnant; I thought I was fat. I burned everything I tried to cook. I kept thinking the stove was broke.

The family we destroy. Alcoholism never gets better. But, when you get recovery and start living the life God wants you to live, things mend. The more I work on me, the better they get. Ain't that something?

I went to lots of psych wards, hospital stays. I remember being in the psych ward, yet again. I was furious with the psychiatrist. Everyone around me got shock therapy. After shock therapy, these people looked different, but I was still the same. Thank God that doctor didn't believe in shock therapy.

New Year's Eve: I'm back in the hospital again. The nurses removed the shackles off of my wrists and ankles. I walked to the window. Everything looked gray. The snow was dirty; gray smoke chugged out of the hospital's chimneys. I was racked with self-hatred, guilt. I'm zoned out on Lithium; remember, they diagnosed me as manic-depressive. I remember looking out the window, thinking, is this it? How did I get here? What happened to me?

My husband came to see me. That night, a smidgen of sanity slid in. I looked at him standing in my room, nicely dressed. He had a career. He had friends. He was off to a New Year's Eve party. He was living life. I was sitting in a bed and everything was hell. The thought entered that maybe there was something wrong with me.

The doctor didn't want to discharge me. I guess he finally pieced together my dilemma and realized that treatment was a good option. Sick as I was, though, I was still running the show. I insisted on going home first; I wanted to cook, clean up the house, do the laundry, and call my kids. You know, get things in order.

The doctor relented. I got home, found a bottle of whiskey, drank the whole bottle, and fell down the steps. My mother found me lying at the bottom of the stairs in a pool of blood. She said, "My God, what did you do to yourself this time?"

Less than twenty-four hours passed. I'm back in the hospital. More X-rays, and then home again. My neck hurt, and thank God I had some medical training. I thought to put a towel around my neck and anchor my jaw with a bandana to keep it from jiggling. The rehab was three hours away, and every time we drove over a bump in the road or hit a pothole, excruciating pain shot from my neck to my head and down my back.

I got to rehab, and this beautiful doctor, I later learned, was in recovery (and you know you can't con a con)—she was so wise. She asked if I had anything on me. I lied and said no. I pulled out a cigarette, and a Valium trickled across the floor. She instructed the staff to search me. "Take everything," she said. She asked about the towel and bandana around my head and neck. I told her I fell down the steps.

She bolted into action, ordered more X-rays, a C collar and whatnot, but all I cared about was, *They took my last Valium. Oh my God, how will I do this? I can't live without something. I cannot live without a pill . . . a drink . . . How do people do this?*

They ended up drilling five holes into my skull. They needed to anchor the halo contraption around my head to immobilize my neck. I had a serious break. A blessed break. What a miracle that I can stand here today, a free woman. I can walk, skip, ride horses, hop on the back of your motorcycle. I get to do it all . . . by God's amazing grace.

While in rehab, we went to meetings, and someone told me to talk to this woman who at the time had ten years sober. My first thought was, *No, I don't want to talk to her. Give me someone with a few days sober.*

God bless those women. I got sober under giants. Walk on the backs of giants. They knew I was a liar. Every time I opened my mouth, those women looked at me and said, "Now is that the truth, or a lie?"

I worked the steps.* My first fourth step, I could barely hold onto a pen, let alone write, but before I finished writing it all out, I decided I would only do the fifth step with someone who was dying. I didn't know at the time, but the lady I did agree to share my fifth step with had cancer, and she did end up dying.

---

* See the twelve steps on page 249–250 of this book.

Work the steps. Steps four and five: leave the garbage of the past on the curb. Steps six and seven, take me out of me. Those two steps helped restore some humility. Steps eight and nine, the amends steps. I will make amends until the day I die. But today, I can look you in the eye.

I lived my whole life looking outside of myself to make me happy. My job, my husband, my clothes, my children. I remember thinking if I went back to college, I'd feel okay, but you know what? I lost my car. Forever, I kept losing that car. I drank before class, and after class, I could barely make it home—that was *if* I could find my car.

I was always looking outside of myself to find the answers. I don't think others long for spirituality like an alcoholic. We're the lucky ones, though. We find it in these rooms. The alcoholic should be labeled with *the disease of searching*. We have a disease of the spirit. To the depth you work that third step is the depth of your program. I am a free woman today.

I have a good life. A simple life. Simple is better, less is more. Took me a long time to figure that out. We all have a job. My job was to raise four kids, be a nurse, and be an alcoholic so I could come out here and help others. I love how you can walk into a meeting and someone tells you something outrageous and we say, "Is that right?" Nothing surprises us.

What I've learned over the years is this: be compassionate. There are lots of young kids coming into the rooms. Will the program still be around and going strong for the babe born today destined to be an alcoholic? You young people have a huge responsibility to keep this going. Keep an open mind. As you get some time under your belt, you think you know it all—it's my way or the highway. Forget it. You still have much to learn.

Quick story about power: the power of God. My nurse friend, Tess . . . We went to nursing school together, but I hadn't seen her for twenty-five years. Out of the blue I decided to call and see how she was doing. She told me she was so anxious she couldn't leave her house. I said, "Tess, do you drink?"

She said, "Just a little. They're putting me in the psych ward. I can't leave my house. Agoraphobia."

I asked her if they had a treatment center near her home. She said yes. I told her, "Take a bottle of whiskey, put a blanket over your head, and have your husband drive you to the treatment center." She listened! Tess died sober.

Lastly, never put money before God.

~ 3 ~
Early Last Call

I BOUNCED BACK QUICKLY from that disastrous marriage. No big deal; just another blemish. As if I had a bad case of acne—what was one more zit? I acquired some street smarts, which was not a bad thing to have in my trick bag. I never loved him anyway.

So by the time I was twenty-one, I'd been married and divorced, I had no children, and I stashed the whole mess in the recesses of my mind. I found out one of my girlfriends from high school was moving to Columbus too. She needed a roommate.

We found a townhouse on the northwest side of the city. It had a health club and a swimming pool. We were all set. The place was clean, sans roaches. I had a new boyfriend of nine months. He stood well over six feet tall and had a laid-back demeanor. I liked that he had a boat too. We used to take trips up to Kelleys Island and partied at Put-in-Bay. The most animated he ever got was when he talked about fishing, a real outdoors kind of guy. I liked his easy-going way, the thick shock of black hair that fell over his forehead, and the dazzling white teeth that crept out from under his slow grin.

He called one day and asked me to pick him up at the police station. "A DUI charge? No kidding? That cop shouldn't have been sitting outside the bar like that. Don't they call that sort of thing *entrapment*? Right. That is so not fair. I'm on my way."

My friends started to graduate from college and secure real jobs. They were moving forward with their lives. I, on the other hand, was still taking classes. I kept changing my major, so I didn't make much progress toward a degree, but I felt productive and well-rounded.

I got fired from my latest waitress job. The manager protested that I had a big mouth and a bad attitude. My boyfriend, cute as he was, started to bore me. He liked to watch fishing shows—for hours.

Getting fired turned out to be a pivotal juncture. First, I worked all sorts of odd jobs. I packed meat, tended bar, delivered invitations to dignitaries around the capital city, trained polo horses, and went back to doing hair for a few months, all the while working toward whatever degree du jour I felt inclined to pursue.

I missed the fast cash of waitressing and found a job at a restaurant that served alcohol. My income tripled. I fell in with an eclectic group of vibrant men who schooled me on how things needed to be done, and they showed me what others who had come before us had taught them: how to pad the guest checks and rip off the restaurant. We found this perfectly justified because we were not ripping off the *customers*, just the restaurant. Hey, we had morals, okay? They also pointed out what waitress I *must* befriend—translation: her husband dealt coke. Got it. I was on it. Most importantly, they insisted I meet Jean-Claude, the scrappy law student. My new friends all swore I would like him.

Trite as it sounds, like does attract like. I didn't realize at the time but learned later that in some ways, he was as nutty as me. He came from a dysfunctional blended family with a total of five siblings. His parents divorced when he went off to college.

What attracted me to him was that I sensed that under all that bravado, there was a survivor. He had gumption and grit. He was optimistic. I liked his swagger and big personality. He was in his third year of law school, partied like crazy, and landed on the dean's list. Nice.

My friends Tommy and Vinney were right. Jean-Claude and I did hit it off from the get-go, so much so that Vinney, with his songbird voice, sang at our wedding. First I ended things with the fishing guy. He freaked, asked me to marry him, and I said no. For a short time he stalked me and my new love, showed up at our after-work haunt (of course it was a restaurant bar), and drove by the townhouse at odd hours of the day or night.

Jean-Claude and I were of the same mold, and after a year or so we started to make plans for the future. The blueprint looked something like this: We'd leave Columbus and move back to his hometown, where he'd practice law with his father. I in turn had been assigned the task of figuring out what I wanted to be when I grew up. Maybe I'd go back to school. I'd been in and out of college for about six years at that point, no degree in hand, but, hey, why rush things?

Once settled in his hometown, I'd be remiss if I didn't tell you that I was none too pleased. I felt I got a raw deal. He moved back to an instant life: family, friends, and a job. I had to start from scratch. A resentment was born.

I found a job at a small company that needed an in-house advertising and marketing person, and I learned a lot at that job. It also was where I recognized that I loved to write. I started writing hotel brochures, ad copy, and any lengthy correspondences needed to rationalize why this man's corporation felt it was above the law. He didn't pay his taxes or most of his bills, and he participated in any number of egregious business practices to skate around the law.

When my husband graduated from law school, an out-of-the-blue job opportunity came up that would send us to Oklahoma. Okay, so at least we both had to start over. My resentment softened.

Oklahoma was in dire straits. This was after the oil boom when everything went bust. We found a great big apartment, and I spent the next four months floating on a raft in the pool with the old lady who ran the apartment complex. She was a delightful person, and she allowed me to wallpaper and paint, but even with all the redecorating, I started to go a bit batty. I needed a challenge or something more to do.

I scoured the want ads in the newspaper every day. My husband's work needed him to travel. At this juncture, even with scads of time to do what I wanted, alcohol was not a significant factor. I only drank on weekends when my husband was home. We scoped out a few good restaurants—our favorite was a trattoria that offered wine by the ounce. We'd taste dozens of samples before settling on a bottle or two of wine with dinner.

One morning I spotted something interesting in the want ads. One of the major airlines that's still in existence today was hiring. They had scheduled open interviews at a hotel nearby. I showed up for the interview and was hired. The only downside was that I had less than two weeks to gather my things and move to Houston for training. I can't remember if training lasted for six or eight weeks, but once I finished training I would be assigned a home base.

That night when my husband came home, I asked him if he wanted the good news or the bad news. The good news was, I'd found a job. The bad news was, I had less than two weeks to get myself to Houston.

During the time I was in Houston, Jean-Claude received a promotion and his company moved him to Dallas. Actually, it was a perfect arrangement. Houston became my home base. The flight between Dallas and Houston was a short twenty minutes, and the commute worked out well.

In Dallas, we discovered Marty's Wine Bar and Café. They had one of the best wine selections in the city, and the food was divine. We frequented wine tastings and bought wine by the case. During the times I was home, we'd spend the weekends drinking wine and exploring the city. We loved the West End Historic District. It was an up-and-coming area filled with trendy restaurants, shops, and bars.

I thrived on the chaos of a flight attendant's life. After training I worked on reserve status, which meant that I didn't have a regular schedule. I also had no clue where or when I'd fly. The phone would ring, and I'd have an hour to get to the airport, whether it be for a short jaunt or a long overseas flight. This was also back in the days when the mini bottles of booze were left unaccounted for on the locked bar carts. The flight attendants held the keys to all that goodness.

Irregular sleeping, irregular eating, bouts of drinking. I felt at home in all that chaos. A life plagued with uncertainty spoke my language. I remember dark cavernous crew rooms littered with bodies in various stages of repose; these rooms, located in the bowels of large airports, became my second home. I loved it. Constant diversion from routine. There was nothing boring or run-of-the-mill. It got to where I'd wake up in some hotel and have to peek at the stationary or the note pad on the desk to remember where I was.

Our first year or so of marriage was like one big date. We met in different cities and had a blast. When I returned to Dallas, he picked me up at the airport with chilled champagne nestled into a silver ice bucket. Back then, Dallas allowed alcohol in the car as long as the driver wasn't drinking. I-30 and I-45 were like parking lots at rush hour. We'd inch through the traffic eating mussels in dill cream sauce and sipping champagne.

My by-then-sober mother came to Dallas for a visit. She noticed a few things. She heard the sigh of a beer can when I cracked the top at ten o'clock in the morning. I sat on the balcony of our apartment, painting my nails. We had a nice view overlooking the pool where they shot a few scenes for the TV show *Dallas*. My mother commented about my morning beverage. I'm sure I said something about being up since 5:00 a.m., so 10:00 a.m. was not so early after all.

Suddenly, my husband's brother died. He decided to take over his father's law practice, and that meant a move back home. Seriously, I didn't want to move. I liked the groove we'd carved out in Texas and saw no reason to leave. I loved flying, and we had Marty's.

Regardless, we moved back to the Midwest. My drinking took off to the next level. I was twenty-seven years old, and I believe this was when I crossed the imaginary line into alcoholism.

If I wasn't drinking, I thought about drinking. *Shall I have wine tonight? Or bourbon and water?* I'd steal more and more single-serving bottles off the planes' bar carts. I had a whole stash of minis in my bag for those nights our flight came in too late to debrief at the hotel bar, or, God forbid, if we ended up at a hotel that didn't have a bar. I transferred my home base from Houston to Denver. When in Denver, I lived in a hotel with a slew of other flight attendants. The commute was supposed to be easier, since I would've had to fly through Denver anyway, but getting to work in the wintertime had become a nightmare. Packed flights, coupled with cancelled flights—well, it was anybody's guess if I'd make it to work on time. After months of spending more time in the airport than at home or having a life, I felt I had no other option but to resign.

I resumed work at my old marketing job, but something was different. The nine-to-five routine sucked the life right out of me. The normalcy and reality of day-to-day living was a grind. I never made the adjustment. No more adrenaline rushes. No more dashing through airports. No more sleeping in dark crew rooms. No more waking up in strange cities and countries. No more chaos. What happened to all the fun?

I needed a diversion. I picked up a shopping habit. Actually, I shopped compulsively. I started hiding my purchases. I felt I needed a "Monday" outfit. My workweek was consumed with finding a new outfit to wear every Monday. I wasted copious amounts of time and money trying to fix my outsides so I would feel okay inside. I thought of no one but myself. I felt anxious, out of place. So, I shopped.

Little did I know at the time that I was playing dress-up. You can gussy up rotten fruit any way you want, but it's still rotten fruit. My dressing up was like covering the outside of a house's cracked foundation with a thin coat of cement. The defect will eventually be exposed.

The Bible talks about building a house on sand. The fairy tale "The Three Little Pigs" warns of the same folly. When the wolf shows up at the door, the houses made of sticks and straw can't withstand the blow. I had to find sturdier building blocks than shopping, drinking, and flirting, but I was still at the place where I didn't know how to fix my problem, and I certainly didn't have the insight to understand it.

At work, I had my own office. I did my thing. I started to crave a cocktail at lunch. That rapidly increased to two or three cocktails at lunch. My craving progressed to thinking and wanting a drink a little earlier each day.

I was still at the stage of rationalization. I drank because I could make time to drink and still do my job. My job required me to drink. I purchased media time from a gal at one of the radio stations. She liked to drink too. I couldn't say no to her offers for lunch and cocktails, could I? *My husband works a lot, so I might as well go have a drink after work. I'm not hurting anyone.*

I got to know everyone in the surrounding bars. I had guy friends, but few girlfriends. Women were snitches and bitches. You couldn't trust them. One afternoon I looked up from my desk, and my office looked like a funeral parlor. I had received five dozen roses and flowers from guys, I guess, that I'd met on my lunch hour in the bars. I didn't know who any of them were. Not to mention that I should have asked myself why I was wasting time flirting with guys who hung out in bars in the middle of the day anyway.

That niggling feeling came back. I found it odd and rather discomforting that guys were sending me flowers. I was happily married, or so I thought. Why would they send flowers? What sort of vibes was I putting out there? I was oblivious. I didn't understand myself, and I sure as hell didn't understand my behavior.

At the time, my thinking was either black or white. I'd like to think that after twenty-eight years of sobriety, I've grown leaps and bounds in this area, and I certainly have grown, but I still lean toward the concrete. It either is or it isn't. You will either do what you said or you won't. I read people well, so don't talk shit either—I have a sharp meter for people who say things just to hear themselves talk.

While drinking, that mistrustful, skeptical, always-dubious-of-your-intentions part of my personality was out there front and center. I justified my brash ways and brutal honesty about people's flaws with the consolation that at least I wasn't fake, and people knew where they stood with me.

My husband focused on building a law practice; poor guy, it took him a while before he realized he was traipsing around town with a live fuse on his arm. He'd get nervous taking me around certain people or situations. He started to ask me things like, “Are you going to go off tonight at so and so?” *I don’t know, maybe. Will they say anything to piss me off?*

I thought it was time for a family. We’d been married about four years and had had loads of fun; maybe a baby would ground me. I was restless and dissatisfied with everything, all the time.

Instead of a baby, we bought our first house, and then I stumbled into the bakery business. I had been fired from my marketing job. Drinking, snorting coke, and fighting with the boss were frowned upon. My husband had a friend, Bruce—they were close as brothers—and Bruce couldn’t seem to find his niche either. Jean-Claude suggested the two of us join forces. Bruce wanted to open a bakery, and he needed all sorts of help. Since I didn’t have a job . . . it was a natural solution. I agreed to become Bruce’s partner.

The bakery was attached to a bar. Perhaps I’d found my dream job after all, but things quickly went south. Bruce had deficient taste buds. He thought cream of shit tasted good. He had a knack for finding the most dysfunctional employees. The man he hired to be the dishwasher claimed he had no electricity or running water at his house. He regaled us with tales of his survival skills. The jolly baker, well, he couldn’t get to work on time. He’d waltz in late with one implausible excuse after another. Mostly his reasons had to do with tales of his wanton love life. I wasn’t buying any of it, since in my estimation he lacked good personal hygiene. He also had no clue what temperature the grease needed to be in order to fry a proper donut. He couldn’t bake a cookie, and I don’t think he even knew what a tart was. He cranked out tough or gummy donuts, depending on the day.

Bruce dragged a cot into the back of the bakery. He was sick of getting up in the middle of the night to come to work, so he devised a plan to just sleep there. He’d sit on the cot, and he’d smoke and smoke and smoke. I was beside myself. Donuts covered in blue haze. Yummy.

I didn’t know how to voice my displeasure appropriately, so I defaulted to hurling trays of sorry-assed donuts toward the plate glass window. The trays always fell a few inches short of creating an epic mess. When throwing a tantrum failed to produce the desired results, I bolted for the bar next door.

A few incidents happened that caused me to take pause. At the time, I drove a Jeep. One morning I woke up to a flat tire—actually, the tire looked slashed. What niggled at my conscience, though, was how I'd driven home without feeling the flat. I had no recollection whatsoever of the car driving off-balance or thumping down the road. How was that possible? It's not like the Jeep had small-enough tires that a flat could go unnoticed. Hmm.

I was the type of person who, if I didn't spend my time well, would find something destructive to do. From his late brother, my husband ended up with a small Honda motorcycle. I took a liking to the machine and cruised around the neighborhood and to the nearby drive-thru, with a Coors Light snuggled in each pocket. It was the way I liked to enjoy spring.

I frequented the drive-thru near our house, a lot, because they sold single cans of beer. I liked buying them that way. I could drink one and toss the can (which I did most times), and I was still on my first beer no matter how many I had drunk that day. Math that makes sense.

After a half-day of cruising around, my buying single cans of beer ended when I went through the drive-thru, yet again. The man selling beer said, "Lady, why don't you just buy a twelve-pack?"

Was he talking to me? How rude! I couldn't believe he'd suggest something far-reaching like that. Couldn't he see I was riding a motorcycle? Was he trying to get me killed?

I assured him I couldn't drink that much. But when I got home, the truth slapped me in the face. Spilling out of the kitchen garbage were cans and cans of empty beers. Wow. *Maybe someone had a party while I was gone. In the middle of the day? Who drank all those?* I was shocked. I think it was the first time I ever came face-to-face with how much I drank.

My best friend at the time had a baby. Her husband played in a band, and he was gone all the time. She spent blocks of time at our house, but now that she had the baby, it started to feel wrong. She liked to party. She had a baby. I don't care who you are—the two do not fit well together. In my mind, perhaps because of my upbringing, alcohol and children was a sure recipe for tragedy.

I started to back off from the friendship. I'd attempt to end our parties at a reasonable hour—you know, put away the beer, toss the empty cans—but she'd respond by laying out lines of coke. I'd periodically ask this friend if she thought I drank too much. Her answer, always, always, was an unequivocal *no*. (This woman went on to have another son. She lost custody of them both when she allowed crack to take her down the path of total destruction—but for the grace of God, there go I.)

More and more, she wanted to run to the bars. I was uncomfortable with my drinking, but not enough to do anything about it, and it fit into my life at the bakery. I was just uncomfortable enough to convince myself I didn't have a problem. I could leave a half a drink on the bar. I didn't get a DUI. I didn't drink every day. I got up early for work. I ran a business, for God's sake. How can you be a partner in a business and be an alcoholic? I knew I didn't have a drinking problem. Alcoholics drink every last drop, and then race around the bar gulping up other people's half-drunk drinks too. I never did that, so, whew, I was good.

But who was I trying to convince? Why was I having these conversations in my head? How come I kept asking myself, and other people too, if I drank too much? But here's where I was brilliant: I thought I deserved a pat on the back. At least I had enough insight to even ask myself these hard questions. Most people who have drinking problems live in denial. So, no, I definitely wasn't an alcoholic.

In January of that same year, 1989, my mother had sent me a book about alcoholism and the twelve steps with the inscription, "With lots of love and prayers." I tossed the book into the closet.

My husband and I met new friends. All of them were young professionals, and they all drank quite a lot. I might've even drank less than most of them. We went to parties and had nice dinners. We bought the *Encyclopedia of Wine*.

I needed to further examine my reality, but at the time, I wasn't capable. If I'd been capable, maybe I would've seen that, although a lot of my friends drank as much if not more than I did, they didn't seem to lose control of their emotions. Other women told me they didn't get up the next day thinking of a drink. Other women confessed to letting loose for a night, but that was the end of it until next month. Other women weren't drinking three to four nights a week, were they? Other women had hobbies and outside interests besides bar hopping, didn't they? Other women weren't consumed with thoughts about drinking. Ouch.

Okay, so everyone is different. I shouldn't judge myself so harshly, right? I was the creative type, and perhaps the problem was that I needed a creative outlet. As I mentioned earlier, while at the marketing job, I'd discovered that I liked to write. I guess when I came back from my liquid lunches I delved into my literary aspirations. I must have started a dozen sappy romances. I wrote pages and pages of pure gibberish. I know it was gibberish because years later, I stumbled over those first attempts. God, I sounded as dark as Poe. Even then, I was searching for an outlet, a release. But the only way I knew to cope was drinking.

My pattern of dysfunctional behavior reached its pinnacle. One night my husband took me to dinner and said something along the lines of, "I don't know what is wrong with you, but you need to get your act together."

My first reaction was *Fuck you. You're drinking right along with me. You've shared all this madness every step of the way!* After that dinner, I continued on my merry way doing what I did, but the conversation took up residence in my mind. I started an internal dialogue full of negotiation: *So, you don't drink every day. You rarely drink before noon. You don't have the shakes. You don't hide booze. So you snort a little coke. When that began to look like a problem, you quit.* (Which I did. I quit coke as soon as it started to get out of hand.) *You're always the designated driver.* True. I was. *So you probably don't have a problem.*

I needed parameters, so I set them for myself. Here's what I came up with to know for sure if I was an alcoholic: first, if I ever got drunk when I didn't mean to get drunk, that would be a warning sign; second, if I ever had the shakes, that would be a sign; third, if I ever wanted more than four drinks in a row, that would be a sign. Within a week, all of my warning signs flashed red alert. That was my bottom. That's what it took for me to stop and take a hard look in the mirror and say, enough already!

I tried to talk myself out of it and rationalize, like we do. My thought was to extend the parameters I had set. Perhaps I needed to give myself more leeway. Maybe the small tremor I noticed one morning was due to too much caffeine.

I believe it was God's grace that allowed me to see what I needed to see. In spite of all the things that hadn't happened yet, the time had come to quit drinking. It didn't matter that I hadn't been to jail—yet. It didn't matter that physically, my health was perfect. I didn't have a DUI—yet. Not many people quit after they burn the toast one morning, but I'd seen how fast my mother deteriorated, and I knew in my marrow that total devastation would be my fate too. The gig was up.

I think a smidgen of relief seeped in once I acquiesced. I had felt for the past two years that something wasn't right. I couldn't put my finger on it, but all that justifying and vindicating that went on in my head couldn't be what normal people did. I found it hard to believe that most people would sit around convincing themselves, on a weekly basis, that they weren't alcoholic. Plus, I never felt settled.

I called my mom and said, "I think I need to come home." Instead of asking why, she breathed a sigh of relief and said, "Thank God. Come tomorrow."

~4~
Raising the Bottom

Lisa. Sobriety date: June 22, 1989

My plan was to stay at my mom's for a few weeks, go to meetings, and, well, quit drinking. I had had enough, or so I thought. I felt miserable, and I hated feeling lost all of the time. So what if from the outside my life looked normal? Husband, house, car, it all looked swell, but behind the facade, I felt chaotic, anxious, crazy—well, I felt like crap, most all of the time. I informed Bruce that I needed a bit of time off from the bakery, and I decided to take the plunge.

My mom lived four hours away. Forty minutes into the trip, I stopped and bought a six-pack. This should have been another red flag for my attachment to alcohol. Sort of like the last meal before lights-out in the electric chair. I cried and drank the whole way home. I wanted to reconsider. Maybe I did have emotional problems and needed medicine instead. Maybe the drinking was the only thing that helped me not unravel all the way. Perhaps I overreacted. Perhaps my husband had his own issues that he was now projecting onto me. Perhaps he was the problem.

I arrived at my mom's in the evening. It was April. I could tell she'd been busy. She had outlined a whole schedule of meetings and coffee dates with women from the program. The women did what they were taught to do, envelop themselves around the newcomer who asked for help. I was bombarded with recovery. Meetings, literature, and women—they were showing up all hours of the day and night just to "talk."

The women were a hoot, including the sweet and flighty nun who was not at all shy about talking about her shocking escapades. She reassured me that feeling and acting nutty were all part of the disease. Another woman confided that in her early sobriety she had kept a folding lounge chair in the trunk of her car because she was obsessed with tanning. She said she could be cruising down the highway, and if the urge to tan hit, she'd just pull off on the berm, set up her lawn chair, and, right there in the grass next to the interstate and whizzing cars and trucks, she'd catch a few rays.

These women doled out snippets of their own insanity, and everyone around the table howled. For God's sake, what did they think was so funny? Okay, I still felt like crap, but I had to admit: listening to their insane behavior made me feel better, if only marginally.

The women came from all walks of life. Some were missing a few teeth and dressed like they had just been released from the drunk tank, complete with requisite tube top and skin-tight jeans. Others had necks, wrists, and fingers so laden with diamonds and gold jewelry I wondered how they could sit up straight without toppling over. But most of them looked like they could've been anybody's mother or grandmother.

This was not a cardboard-cutout disease. An alcoholic could look like anybody. I never thought my mother fit the alcoholic stereotype of the man under a bridge wearing a trench coat. Alcoholism is an equal-opportunity disease. It likes all demographics. I liked that. I didn't have to fit into a frame. I also had a rebel heart, and I knew if I had to look or be a certain way, the deal was off. I would've failed without even trying. I would've split.

I wasn't nervous about going to the meetings. I knew what to expect. I had been to that one meeting in Columbus with my first husband seven years prior. The last two years of my drinking, I bounced around other recovery rooms. Here and there—okay, twice—I popped into an Al-Anon or Adult Children of Alcoholics (ACOA) meeting. They weren't the right fit. The people seemed a bit dour, and they had real tragedies to discuss. I left those meetings jubilant that I didn't have their problems. I celebrated by zooming through the nearest drive-thru.

The year before I quit drinking, I had bounced into a twelve-step club just to see. The room was full of men—older men, men who had drunk bottles and bottles almost their whole lives. But fate intervened when I heard someone read the words that leapt off the page and stuck in my craw. "To be gravely affected, one does not necessarily have to drink a long time nor take the quantities some of us have. This is particularly true of women. Potential female alcoholics often turn into the real thing and are gone beyond recall in a few years."[2] *Wow. No kidding.* I felt like I'd been slugged. The reader went on to say how potential alcoholics litter the planet, but how few of them want to quit while they're still young. "Certain drinkers, who would be greatly insulted if called alcoholics, are astonished at their inability to stop."[3]

Most dragged themselves and their families down before stopping. I didn't want to be that person. I watched my mother completely destroy herself with alcohol, and it happened within a span of five years. There was no reason why I had to follow suit. I believed those lines I'd heard because I lived it. I saw what happened to people who allowed their pride to step in the way. Sure, Mom started the whole ball rolling with prescription medication long before her drinking got out of control, but still, I knew her fate would be my fate. I saw first-hand just how wrong things could go.

I don't recall overt resistance, though I do recall that I wasn't 100 percent on board. I started to feel better after a few days without booze. Then I did what so many do: I started to reconsider. Perhaps I wasn't an alcoholic after all. I was only twenty-nine years old. Nothing bad had happened. I was a law-abiding person. How could I be an alcoholic? And the most troubling thought of all was, how could I possibly not celebrate with wine or champagne on my birthday? It was April, and my birthday is in December. New Year's Eve, to be exact.

That right there should've been another tip-off—but doesn't everyone think like that? Doesn't everyone worry about what they will have to drink eight months down the road, and sob and cry and carry on if they think they will have none?

After ten days of twelve-step immersion, along with scads of women chirping in my ear, I decided that I needed to go back home. It wasn't all that hard staying sober at my mom's. I had no responsibility, I felt nurtured, and I liked her crew of friends, but it wasn't my reality.

I needed to go back to my life. I needed to figure out me. I wanted to learn to live instead of just react. I had to get out of that primitive survival mode. I had to learn to respond appropriately. I was done smearing salve on my open wounds; it kept washing off.

I went home and told my husband my plan to quit drinking—for good. He looked aghast. I was his best drinking buddy. He tried to talk me out of it and said things like, "I don't think you're an alcoholic. You just need to learn how to control your emotions." Well guess what? I can't deal with my emotions when I drink because alcohol affects me that way.

Alcoholics are allergic to alcohol. People that are allergic to peanuts or strawberries don't run around eating up those foods. They avoid them. Well, alcoholics are allergic to alcohol, but we still want to drink! Alcohol makes our brains react differently. The reward section of the brain, located in what researchers call the *midbrain* or *limbic section*, is different in an alcoholic than in someone who's not an alcoholic. Addiction nestles into that part of the brain and sets up house. It lives indefinitely, rent free, and, like any good moocher, when it gets a taste of something it wants, it screams for more. Think of it as a switchboard or a neon sign. Someone flips the switch, the phones ring, and the lights come on. Give an alcoholic alcohol or drugs, the switch goes on, and the brain wants more. That is why an alcoholic can't just have one beer or one glass of wine. With us, it leads to another, to another. It's that first drink that gets us every time. Once I ingested alcohol, my emotions ran amok. Then I wanted more. I liked the feeling of not feeling. I didn't care that I became irrational and argumentative. Just give me more of that feel-good juice, and I was good. Therein lies the malady and the heartbreak of alcoholism. We want what can kill us. We crave more poison. In one sense, alcoholism is the disease of more.

I told my husband I didn't care what he thought. None of it mattered. What mattered was what I thought. I was resolute. I informed him that if he didn't like my choice, he could let himself out the door at any time. That shut him up. He knew I wasn't playing.

He was cooperative for a short time. We devised a plan that he had to keep whatever beer or wine he had in the house somewhere where I didn't have to look at it every day. We bought a second refrigerator, and most of the alcohol went in there. I asked him not to drink in front of me, at least until I found my sea legs. He obliged. I asked him not to drink a cold beer on a hot day unless it was in a Solo cup. I didn't have the strength to look at icy, cold bottles sweating in the noonday sun. I changed my route to and from places so I didn't have to pass by the drive-thru. Those blinking neon beer signs called my name. I went to meetings—lots of meetings. I listened to what people said, but that's about all I did. My mother called frequently to check up on my progress.

I think my husband thought I'd be over my sober phase after a month, and we could get back to wine with dinner and whatnot, but that wasn't to be, at least not yet.

In order to get sober and stay sober, I had to make some changes. People in recovery would laugh and say, "You only have to change one thing, and that's everything."

Well, I wasn't ready to change everything. I wanted to not drink but still go to bars and hang out with my partying friends. I wanted to continue living a double life—doing what I wanted when I wanted, without the risk of consequences. I felt I had to run my life and parts of other people's lives too. I didn't work the steps. I didn't get a sponsor. I didn't talk to anyone. All I did was show up at meetings. I stayed sober three months, and then I relapsed.

It was the darn beer drive-thru that got to me. I remember the day well. I was at a meeting, and at the end we all stood, held hands, and said the Our Father. I decided right in the midst of that prayer that on my way home I'd swing by the beer drive-thru across the street and get on with my life. I did just that.

I bought and drank a whole bottle of wine. For some odd reason, I got commode-hugging sick, and then the light of surrender flipped on. Clearly, the one-day relapse showed me that the fun was over. I no longer wanted to keep doing what I was doing to keep getting what I was getting, which was nowhere. I was sick and tired of being sick and tired.

My mom was seven years sober at the time. She had morphed into this amazing, wonderful person. She was living life, was riding horses, had made a vocation of helping others, and traveled the world with my dad. Sobriety started to look darn good. I just had to get over the hump of thinking that alcohol was so damn important.

What is it with alcoholics? We'd rather have any number of horrible diseases—as long as no one takes our wine. I know of women who'd rather be diagnosed with major depression or bipolar disorder than quit drinking. That's how sick some get. I had to realize that normal people don't want to curl into a ball and sob uncontrollably if someone tells them they can't have wine. Or beer. Or Jim Beam. Or Glenlivet. Someone without a problem will shrug and then head to the store in the next few weeks to scope out the new lemonade, juice, or ice tea flavors on the market. You tell an alcoholic they need to quit drinking, and prepare yourself for pushback and heaps of denial.

Then the bargaining started: *Alcoholism helped me feel better.* No it didn't. *I was having fun.* No I wasn't. That was another lie I told myself. What is so fun about drinking, feeling sick the next day, not engaging in life, not having hobbies, and feeling bad about yourself because you know deep down that you drink too much and too often, and that you're a control freak and feel stressed, and that is not the person you're supposed to be?

June 22, 1989. My one-day relapse was behind me. I went back to meetings. This time, though, I listened. I stopped criticizing, and instead, I tried to relate. Before each meeting someone in the group always read "How It Works." I used to get so annoyed that they kept reading the same stuff over and over. I finally understood why. I heard another line that was instrumental in my sobriety: "The result was nil until we let go absolutely."[4]

So there you have it. Surrender is a must. I had to be willing to let go of old ideas. I had to be willing to let go of all the people I thought were friends, when in reality, they were nothing more than drinking buddies. Nobody, at least in the beginning, wants to drink alone. People always welcomed someone who bellied up to the bar with them. And by the way, none of those so-called friends ever called to ask why I quit coming around. Next.

I scoped out a sponsor. I wanted someone who was at least as smart as me, because I'm brilliant, remember? I wanted someone educated and solid. I wanted someone who was living a good life. I found the perfect person: Patricia. She's since passed, but she was instrumental in the first thirteen years of my recovery. I still had gargantuan trust issues, so I wanted someone stable but who wasn't all sickly sweet. I didn't trust that fake kind of nice. I wanted a woman who had inner strength and who wasn't a gossip.

My instincts were correct. Patricia was a class act. There was nothing warm and fuzzy about her. She was rather cut-and-dried, and she had some of that black-and-white thinking that I could relate to. She was a college professor who taught anatomy and physiology to graduate students at a premier university. She was smart and educated. She had a good long marriage to an orthopedic surgeon. They had two sons. Check. Check. Okay, her life was stable and happy. Check.

She walked me through the steps. She made suggestions. It was my choice to follow her directions or not. She didn't let me whine, and she told me to shut up about my dog—I was obsessed, like broken-record obsessed, with every aspect of the basset hound I had at the time.

Patricia was a great example of someone who came to terms with her alcoholism, did what she had to do, and moved back into the mainstream of life. I wanted what she had. She had been sober about seven years, which, at the time, seemed like forever. She still went to three meetings a week. She worked with other women. She was involved in service. She had a career, she had a family, and she was peaceful. In other words, she did life remarkably well.

I started making friends. I started to see that the rooms weren't just full of weathered old men. There were women all over the place. There were professionals, PhDs, and judges, and there were housewives and grandmas. It blew my mind. I still thought I was younger than most, until I met a woman who got sober when she was seventeen and had been sober twenty years already. That ended my preoccupation with age comparisons. But I still felt cagey as hell. And then, two weeks into my newfound serious sobriety, I was standing in the bakery, spatula in hand, when I became so dizzy I had to sit down. Bruce laughed and suggested I might be pregnant. A few weeks later I learned the truth.

~ 5 ~

I'm Supposed to Be Happy. So Why Am I Crying?

So, I WAS TWO WEEKS SOBER, and not just pregnant, but pregnant with twins. This shit was getting real. Talk about sheer terror. I had no clue how to live life, and now I needed to be responsible for two other lives.

What did I do? I kept going to meetings. I talked to my sponsor, and one day at a time I didn't drink. I struggled daily with the first step. I knew without a doubt that my life had become unmanageable, but I didn't yet believe that I was powerless over alcohol. When you're not a daily drinker, and you don't drink much more than a lot of other people, how can you possibly label yourself an alcoholic?

My biggest hurdle was accepting that once I ingested alcohol, my reaction to life changed. Alcohol changes an alcoholic's brain. If you start to pay attention, I am willing to bet that nine times out of ten, when there's drama in the room, the person who drank too much is causing the ruckus. Quantity does not have to be the deciding factor. People do not realize that the quantity and length of time someone drinks does not determine who is and isn't alcoholic—but both can be factors. It's a complicated disease.

For women who start drinking in high school, by the time they're twenty-five, they already have a decade of hard drinking under their belts, and keep in mind that emotional growth stops when a person starts drinking. Do all of them become alcoholics and stay emotionally immature? Not necessarily, but it pays to be mindful and to realize that, at the very least, the frequency with which they drink can increase their chances of acquiring an alcohol use disorder, if they haven't acquired it already.

At the time, I didn't know anything about alcohol use disorders or emotional immaturity, nor was I convinced I was an alcoholic, but I can say with certainty that my life was unmanageable, and acknowledging that my life was unmanageable was what kept me in the recovery rooms.

I knew that I felt better and liked myself better when I didn't drink, and my emotional equilibrium returned. Yes, I still had a bit of a temper, but that is who I am. I have enough Italian and gypsy in me to be fiery, even when stone-cold sober!

I had a rough pregnancy. I was put on bed rest, and bed rest became a theme. I was in and out of the hospital and in and out of bed the last four months of my pregnancy. To the best of my ability I kept working the steps. I let go of my pride. The hospital where I had my twins had an inpatient treatment center. I told my doctor he'd have to arrange for someone to wheel me downstairs to the weekly meeting held in another part of the hospital.

Hooked up to IVs and sitting in a wheelchair, I went to meetings. I had become willing to do what I needed to do to stay sober. Not that I would've drunk at the hospital, but the noise in my head was still too loud.

I didn't know where that strength came from to say the hell with it all, or where I found the ability to don blinders and do my thing—that right there is God's grace in action. I felt blessed. I've watched so many women implode because they care too much what others think. They care that their family will judge them. They fear they will lose friends. The truth is, some friends need losing. What sort of friend wouldn't want what's best for you? Only a sick alcoholic friend would want you to stay sick, miserable, and alcoholic and drink with them. It's their selfishness that doesn't want you to get well. They want a drinking buddy! Wake up.

Look at your relationships with your friends and family for what they are instead of what you'd like them to be. Ladies, that's how it works. If you question your drinking, look around you. I promise that most everyone you associate with, including your family, drinks as much as you do. Of course, they will all reassure you that you are fine—but remember, we have learned that *FINE* means: Fucked-up, Insecure, Emotional, and Neurotic.

As I mentioned, my first attempt at sobriety was in April of 1989. I lasted a few months and then had a one-day relapse. During the few months I was sober, my mother had orchestrated my attendance at a twelve-step recovery retreat. The retreat lasted all weekend and was held at an old convent, the bucolic grounds a balm for my battered soul. I did my first fourth step with a priest. At that time in April, I didn't yet know that I'd end up pregnant with twins or that I'd land on bed rest.

What a blessing it was to have so much of my garbage cleared out of my head. I also didn't know then that I wasn't committed to the steps or the program or anything about sobriety. I had no idea that a few months down the road I'd relapse for that one day, but it didn't matter. I still gleaned the benefit of coming clean. Doing that first fourth step helped me to let go of a lot of rubbish; some, though not all, of my anger was gone. It was easier to be on bed rest without the committee holding court in my head.

My obstetrician was a gem, but he'd gone on vacation, and during one of my hospital stays, his partner took over his rounds and paid me a visit. We had a few words. He didn't like that at the time, I smoked a few cigarettes a day. My doctor felt it would be more stressful for me to completely quit smoking while still so early in my sobriety. He was fine with two cigarettes a day. The women in sobriety supported the theory that we can only address one issue at a time. It was far more important that I stay sober than not smoke two cigarettes a day.

This doctor lectured me and accused me of abusing my unborn babies. I threw a potted plant at him and told him to get the hell out of my room. My doctor came back from vacation and said something like, "I heard things didn't go so well."

First off, yes, my behavior could've been better. Second, I believe professionals need to remember to meet people where they're at. That doctor had no idea that I was only six or seven months sober. He had no idea that I had few coping skills. Physically, I felt fine. I'm a high-energy person. Lying around in bed all day was hard. I was bored out of my mind. There were no iPads, and Pinterest didn't exist yet. I had few distractions and lots of raw emotion bubbling to the surface. That doctor couldn't have known. Nevertheless, it's important for professionals to not make snap judgments, and more importantly, it's crucial they not be assholes.

Women brought meetings to my private hospital room. One of them taught me how to do needlepoint. I made bibs for the babies. Lots and lots of bibs.

~

Three months after I delivered my healthy twin boys, I ended up with a blood clot in my leg. Back to the hospital. But this time, it was a bit of a reprieve. Those twins never slept! Something about colic. I was exhausted.

One morning a woman that I knew from the program waltzed into my room to deliver a pitcher of water. I asked her what she was doing at the hospital. She said she worked there because she was going to nursing school. *Nursing school. Hmm.*

As soon as she left the room, I rolled over in bed, picked up the phone, and set the ball in motion to enroll in nursing school. That September, when my sons were six months old, I would go back to school.

The birth of my twins startled me into reality. I felt an overwhelming need to be capable of supporting my children. The fog had lifted, and I couldn't believe that although I had been in and out of colleges for a decade, I hadn't finished a degree, though I had amassed hundreds of credits. I also realized I couldn't handle feeling dependent upon my husband.

I didn't want to go back to a marketing job. It involved too much travel, and drinking seemed to be a staple in the business world. Plus, I had no intention of returning to the bakery. Nursing seemed like the perfect fit. At the time, I couldn't think of another career that would offer as much flexibility. I wish I could say I had more altruistic motives, but for me, it was about being practical.

I informed my husband of my plans to start nursing school in the fall. He was livid. He berated me with all sorts of *could've, should've,* and *would've.* Why didn't I finish college when I *should have*? Why didn't I get my act together when I *could have*? I fought back hard. I was still operating in survival mode, but I'd also cleared up enough to realize, yes, I had pissed away a whole decade, but he knew that when he married me. I was not going to spend the rest of my life beating myself up for things I didn't do. If I *could have* focused and stayed in school, he could bet his ass I *would have.*

The dynamics of our entire relationship changed. I took back my power. He could no longer manipulate me. I debated against his legalese. I remembered what I did and didn't say. The battle of wills had begun. He berated me for studying; he couldn't accept he was not the center of my universe. He had lost his best drinking buddy. He felt betrayed. During those years, I ignored him the best I could, and I forged on.

I had a new resolve. I had support from my new sober friends. I refused to worry about what anyone thought, including my husband. It dawned on me very early in my recovery journey that I had to let go of everything. Whatever shook out in the end was what I was supposed to have. This line of thinking mirrors step three. I had to believe that God could and would do a much better job of running my life than I had done. I had made an art form out of floundering. No more. I had to change my thinking. My best thinking took me right down the road of alcoholism. I knew nothing.

What I most cared about was getting well so that I could mother my children and get on with my life. I adored, and still do adore, my sons. They are my best accomplishment. I refused to make the same mistakes my parents had made. My sons would not be raised by wolves.

At that time, I was more intent on staying sober and learning to navigate life than I was worried about my marriage. I've never feared being alone. I'm independent. Thank God for that. I was perfectly willing to accept that my marriage either would or wouldn't make it. Either way, I'd be okay.

I'd always felt a bit misunderstood too, but that's okay. I realized I no longer needed approval. I began to see that my dysfunctional childhood and my rage-aholic father had battered my self-image and self-esteem. I think on some deep level I had always wanted his approval. I got to the point where I didn't care if I had his approval or anyone else's. I had to accept that my father had his own demons and probably did the best he could. What mattered was that I stayed sober, worked on me, and focused on the next right thing.

During the years I went to nursing school, life was a constant struggle. My husband continued to bubble over with resentment. My twins were a handful. School kicked my ass. I had little time to do more than babies, books, meetings, and the grocery store. That was my life for almost three years, and it paid off: I stayed sober, I graduated valedictorian of my class, my kids continued to thrive, and somehow my marriage stayed intact. It was only in hindsight that I realized that was God's plan.

Prior to this time, I lacked any sort of discipline. The last time I'd had any discipline was when I had my horse. I believe God gave me the struggles I had because I needed all that structure to keep me focused. I started to learn about me, and I realized that for me, free time was my enemy. At this early juncture in my sobriety, surrounded by neighbors and friends who drank, it would've been all too easy to slip back into my old habits.

I got sober so I could jump back into the mainstream of life. I didn't get sober to quit living. I got sober so I could live life—on life's terms.

That meant I was free. Sobriety is about living—not hiding. Some people have the misconception that if they get sober, their life will be over, and they can't ever be around alcohol. But that's not true. When you work the steps, all twelve of them, you become a free person. I go where I want, travel where I want, and do what I want without the fear of picking up a drink. As long as I stay close to God, I know I'm protected. At the beginning of my sobriety, my life was just beginning. Alcoholics are so lucky; we get to live two lives: life before sobriety, and life in sobriety.

I needed structure. I had to stay focused and stay out of self-pity. School kept me out of a bad neighborhood—the space between my ears. Plus, I loved learning. I didn't know that about myself.

There were times when I was so exhausted that I did sink into self-pity. All these emotions bubbled to the surface, and I was clueless about how to deal with them. I'd look around me and see other women who never worked a day in their lives. They spent their days at their kids' school or the gym, having lunch with girlfriends, and cooking dinner in the evening. Really? How hard was that?

I was so jealous of these women's lives. One of their kids would puke, and they'd have hubby on speed dial, and he'd run home from work with medicine and help. Seriously, their biggest challenge was a few kids with the flu. Were these women that weak? Or were they just lucky to have all that support?

When I felt those icky emotions, like jealousy or envy or exhaustion, I called my sponsor or a friend in the program. I'd fly out of the house and head to a meeting. I talked to other women about feeling overwhelmed and jealous, and they'd say things like, "Where's your gratitude?" or "If God wanted you to have an easy life, he would've given you an easy life. Deal with it." Wow, isn't it mean to talk to someone like that? No, it isn't mean. They were teaching me to grow up. Those women taught me to make the best of my circumstances and quit looking around and comparing my life and my insides to what I only could see from the outside. And the truth was, I had a pretty great life. I just couldn't see that. My perception was still skewed.

I had feelings that I had no clue how to handle. I wanted to jump out of my skin. I'd think about having a drink to make all that icky go away, and then I'd play the tape forward and remember that for me, one drink would flip the switch. Not a good idea. So I'd pick up the phone, or take the babies for a walk, or go to a meeting. For a while, the meetings were my only coping skill.

I still struggled with the notion of whether or not I was a real alcoholic. I kept ruminating about the fact I could walk out of a bar and leave that unfinished drink sweating on the table. Talk about obsessive thinking. I obsessed over the fact that I was probably not an alcoholic and asked myself why was I making myself not drink and go to meetings. I wondered if I maybe overreacted and if perhaps my mother didn't know what she was talking about either. Perhaps I did just need to calm down and get it together.

In spite of all of my reservations about whether or not I was an alcoholic, I kept going to the meetings. They say you have to work the first step perfectly and admit powerlessness, but I am proof that even the first step leaves some wiggle room. At least in the beginning you don't have to swallow it all. I clung to the second half of the first step. My life was most definitely unmanageable. Powerless over alcohol? At the time, I wasn't convinced.

Alcoholics have a thinking problem. Drinking is but a symptom of the distorted, delusional thinking that plagues every alcoholic and abnormal drinker. My thinking was messed up. My reaction to life was unnatural. It is wholly unnatural for any person to use alcohol as their coping mechanism. It is wholly unnatural to drink to suppress feelings that you don't want to feel, much less deal with. It's wholly unhealthy to nurse resentments instead of deal with them. It is wholly unnatural to drink, get drunk, wake up remorseful, suffer a hangover, remember only sketches from the night before, and then by noon forget all about the negatives and commence to have a Bloody Mary or mimosa at brunch. Non-alcoholic people don't do that.

I was sober almost a year when I heard a woman give a talk and I felt like she was telling my story. She too had quit drinking when she was rather young. At the time she told her story, she had a dozen years sober. I can still remember that she wore a Kelly green blazer, a white blouse, and a black skirt. She talked about working the steps, getting sober, and staying sober. She had a job she loved in corporate America.

We can argue and debate opinions all day long, but I couldn't argue with her experience. She wasn't standing up in front of the room telling people what they needed to do. She talked about what happened and what her life was currently like. She talked about growing up with an alcoholic parent. She talked about her emotional bottom. She talked about coming to terms with her drinking. When I heard her talk about herself, I knew she was also talking about me. That's how the magic of recovery sprouts hope. We see ourselves in others. We listen to how they got to the other side. If you want what we have, do what we do. It's so simple, yet the surrender part is so difficult. I started to love me. I started to smell the rain and enjoy the moon. I started to acquire the gifts of a quiet mind and a peaceful heart.

My sons were four when I went to work. My husband and I drifted apart. He was doing his thing, and I did mine. He was a wonderful dad, but our schedules were such that one of us was always coming while the other was going, and he drank with the crowd.

Once the boys started kindergarten, we socialized more. Everyone in our circle drank. We went to all sorts of events, and that's when I began to realize that I was more of an introvert than I thought I was. Sobriety will do that to you—no, it won't make you an introvert, but as I started to get to know myself, I realized that my drinking persona was not at all who I was. I realized I liked being at home with my sons. I liked animals. I liked books.

After years of feeling drained from going to party to party to party, I told my extrovert husband to pick a few of the parties he really wanted me to go to with him and that he'd have to go to the rest alone. I just couldn't do it anymore. I didn't want to do it anymore. I'm not fond of meaningless small talk. I hated getting a babysitter. I preferred staying home with my sons.

I have to interject here that I've worked with many women who tell me they can't get sober, even though they know they desperately need to, and they say they can't because their husbands, boyfriends, or families drink. I tell them that's an excuse that you tell yourself in order to keep drinking. If you want to get sober, you can get sober in spite of the madness around you. If you surrender and find a God of your understanding, and if you ask that God to help you stay sober, all while doing your part, anyone, and I mean anyone, can get sober. It all boils down to how willing you are to do what it takes. How willing are you to let go of people, places, and things? How willing are you to maybe be shunned by—or to shun—the people who don't support your decision to save yourself?

When I had been out of nursing school for all of two days, I stood in my kitchen cleaning up after the boys' snack, and I heard a voice telling me to write a book. The details of that experience are for another book at another time, but the voice led me away from contemplating divorce, and I started writing.

I toyed with the idea of going back to school, yet again. I had to work through some resentments toward my parents and myself; I felt my life would've taken a different course if I had had some solid guidance and a clear mind when I was younger. Perhaps I might have moved to horse country in Kentucky or stayed in Texas and gone to vet school, but I had to let all of that go and learn to deal with life as it was, not as I wished it could've been. I guess my drinking career, though relatively short, had still sprouted a few regrets.

I prayed and prayed for God to show me what to do with my marriage. I felt like a butterfly stuck in a cocoon.

I remember my husband saying, "Didn't you think about what marriage was about before we got married?"

No, of course not! I never gave anything much thought. At the time it seemed like a good idea, but five years into it, I wasn't so sure. I continued to pray for guidance.

Three years later I got my answer. I was on my knees at the side of my bed. Some clear insight popped into my mind. *My God,* I thought, *I'm still in the marriage, and I've finished a novel.* I guess that was his answer: *Stay.*

I had grown. I knew my wants and desires had to take second place to what was best for my sons. Alcoholics are notoriously selfish people. That selfishness has got to be reined in, and reined in hard.

Selfish, self-centered behavior breaks up countless families and damages countless children. When the decision to divorce is made in haste or is made because you're not happy, stop before you take action and think again. Find a way to get happy. I had to fix what was broken in me first. It would've made little sense to abandon my marriage and rush out, only to repeat the same dysfunctional patterns. The steps help point out patterns. People tend to do the same things over and over. They change the players, but the pattern stays the same, and they reap the same results: unhappiness ensues. Wherever I go, there I am. Some people never get that.

It was suggested to me to not make any decisions in my first year of sobriety. Women always tell other women who are in early sobriety and who are hell-bent on getting divorces to wait. We tell them to get rid of the guys that they're having affairs with and focus on their marriages. Quit drinking. Find a God or a power bigger than you. After you clean up your life, if things don't start to turn around after a year or two, then make a decision. Invariably, it has been my experience that many couples stay together after one spouse gets sober. Sometimes the other spouse will also get sober or get into Al-Anon. Beautiful relationships based on love, respect, and, yes, sobriety develop.

A year or two into sobriety, my mind was clear and sharp, and bits of gratitude seeped in. I was grateful to be a sober mother to my twins. I was grateful that I could feel so much love. I was no longer numb. The dull haze was gone.

The downside to my clear vision was that I saw all these thirty-something couples drinking themselves silly—and half of the time, these couples were fighting like crazy. One partner was always upset due to something the other partner did or didn't do. Alcohol was the one common denominator. Couples were hurt and angry over who was flirting with who. Couples fought over such and such bad behavior, all while sloshing back drinks.

I was glad to be out of the chaos. I noticed that when we went to parties, the first hour all the women looked lovely, but by the end of the night, not so much. There's nothing classy about a woman staggering around and slurring her words, mascara smeared around her eyes. One time I saw a woman wearing a cocktail dress lying on her back in someone's mini-mansion living room doing the alligator dance. I was grateful it wasn't me.

If you're someone who can't just drink a few drinks and be done, then maybe you can at least consider mindful drinking. I don't want to suggest that everyone needs to be a teetotaler. The truth is, if I could drink responsibly—one or two glasses of wine or a cocktail and then that's the end of that—I can tell you with 100 percent certainty I'd still drink. However, I had to get honest with myself; that sort of restraint was not to be for me, and it won't be for any alcohol-dependent person. When alcohol adversely affects your behavior, your decisions, your relationships, your marriage, or your parenting skills, it's time to face the truth and stop drinking.

No woman in her right mind would wear a pair of pumps over and over again if they created large blisters. Eventually, she would toss those babies out. It's the same with alcohol. When drinking blisters you up over and over, how insane is it to keep drinking? If drinking makes you a lesser person in any sort of way, why drink? There is nothing classy or fun about degrading yourself. It is so cool to be in control of your mouth and your manners. Now if I shoot my mouth off, I do it because it is a conscious choice. If I am wrong, I can make amends. I own my behavior. You don't have to keep giving away your power.

If you fight with your spouse or your friends, force your will onto your children, or make poor decisions when you drink, then why drink? Maybe the reason you keep drinking in spite of bad results is because you can't quit. Or maybe you can quit—for a while—but you can't stay stopped. All sorts of people quit drinking for a week, a month, or even many months. But if alcohol is a problem, you will always find your way back to the bottle unless you commit to sobriety.

If you go a step further and tell yourself the truth, you may even admit that your life revolves around alcohol quite a bit. When alcohol is front and center of every activity, that's a problem. When you find you have few hobbies or interests, that's a problem. When the thought of not having a drink sends you into an emotional spin, hmm . . . I thought you said it wasn't a problem?

I wasted a whole decade partying. I thought it was fun, and it was for a while. Eventually, though, I stifled my creativity, lost my dreams, and did nothing but talk about all the things I planned to do but never did. Drinking, bar hopping, brunching, or lunching usurped copious amounts of time. It wasn't until I got sober that I realized just how much time I wasted.

Early sobriety is raw. All these emotions that have been stuffed down and glossed over beg for some attention. That's where the steps come into play. There is a step to help you deal with every aspect of every situation in your life. Wow.

I had to learn how to apply those steps to my life—and slowly but surely, the steps became *part* of my life. They were as much a part of my life as breathing. I retrained my brain to think differently. My old thoughts and ways of reacting slowly dissipated. The women who entered my life, and all the friends that helped me find a new way to live and think, were keepers.

I loved taking a night or two to spend with a bunch of women at Marilyn's cabin. We all called it the farm. Scads of us piled into the place. We laughed; we cried—all of us were in various stages of sobriety. One time, a new woman came for the weekend . . . and we all knew she had struggled with sobriety. There she was, her big liver jutting out from underneath her blouse, trying to convince a room full of sober women that she'd been on the wagon and was doing a fine job. It's tragic, but funny, how alcoholics always think they can fool people. The only people they fool are themselves.

I continued to struggle with my marriage. I thought my husband needed to grow up. I felt he made decisions based on himself that were not always the best for our family. I ended up being the disciplinarian for our sons. I hadn't expected that.

Here's one example of our constant conflict: Our sons were seven years old, and we took them to Jackson Hole, Wyoming, to ski. For the skiers reading this, you know Jackson Hole is no joke. Half the blue and green runs are wicked enough for the average skier like me. My husband took our sons up the tram, dismissing all the signs that warned only expert skiers get off.

The boys learned to ski when they were three years old, and when they were around five or six years old they switched to snowboarding. They'd been all of a half dozen times in two years. Jean-Claude promised me he was taking the boys up the tram to have a look. I was done skiing for the day, so I sat at the base waiting for their return. A few hours later, I began to worry. The sunlight waned. Exhibition Run was the only way down the mountain off the tram—it was a steep black-diamond run. *Certainly he wouldn't take the boys down that. Plus, he doesn't ski that well.*

By five o'clock, it was almost dark. The scenario in my head told me they'd all slid off the mountain. They were buried under a drift. They were hurt somewhere. I needed to alert the ski patrol. If I still drank I would've raced into the lodge, swigged back a couple shots of Jack Daniels, ordered one more shot for the road, and then started screaming for the rescue helicopter.

I was furious. I was stunned at Jean-Claude's selfish behavior. *How could he cause me to worry like this just because he wanted to go down that run? What sort of a person would take inexperienced seven-year-olds up a mountain like that?*

Now sober, I found I had little tolerance for bullshit. Jean-Claude needed to grow up too. The difference was that he didn't have a program to help him. He wasn't changing as fast as I was. My problem was living with someone who now seemed reckless, irresponsible, and self-seeking. As of yet, we had little symmetry.

The sun slid behind the mountain. I stood and paced at the base. Through semi-darkness I heard loud whooshes. "Mom!" There my boys were, with ruddy cheeks and mile-wide smiles. Thank God. I gathered them up like a hen does her chicks. "So where's your father?" I asked.

"We lost him. He kept falling, and we couldn't stop."

Fifteen more minutes passed. Finally, Jean-Claude slid to a stop inches from my face. He was covered in snow, breathing hard, but exhilarated. I wanted to strangle him.

It was hard staying married. I'd watch him do things like pull out of the garage with a beer can between his legs and the kids in the car. I'd blow a gasket.

That sort of nonsense had to stop. When two people are drinking, poor decisions are made every day. When you have clear eyes and you watch the outrageous behavior swirling around you, it's hard not to judge, and I'd say to myself often, *But for the grace of God there go I.* Sometimes I felt like a policewoman, always working to stay one step ahead of people, like my sons' father, who sometimes made stupid decisions that could've had catastrophic endings. When you're in that mess, you don't see it. You think it's normal because so many well-educated, successful people exhibit unbelievably selfish behavior, and everyone cosigns on everyone else's bullshit.

I'd hear people say things like, "You're so much fun, but I bet you were really a riot when you drank. I wish I'd gotten to see that!" Such is the mentality of so many. Why is that?

Why do people love debauchery so much more than sanity? I don't get it, and perhaps I never will. I believe we need to quit glorifying all the destruction that heavy drinking leads to. We need more people to stand up and say, no, it is wrong to enjoy watching young women lose their power to drinks. We need more women to stand up and say, no, I prefer to act like a lady instead of a lush. There is nothing attractive about a drunk woman, yet too many people encourage and even long for their friends and family to drink with them.

I learned that it is none of my business what other people think about me. That right there is so true, and so freeing. The stronger I got, the more I learned to love me, and the less I cared what others thought.

I've worked with some women who say they want to get sober, but they stay stuck. They care too much about what their friends think. They don't understand the steps and can't figure out how doing the steps will help them. They recoil from heading down a path of which they can't predict the outcome. It's all about letting go. You have to at least believe that you don't know what's best and that you don't rule the world. Surrender is the epicenter of recovery.

Women worry they will lose their spouses and/or their friends if they sober up, and they also worry what their kids will think. (Your kids already know you're a lush. They will be thrilled to have sanity in the house. I promise.) Women have a hard time letting go. My pat answer is always: if your friends don't want what's best for you, you don't need those friends.

One day, my husband looked at me and said, "You're nothing like the girl I married." At the time, I'm not sure he meant that statement as a compliment, but I was beyond thrilled. That was the best compliment I ever received.

Anyone who wants a different life and is willing to work toward something better can have better. Change is possible, but it comes with a price. You have to be willing to pay the price of losing friends, maybe losing your marriage, and maybe losing everything. Most of the time, that doesn't happen, but you have to have that kind of willingness to succeed. Lack of willingness is one of the primary reasons people fail to recover. They want to do things their way. They don't believe or trust in a higher power. They want to run the whole damn show and orchestrate every last minutia of how things should play out, but, of course, they continue to get the same lousy results. You won't get different until you do different.

As the years slipped by, my husband changed too. He adjusted to the new me. He adored the new me. He was the first one to admit that had I not gotten sober, there would be no us. I never doubted how much he loved me, and we were both so grateful for all of the positive changes that had occurred. We went through a lot of turmoil, and we had to adjust, and readjust, and readjust some more.

It's amazing what you can do and understand when you don't have the addition of alcohol clouding your perspective.

My husband knew I didn't have a close relationship with my father, yet they got on well and bonded over their shared love of golf. By the time my husband met my parents, there were no more stampedes at home. All was calm, and my family appeared as ordinary as any other family, I guess. My father had changed, or perhaps he just kept a better lid on his rage. My mother was beautiful and strong.

My husband didn't, or maybe he couldn't, grasp how crazy my childhood was. It's one thing to listen to sketches of the past and another thing entirely to live it. How could he really know?

Recovery truly is a process. You don't wake up one day recovered. It may take years to recognize all the ways we can self-sabotage. Those destructive patterns and behaviors have to be recognized before they can be changed. I also had come to understand that I couldn't change all that I needed to change at once. I was told to release one objectionable behavior at a time, and of course, I had to ask God for help. I had run on self-will for so long, but slowly, I began to chart a new course.

~ 6 ~
Women and Alcohol: It's Complicated

ADDICTION OCCURS FOR A PLETHORA of reasons, but for me, the predisposition for addiction came from several directions: genetics, early childhood trauma, and the dysfunctional and flimsy bonds I had with my parents. However, I know alcoholics who came from stable loving homes; women have told me they had great parents, and still, for unknown reasons, they turned to alcohol.

The feeling of fear predominated my childhood. The intense, negative emotions I felt as a child with no coping skills demanded relief. Is it any wonder that when I discovered beer at the age of twelve I liked the feeling of escape it lent?

Here are four questions you can ask yourself to help you decide if you drink too much:

- When I drink, can I predict the outcome?
- When I drink, do I get into arguments?
- When I'm not drinking, do I think about drinking?
- When drinking, do I behave in ways that don't align with my morals?

Honest answers to those four questions will help lead you to the truth.

What would a grown-up do? Sometimes we roar through life and have no idea how to show up as an adult. All of the women in this book showed up for life in a less-than-adorable manner. It's not so much the things that happened to us in life that hurt us, it's our reaction to those things and the way we think about our struggles that caused all the pain.

If you think you'd benefit from not drinking but the thought of not drinking elicits a loud groan and an overwhelming sense of panic, keep reading. Maybe you will discover some shadowy but necessary truths about yourself.

Women who drink too much or abuse prescription or illegal drugs seem to possess one of several unhealthy mindsets, and most of those mindsets are governed by fear. Fear wears hundreds of different outfits: Fear may show up as a control freak who tries to micromanage everyone's life, including family, coworkers, lovers, spouses, and friends. This woman wants to control the uncontrollable. She is terrified of letting go. Fear may also show up as a perfectionist. This is the woman who fears she won't be good enough and genuinely wants people to like her. However, she may go about it the wrong way. She forces her will on people, places, and situations that she has no business trying to control. Then, when people push back, this same woman cries and wonders why everyone is so mean!

Fear may show up with low self-esteem, and it can manifest in other ways too. For example, I felt entitled to bitch about everyone and everything, without ever looking at my part in the chaos. Other people crave special attention just so they can feel normal.

Sure, women who don't drink may have some of these personality defects, but we need not worry about the women who can have one or two glasses of wine and be done for the month. We're talking about the woman riddled with deep-seated fears, emotions, and/or unresolved longings who has found her solution to be alcohol. This is the woman who has made alcohol an integral part of her day, an integral part of her life. In all of her relationships it is the third wheel. In all of her activities it is the one constant. At the end of the day, it is her anticipated reward. This is the woman who looks for ways to kick everything up a notch.

So what of the warped thought processes? There's the woman who may not even be aware that she allows others to make her decisions and then heaps blame on everyone's unsuspecting heads when things don't work out to her liking. Fear lives at the bottom of this behavior too. This woman fears she will make a mistake or make the wrong decision, and then what will people think? Part of the problem is this self-centeredness that tells her everyone is paying attention to what she's doing, when in fact they are not. People are preoccupied with their own lives. Most don't have time to worry about you.

The woman who fears taking responsibility for her decisions will claim the victim role because it frees her from accountability. She is the person of seemingly hollow bones—there's no substance there. This is also the woman who may even acquire vague ailments and go to the hospital. As long as she has an ailment, she doesn't have to take responsibility for herself—or, in some cases, for her children either. She has her own civil war raging inside her mind, and underneath all the drama is a scared girl who needs help. To the outside world, this woman appears childish, superficial, and immature.

Then there's the gal who fears she will never have enough security, stature, or contentment, so she grabs for more and more to help her feel secure. Her expectations are off the charts—she demands the outcome of her choice, and when she doesn't get it, you will pay. She hasn't learned to ask for what she needs, and instead she expects you to intuitively know what she needs and then provide, *tout de suite*!

She also believes that she deserves to have attention, all the accolades, all the help, and all of your time and energy. She wants the best house, the best car, the best jewelry, the best job, the best spouse, the best kids. Enough will never be enough. She takes the disease of more to a whole new stratosphere. No one can live up to her impossible standards. Eventually exhausted, even *she* can't keep up with her high standards. To the outside world this woman may appear entitled, vain, and narcissistic, when really she battles a deep insecurity. She thinks that having more of everything will fill the hole in her soul. She is also the mother who pushes her children to succeed so she can brag endlessly about their every small accomplishment in order to feed her otherwise low self-esteem.

A skewed perception of reality screams alcoholism. Alcoholics and addicts have a physical craving for alcohol in addition to a thinking problem that tells them they are fine. For the alcoholic or problem drinker, once the first drink is drunk, there is little hope that she will always be able to control the amount she will drink. Once that switch is flipped, she cannot always predict the outcome.

Alcohol easily passes over the blood–brain barrier and goes right to work on the cells in the central nervous system. For different people, the reaction and reaction times differ. Some women become mellow; others become more animated; still others become pushy or argumentative. Over time, tolerance increases, and it takes more and more alcohol to feel the desired effects.

The twisted mindsets and behaviors described play out in relationships and families all over the world. Most all of the hundreds (maybe thousands) of women that I have known, met, and listened to all agree that in order to recover, they had to first open their minds to the possibility that maybe they drank too much and maybe they had a skewed sense of reality.

Now on to the martyr: This is the woman who runs herself ragged. She does it all! She works too many hours. She cooks, cleans, chauffeurs kids, and does far too much for her family and for others, and the entire time she moans about her heavy workload. Poor me; pour me another drink. Life feels hard. She is overwhelmed with responsibility and feels that nothing will get done right if she doesn't do it herself. This woman needs a helping hand, but she won't ask for help. She never learned to stand up for herself or set firm boundaries. She never says no. The less time she has, the more she takes on and the more angry and resentful she becomes. Her overachieving ways send her racing toward a drink or a pill.

Some say *normal* is a setting on the washing machine, but I do know people who seem to have an innate grasp of life, like my friend Kim. I had no idea how to cope without having a drink at *it*, whatever *it* was. I had to learn to live life in small increments. Much of recovery is a matter of retraining your brain to think differently. I had to work at not projecting into the future. I had to work at letting go of everything that I had no control over. Most importantly, I had to get honest about my drinking. I had thought that drinking made my life easier and more fun. And for a short time, perhaps it did, but the reality is that drinking makes everything infinitely harder and sadder.

I know that in my family, just about all of the women are alcoholics. The two times in her life that my maternal grandmother drank—well, she drank the whole bottle and passed out. We've always known drama of some sort in our family, but it's amazing to see that as sobriety takes hold of us one by one, the drama recedes like water flowing through an unclogged drain.

Once my mother sobered up, the entire tone of our family dynamics changed. As she became strong, as mentioned, my father simmered way down. Sometimes it saddens me to think how different a trajectory all of our lives would've taken had my mother been sober and strong when we were young. I know my father's anger came from a place of fear. He couldn't accept his powerlessness over my mother's disease, and he became as sick as she was.

Women from affluent homes or those married to wealthy spouses may have a harder time getting sober and staying sober. Unless they have a coveted career, like the doctors in the forthcoming stories, people with money can take longer to hit bottom (though sometimes even a coveted career is not sufficient motivation to quit). When you have a financial structure that never collapses, there can be little motivation to change.

Money can be an alcoholic's or addict's worst enemy. It will keep her doing her thing until her liver goes out. She may quit if she has other consequences that mean something to her, or she may decide to act when that moment of clarity dawns, but most times, she'll just keep drinking.

All of the women that I selected to share their stories had relatively high bottoms. None of us were homeless. None of us went to jail except Marilyn, who spent one night there for a DUI. There is still the misconception that alcoholics are people wandering the streets wearing layered clothing and pushing shopping carts. This is not true at all. As I've mentioned previously, most alcoholics are functional and have jobs.

The women you'll meet in the stories all had jobs, relationships or marriages, homes, and cars, and, yes, even some had lots of gold jewelry and closets full of shoes. Some of our bottoms may not seem so low, but keep in mind that alcoholism, at least for me, was more about disintegrating internally while all the outside props still appeared in place. For most of us, from the outside looking in, you'd never guess that we led double lives.

Women like Lee and Grace sought out men to validate their existence. So many women get involved in bad relationships and pick the same type of man over and over again because they fail to realize that nothing changes—nothing changes. They continue to take themselves into these relationships, and the same insanity ensues.

My undocumented research in working with scads of women led me to conclude that most women who marry three or more times, if they're honest, will see that alcohol probably had a dominant role in all of those relationships.

Why is that? It's because most women with drinking problems refuse to look at themselves. They refuse to look at their behavior and would rather leave a relationship than quit drinking or change. Infidelity often is a part of the alcoholic's story.

Most women who drink too much can't stop on their own volition. However, if women understand what the early warning signs are, and if they can understand that the anxiety, depression, and lack of zeal for life could stem from the core issue of alcohol or pill misuse, they can seek help and recover before the destruction mounts.

I've worked in emergency rooms and psych wards for over twenty years. That's a lot of undocumented research; I have friends who work in hospitals all over the country. Their experiences mirror my own—substance abuse in one form or another contributes to an overwhelming amount of hospital admissions, either directly or indirectly.

What I've seen is that people end up in emergency rooms and psych wards because of substance abuse. The traumas, the wrecks, the falls, the esophageal varices, the bad livers, the cocaine-induced heart attacks, the fights, the shootings and stabbings, the depression, the anxiety, the generalized malaise that seems to overtake too many young people and sends them in search of antidepressants and disability checks—all too often, these have the common denominator of alcohol and/or drugs.

Women who complain of hypoglycemia (low blood sugar) might want to look at their drinking. Alcohol turns to sugar in the body. When your blood sugar suddenly drops, that's your body's way of saying, "give me sugar." For women who just quit drinking, we tell them to drink orange juice and put some honey in it. That craving they have for booze will lessen if they feed their bodies some sugar. Binge drinking can be one of the causes for hypoglycemia in women who aren't diabetic, and diabetics who drink uncontrollably court disaster, especially if they're brittle diabetics.

Recovery meetings can be found all over the world. They're free, and they work. Some people find sobriety in the church. Others have tried programs such as Moderation Management (MM), which asks people to set guidelines and women to keep to no more than nine drinks a week.[5] The National Institute on Alcohol Abuse and Alcoholism's guideline for women is no more than seven drinks a week. MM says they want to reach the early problem drinker who doesn't want to be labeled an alcoholic—but that panders to the denial and alcoholic ego that needs to be checked anyway.

Not labeling yourself an alcoholic when in fact you are an alcoholic nixes any chance for real recovery. Recovery is about getting honest. It's about squashing that inflated ego and scraping off the hubris that hides those character flaws that create mounds of havoc, and it's about breaking through the thick layer of denial. If a person could moderate, he or she wouldn't have an issue. Audrey Kishline, founder of Moderation Management, killed two people while in an alcoholic blackout.[6] Not calling problem drinking and alcoholism what they are kills innocent people.

Addiction causes changes in the brain. It's a real problem that has nothing to do with willpower, which is another misconception that must be smashed. There are people out there, many working in medicine, who still think alcoholism or drug addiction is just a matter of will power, morals, or the ability to say no. That fallacy does nothing to help the suffering. As chemical dependency counselor John C. points out in his upcoming story, "The saddest thing is when a person asks for help and they're pointed in the wrong direction."

Most addicts and alcoholics are engaging, bright, strong-willed, and irrepressible people. Who else could do what we do and keep getting back up for more? Unlike the bloody fighter in a ring who eventually goes down and stays down, we keep getting back up and back up and back up, ready to face off for yet one more round.

I believe that every addict and alcoholic is blessed with a moment of clarity. A sliver of sunlight will make a flash appearance, and the addict/alcoholic will either rise up and make changes or snuff out that moment of grace and keep going. I believe a miracle allowed me to see what I needed to see when I saw it—and I think it's even more remarkable that I took action. It still blows me away that I chose to get sober and stay sober before I became a daily drinker. I never had to *try* to quit drinking, because I quit drinking long before it became necessary. I thank God that I quit before I had consequences. I can tell you this: I didn't have much to do with it. I believe God wanted me sober so I could be a sober mother to my twins and a decent wife to my husband, and because he had books for me to write.

Though more and more knowledge is spread and as much as Hollywood has brought addiction and alcoholism into the light—and now we have the heroin epidemic plastered all over the news—it is still not enough. I'd like to impart that you don't have to wait until you're *tore up from the floor up* to seek help and make changes. You don't have to wait until your health has failed; your kids are embarrassed, disgusted, or harmed in some irrevocable way; and your second husband is racing out the door.

I sobered up because in that moment of clarity, I believed what my mother pointed out to me that morning in Dallas: I seemed to have the same problem she had. She noticed my love affair with alcohol before anyone else would've noticed. It takes one to know one. We see the drink problem in others long before they do or anyone else does.

I will always be grateful for my mother. She absolutely saved my life when she nudged me to question my drinking. She said something to the effect of, "Why not stop now and save yourself years of self-manufactured hell?" Great idea. Yes, I think I'll do that. I know she said as much if not more to my sister Violet, and the difference was that Violet refused to listen.

Granted, I didn't take to my mother's prodding right away, but she planted the seed. I've peppered the book with some trite but true sayings, and as repetitive as some words or phrases may sound, these short snippets can be the seeds of recovery that sprout, maybe even years down the line; people will recall phrases like "tore up from the floor up" more than they will remember eloquence. I drank for another year or so, but her words played in my head. Why go through life doing damage? Eventually, by the grace of God, I realized I could hop off the stage and end the show.

I know I'm the exception rather than the rule. For most, if you mention to them that they might have a drinking problem, you'll be met with resistance and even anger. That right there should tell a woman all she needs to know. Women who don't have a problem with alcohol won't get defensive when you talk to them about their drinking, nor will they axe you from any future gatherings, nor will they inwardly seethe or try to justify their drinking.

I have come to learn one truth: women who don't have drinking problems never get accused of having drinking problems. Twenty-eight years ago, when my own mother mentioned my drinking, she recognized a shift—it was in my behavior and the way I drank. When people start to mention your drinking, it's because they've seen a change; your actions are no longer isolated.

Your family, your friends, your employer—no one is going to tell you that they think you drink too much, unless of course it's true that you do. And when they do speak up, what other motive would they possibly have other than that they care?

Drinking and breast cancer: the correlation and adverse relationship between alcohol and the increased risk of breast cancer is not talked about enough. According to the Susan G. Komen foundation, ninety-eight studies have shown that women who drink alcohol have an 11 percent higher risk of getting breast cancer than women who don't. Women who have two to three drinks per day have a 20 percent higher risk of getting breast cancer than women who don't drink.[7]

According to the Center for Disease Control and Prevention (CDC), excessive alcohol use can lead to fertility problems, miscarriage, stillbirth, and premature delivery. The CDC concurs that heavy drinking increases the risk of many types of cancer, including breast, colon, and liver cancer.[8] Because of our body chemistry, women can't break down alcohol as quickly as men. Alcohol abuse in women can cause long-term health problems. Why don't we talk about the truth more than we spread the lie that drinking is "fun"?

The media talks quite a bit about the violence and rapes that happen on college campuses. In 2015, Kelly Wallace of CNN did a story about incapacitated rape on college campuses, and she stated that "Nearly one in five women on college campuses in 2015 have been raped either by force or while incapacitated."[9] With this sort of knowledge firmly documented, why does society continue to glamorize excessive drinking? I know families who still play drinking games—parents partake with their grown children. Why encourage what can kill and destroy so many families? And what's with all the mother-daughter drinking? These are the sorts of questions we need to ask.

The core issue behind much of the violence that happens in society is due to alcohol abuse. Why isn't more said about ways that women can protect themselves? I'm not talking about karate or concealed-carry permits; I'm talking about the simple solution of not drinking to the point where you can't function. When one is incapacitated, there is zero equality. Once you've reached the point of slurred speech and stumbling gait, and even before those outward symptoms appear, you've handed over all of your power and rational thinking to someone who may be even drunker than you and who may lack scruples.

What could possibly be fun about a woman drinking to the point where she is helpless and has handed over all of her power, self-respect, and self-control to the vultures in society who can then do as they please? When you see it in black-and-white, it's outrageous, but no one wants to talk about how alcohol and drugs are the one common denominator in much of the terror and mayhem that occurs on college campuses and across our country. If a person cannot go out and have a *few* drinks and enjoy their friends and the evening, if he or she only drinks to get drunk or drinks more than he or she intended, then there is a problem with the way that person drinks.

Our culture supports ubiquitous alcohol consumption. Advertisers have convinced the masses that without the adjunct of alcohol, they will have little fun. Why do we have to continue to believe that lie? Why can't the script be changed? Instead, let's tout the slogan, *Do life!* Get out there and live. Plant a garden, read a book, engage in physical activity, ride the rapids, take a class, learn to sculpt, or go to the range and work on your marksmanship.

We, as a society, have ignored the fact that when women abuse alcohol, it acts as a violent oppressor. Would society tolerate another person incapacitating women the way alcohol does? Surely not. Society encourages drinking and binge drinking through the constant ads portraying slim, pretty caricatures of women touting alcohol. Advertisers want women to associate alcohol with fun and romance. We see drinking all over television and in the movies. Parents condone and even partake in drinking with their teenage and adult children, even with toddlers running around. Moms get together for playdates with their small children and sit there drinking wine. Advertisers portray alcohol as seductive and chic, but the truth is—I'll say it again—for many people and families, alcohol demeans, destroys, and debilitates.

Videos of inebriated women are splashed all over YouTube. People watch these videos and laugh. But why do we laugh when we should be crying that anyone would think it's funny to see a beautiful woman or young teen passed out with a piss-wet crotch? These women went out for the night expecting glitter and unicorns but ended up with a ghoul. Time and time again, they end up vomiting at the curb, passed out, or in some compromised position, and no one bats an eye. The behavior is brushed off because they're "just having a good time."

Women justify their behavior as harmless because they maintain their grades, or because they still get up and jog. (This is a big one. Many women feel that if they can get up in the morning and jog, then there is nothing wrong with their drinking.) It's one thing to look okay, but at some point, wouldn't it be great to feel okay too?

St. Patrick's Day on college campuses is the high holy day of them all, the feast of the deep chalice and green beer. We glorify these drinking holidays, but the misery that comes to those who don't have an off button can impact them for the rest of their lives.

When I worked in the ER, on weekends we'd see numerous college students come in with alcohol poisonings and drug overdoses. There were rapes. Car accidents. Always, drugs and/or alcohol was/were onboard. A few times the endings were tragic.

During the first few years of my sobriety, I used to go to the women's workhouse. There I saw why my decision to quit drinking at twenty-nine was indeed a great decision. I got to see and hear first-hand what happened to women who refused to acknowledge their substance-abuse problems.

It's a well-known fact that alcoholism and addiction ends one of three ways: jail, institution, or death. My mother and sister had multiple stints in mental institutions. The women I visited were in jail. I talked with many of them who had already lost mothers, sisters, and daughters, all due to substance abuse—the unlucky ones who died before they landed in jail or the psych ward.

We took meetings to these women, and I got to know their stories. Some came from affluent homes, and some had known good careers and loving families, but somewhere along the way, they took a wrong turn and never found their way back. Others were raised in drug-infested environments and never stood a chance. Others suffered abuse of some sort, and those that had been sexually abused seemed to have the most difficult time finding peace. The alcohol and drugs were the only way they could cope with what had happened to them.

Prostitution was another reason many of the women were in jail—they needed money to fuel their habits. Some inmates were drunk when they stabbed their baby's daddy, drunk when they killed two people in a motor vehicle crash, drunk when they set fire to their spouse's car, drunk when they beat the hell out of their lover. These women had already hit low bottoms, but sadly, few of them were done drinking and drugging. I'd hear them say they wanted to get sober, yet they'd do their time, get out of jail, and a few months later they cycled through again.

To think bad things only happen to women who come from impoverished backgrounds is to think the tides aren't governed by the moon. Alcohol is that jealous lover who becomes selfish to the extreme and consumes all of your time. Alcohol gives you false courage, strength, and a feeling of power. It tells you it's not hurting you. This best friend will allow you to lose everything of value and not give a care. Perhaps it is time to find a new best friend.

~ 7 ~

Flag's A-Flyin' and I'm Still Lyin'

MOST PEOPLE THINK that if you have a problem with alcohol, or with life, it means you're the forty-year-old who rides a bike through the drive-through window, or that you're the drug dealer whose only overhead is baggies. Though that's what people picture when they think of drug addicts and alcoholics, as previously mentioned, the vast majority of alcoholics have lives that look nothing like that at all.

For example, a lot of women only drink after their children are in bed. And there are a number of women who believe that since they can put drinking off until late in the day or early evening, they don't have a problem.

If you've ever tried to control, conceal, or limit your drinking in any way, you probably already have reason to be concerned. If you're wondering if you may drink too much or if alcohol or drugs plays an important role in your life, ask yourself questions such as: Have I tried to limit my drinking to weekends only? Have I already switched beverages? (Maybe you stopped drinking tequila and switched to beer or wine.) Or have you sworn off the bourbon and switched to vodka because you believe it doesn't smell? Are you overly sensitive and make everything about you? Is your only hobby sitting at cafés and restaurants? And (this is a big one) at family gatherings, do you always have to have an emotional outburst? Are you mean-spirited and controlling? Emotional immaturity is part of alcoholism.

What precedes complete demoralization are the symptoms and patterns of alcoholism or problem drinking: cloudy perceptions of reality, erroneous thinking, and plenty of rationalizing will already be present. You may not be aware that more and more of your thoughts are preoccupied with thoughts of drinking. By Wednesday, you can hardly wait for the weekend, because at this point you only drink on weekends, but almost every day, you think about drinking. Eventually, on Monday, you'll start to salivate.

Early warning signs are sly and insidious. Just like that morning in Dallas when I sat on the balcony, popped a beer, and painted my nails; I saw nothing wrong with the behavior. However, my mother saw plenty wrong. She'd been there and done that and had no choice but to sound the alarm.

I can't say that I remember ever attending a party, a wedding, or any sort of function that didn't involve alcohol. If offered the choice between a restaurant that did or didn't serve alcohol, regardless of the food, I'd pick the place where I could have a drink. Even though I'd rarely refuse an offer for a cocktail, I had yet to consider that my relationship with alcohol was abnormal.

Women have pressures firing at them from all sides and can use those pressures as an excuse to justify their drinking. Some women find parenting stressful. Others have to deal with small or sick children, or aging parents. Still other women believe they have to drink to fit in socially, or to fit in at their jobs. Professionals and sales reps make excuses for why they drink: Everyone drinks at functions. It's hard to go to conferences and socialize if you don't hang out at the bar. But the truth is that most people wouldn't notice, nor would they care if you only ordered club soda. Believe it or not, people are not focused on you. I was amazed when I quit drinking how few people cared if I drank. The only people that ever had an issue with me not drinking were those who drank quite a bit themselves.

Other early warning signs may be:

- You obsess over alcohol and frequently crave a drink.
- Vacations are a good excuse for all-day drinking.
- Amazon packages show up at the house, but you have no memory of ordering anything.
- You wake up and check your phone to see who you drunk dialed or drunk texted last night.
- You complain of hypoglycemia.
- You don't have any sober friends. All your friends drink just like you.
- You're smitten with wine, and, no, you don't work as a sommelier.
- You frequently drink in front of your young children, and you think nothing of polishing off a bottle or two of wine with your friends while your young toddlers play at your feet. (Alcoholics think this is fine, but social drinkers do not mix wine with child-rearing.)
- After a few drinks your personality changes.
- You spend a lot of money on wine.
- You keep getting divorced and remarried. (Anyone can make a mistake . . . but three, four, or five of them?)
- You find yourself drinking earlier and earlier in the day, and you waste precious days each month nursing hangovers.
- You frequently post on Facebook, and in every picture you're drinking or drunk.
- Every occurrence under the sun demands a celebratory or conciliatory cocktail.
- You cannot go to your child's sporting event without a Solo cup or travel cup filled with some alcoholic beverage.

- You've gained weight, but you refuse to stop drinking all those calories. You'd rather be miserable, overweight, or starve than give up the wine or cocktails.
- You go to the doctor in hopes of scoring Ativan, Xanax, or Klonopin. You then schedule lunch with your girlfriends to talk about your anxiety disorder and PTSD.
- You dread going places where you can't drink with impunity.

All of the above scenarios don't have to apply for you to consider the possibility that you have a problem. Alcoholism/addiction is self-diagnosed, because someone else pointing out that you may have a problem will most always be met with resistance.

If you are the woman who makes excuses for unacceptable behavior (such as, "You'd drink too if you had to deal with my kids, job, spouse, significant other, and parents"), perhaps you may want to be honest with yourself and admit that the real cause of your drinking is that you like the way alcohol makes you feel, and that even though you need to quit, you don't want to.

Another way to know if you're sliding downhill is when you promise yourself that you'll never do certain things, but you fall short of the standards and keep lowering the bar. When you miss the mark, you rationalize and say, *Well okay, it was only that one time.* When your life tends to get smaller and smaller and you spend less and less time on your hobbies—sports, scrapbooking, going to the gym, baking, cooking, gardening, reading, running—all because you need to make more time for drinking and wine tastings, you may be in trouble.

I know women who convinced themselves they drank because they had problems, when the truth is they had all those problems because they drank. Still other women admit they like to drink because it makes them feel better, prettier, funnier, smarter, skinnier—whatever the case may be. After the first drink, whatever bugged you a minute ago has fled, and the hole in the soul doesn't feel so gaping.

When you turn to NyQuil, Benadryl, or sleeping pills because you ran out of wine and you need to get to sleep, that's not a good sign. A lot of women complain that they can't sleep at night. We tell women in the program that no one has ever died from lack of sleep. Your brain will eventually learn to shut itself off. That committee in your head will quiet down. Be patient. If you exercise, avoid caffeine, and maybe listen to some soothing music, eventually your body will heal and learn to fall asleep rather than pass out. It's a wonderful thing to fall asleep and wake up, rather than to pass out and come to.

Here are some other indications that alcohol may be a problem:

- There is drama in all of your relationships. (The one common denominator is you.)
- You think all women are bitches. Your close friends are all males.
- You have an acute fear of failure, and you drink to erase that feeling of impending doom.
- When people don't do what you want them to do, your go-to coping skill is to have a drink *at* them.
- You feel inferior in spite of great accomplishments.
- Enough is never enough—of anything: money, love, attention, success, etc.
- Everything you do is full speed ahead.
- You like that buzzed feeling. You chase that buzzed feeling a lot.
- You assume the victim role often. You like the attention you get from being the victim, and you wallow in self-pity.
- You mask emotional pain with alcohol/drugs/food/sex.
- You understand the sentiment *treat me special so I can feel normal.*
- You are selfish and self-centered.

- You participate in activities such as art and wine, volleyball and beer, painting and vodka. You do these activities because of the alcohol involved, not because you love the activities.
- You bring your own stash to places and functions that don't serve alcohol.
- You promise yourself you will only have one or two drinks, but you frequently miss that mark.
- You can't quit drinking even for a few months. If you do manage to quit, you think about alcohol every day.
- You hide alcohol in your purse.
- You pre-drink/pregame, and you justify those pre-party drinks.
- You lie to cover up mishaps that occurred while drinking.

Alcohol is not the sole problem. As you can see from the list above (and believe me, this list is not all-inclusive), the behaviors have more to do with thinking and craving alcohol than they do with actually drinking alcohol. It's helpful not to focus on quantity.

Alcoholism is just a symptom. The disease is nebulous because it can't be pinpointed on an X-ray. Alcoholism manifests as a pervasive soul sickness of sorts. The disease causes people to constantly lower the bar. Each one of us has a moral compass, but the alcoholic's moral compass goes haywire. Remember the reports of navigational equipment doing odd things while going through the Bermuda Triangle? For alcoholics, alcohol is our Bermuda Triangle.

In the untreated alcoholic/addict or problem drinker, unhealthy emotions pile up: unresolved anger, resentments, unmanageability, unforgiveness, fear—whatever the case may be. All of this emotional baggage and misguided thinking grows and swells in the mind. Someone with the inclination to become alcoholic will do what comes naturally; they'll drink to quell those ill feelings.

The first step of any twelve-step program is to admit that you're powerless over whatever vice it is that you want to squash.

The first step reads, "We admitted we were powerless over alcohol—that our lives had become unmanageable."[10] I knew without a doubt my life was unmanageable, but it took me a solid year of going to meetings and choking on the idea of alcoholism before I could get honest enough with myself to see that I was also powerless. Drinking was a symptom of my disease. Alcohol was not the total sum of the problem.

The myth that alcoholism has to do with quantity is just that—a myth. Most people, through no fault of their own, are ignorant to this important distinction. People talk to me all the time about their wayward friends and family members who drink too much, but they almost always caveat their concern with, "But they can't be alcoholic because they don't drink every day," or, "They only drink beer." By now you know that all of those protests are flawed thinking. Loss of control, or the maddening quest to try to control one's consumption, is far more indicative of alcoholism than quantity.

Alcohol shaped all of my decisions. It determined where I'd go and who I spent time with. It turned me into a snarky bitch. It robbed me of my resolve, determination, energy, and direction. I kept drinking because I liked the way alcohol made me feel: better. Alcohol numbed whatever feeling I didn't like at the time. Plus, I thought that to quit drinking meant a dull life. I couldn't have been more wrong.

The twisted personality traits that turn us into problem drinkers and alcoholics are present *long* before the alcohol takes over. Normal people have some of these feelings too, but again, they do not use drugs/eat/screw/drink over them. Normal people also don't question their drinking, and they don't feel shame and guilt over their drinking. Family members don't whisper about their drinking. Normal people don't sit in bars contemplating whether or not they drink too much. Normal people are out doing things that alcoholics only think and talk about doing but never get around to actually doing because they're too busy drinking, brunching and lunching, and talking about their big plans. Normal people find healthier ways to manage their feelings. That is where the alcoholic or potential alcoholic is different. We don't manage anything; instead, we drink, and we only think we are managing.

Most problem drinkers are controllers. They want to control the people, places, and things that they have no control over. If everyone tells you you're a control freak, you may want to have a look at your drinking/eating/gambling. I have yet to meet an alcoholic/addict who wasn't beaten down and exhausted by trying to control the uncontrollable.

I've known women with alcohol problems who will cling to so-called hobbies or run a marathon just to prove they don't have a drinking problem. Those heroic efforts should tell you something right there. Normal people don't get defensive about their drinking. The woman with a budding problem gets extremely defensive, and then sets out to prove wrong everyone who ever questioned her drinking.

Potential alcoholics lie to themselves, but most don't even know they're lying. Here's a glimpse of how denial might work: Walking between the motorcycles at bike night while drinking a beer is not a hobby, but the alcoholic or problem drinker will say, "Oh, but we must go to bike night. I love looking at the bikes. I want to learn how to reupholster the seats and tear apart the engine. Just being there inspires me." *Gulp. Gulp. Gulp.*

Or, "My hobby is cooking. I must go to brunch! I must go to lunch! I must go to dinner! They serve wine, right?" And all the while this person pretends to deconstruct the various dishes while drinking mimosas, Bloody Marys, gin and tonics, wine, or beers. That, ladies and gentlemen, does not constitute a hobby. We can lie to ourselves in a million different ways. Those are just two examples.

Alcohol is often the underlying reason why people become disenchanted with their spouses, hence the reason some alcoholics have multiple marriages. The alcoholic personality will blame everyone and everything else on the unhappy state of their affairs, but they fail to look first at their drinking, or themselves. So many young couples start off their relationships and marriages saturated in alcohol. A few years later the novelty wears off, the drinking is a staple in their lives, and both parties view the relationship through pickled vision. There's no clear direction or solution. They start blaming each other. Unhappiness ensues, along with resentment and unreasonable expectations.

When the reality of marriage doesn't match the idyllic visions in their heads, alcoholics may want to bail, or worse, find hook-ups to reassure them they are still so wonderful. If you need to blame something for your unhappiness, look in the mirror and look at your drinking. Start there first.

I'd encourage anyone thinking to end her marriage and fracture her family to first remove alcohol and drugs from the equation. If you can't give up your alcohol for six months to a year (without thinking about it every day), then you have your answer right there as to why the relationship or marriage is probably failing. Alcoholism breeds unhappiness. So often alcohol is the culprit behind the visit to the attorney's office, but women will search for any number of things to blame except the drinking. Heaven forbid they give up the wine.

My God, what will people think if I don't drink? Why does society continue to encourage drinking when for so many it does so much harm? Why don't we ask these sorts of questions more often?

We can't talk about early symptoms of alcoholism without talking about anxiety and depression. So many budding alcoholic women complain of depression. They run to the doctor, he or she starts them on antidepressants, and a long and often-maddening cycle begins. Some women become suicidal. They have these thoughts while ingesting alcohol, Xanax, Ativan, Klonopin, and Adderall. Women blame their depression on everything—and I mean everything—but the alcohol and pills. They so badly want the diagnosis of anxiety or depression, which gives them a green light to keep using.

Alcohol acts as a depressant. Why would a sane person continue to drink if she feels depressed? This is one place where the alcoholic riddle starts. The person would much rather run to the doctor, get on antidepressants, then race back to the doctor—multiple times—to whine and complain that the antidepressants don't work, but it never occurs to her to stop drinking. There are women out there who believe they are depressed because their son or daughter has ADD. There are women whose mothers died—many years ago—but who are still depressed over those deaths, or they say they have anxiety or PTSD.

Women expect doctors to fix them, along with their bad marriages, difficult children, and generalized unhappiness, or they expect doctors to quell the raging thoughts in their heads. Doctors are not magicians. They cannot rid anyone of the hundred forms of unhappiness they feel. The list of symptoms and complaints can get quite long. The doctors write prescriptions because they don't know what else to do. This practice of throwing pills at the problem is often the start of a long and painful journey, just as we saw with my mother.

Of course some women do suffer from depression, and for some, medication is necessary and helpful. However, what I've seen far too often is that women who drink heavily also complain about depression, and doctors rush to start them on antidepressants or anti-anxiety medications instead of suggesting that they quit drinking. Alcohol is a depressant. If you suffer from depression, it only makes sense to eliminate the obvious. In addition, I believe that women with depression would benefit if doctors took a more holistic approach.

If the person is an alcoholic or a potential alcoholic, it's almost a guarantee that they will lie about their drinking, so this compounds the problem for the doctor. These women will blame their depression on everything but the primary cause—alcohol or antianxiety medication. The cure for this sort of depression should be a prescription to go volunteer, go help someone else, go exercise, eat right, do anything to get out of yourself and out of your own head, and, for God's sake, leave the cork in the bottle.

In other cases, such as situational depression, it can be perfectly normal to feel depressed: death, job loss, injury, family problems, grief, sickness, severe disappointment—any significant life upheavals can cause depression. In most people, the depression eventually lifts, and life goes on. Or maybe they do need to see a doctor to help get through the crisis. There is a difference between situational depression and being depressed *just because*.

Only you can determine the cause of your depression, but keep in mind that lying to yourself about any substance abuse can set a lifetime of misery into motion.

~8~

What Your Kids Say about You and Your Drinking

DO YOU WANT TO PARTY, or do you want to parent? It's a fair question that every woman should ask herself before she makes the decision to become a mother. Honest answers to that question would produce fewer unhappy, confused children in the world. You can't be present in the world and not see the dysfunctional, ineffective parenting that takes place. Our children need role models and continue to suffer because of poor parental decisions.

Women fill multiple roles. We are the mothers, the nurses, the teachers, the chauffeurs, the troubleshooters. Women are more valuable than any CEO. The task of shaping the next generation is monumental; it takes creativity and stamina to run a family. We are the glue, and when that glue melts, the family often melts too. We need to restore the idea that there is no more important job than that of shaping the next generation. How did we as a society get so far off the mark that we continue to belittle women who choose to stay home with their children? There is no more important role.

Of course there are children who go astray in spite of decent parenting, but we can't neglect the fact that parenting plays a huge role in how our children will function as adults. Somewhere along the way, the role of mother has been minimized and marginalized. Here again, we need a shift in the way we think as a societal whole.

Take Fiona, the ER doctor who you'll meet in one of the upcoming stories. She knew she had a problem with alcohol, but she rationalized that her drinking and use of anti-anxiety medication wasn't hurting anyone.

Alcoholism/addiction, even just problem drinking, affects the whole family. A broken bicycle spoke causes the wheel to wobble, just as an ineffective or sick mother causes the whole family to wobble.

One woman I know lived the good life—she didn't work a day outside of the home. She had the resources to stay home with her brood of children, but because she had the money, she opted to hire babysitters to raise her children while most days she ran off to hobnob with her gal pals. All of her children have substance-abuse issues or are medicated for one reason or another. There is no pill that will fix poor parenting; addictive, dysfunctional, and selfish people do not, and cannot, raise emotionally and mentally healthy children.

There are women who appear to lead stable lives, but they're only sleepwalking through life because so much of their time is spent in their own heads. Fiona was the mom who transported her kids to all the necessary places: she made sure they got to soccer practice and music lessons, and she showed up for the school play. She thought she was a good parent. However, once she got sober, she realized that ferrying kids to functions didn't constitute parenting.

I know countless women who felt they were decent parents until they quit drinking and realized they had been emotionally unavailable and self-absorbed to the nth degree, and they regret that they were never fully present in their children's lives. Like Marne says in her story, "I had regrets, and of course, the most painful regrets had to do with my children. Although I didn't drink all that much during the years I raised them, I wasn't fully present. I was so mired in my own misery, licking my own wounds, that I wasn't present emotionally for them."

Grace, in her story, makes a point of saying she was glad she didn't have a child—with all the moving around and men in and out of her life, certainly all that drama would've scarred any kid.

We need to be mindful and honest with ourselves. The world needs more adults; there are a lot of people running around dressed up as adults, but they don't act like adults. I can say from experience that neither one of my parents knew how to be the adult. Neither one of them had good coping skills. It wasn't just my mother's alcoholism that was detrimental. It was all of it—and although I believe my parents did the best they could, they were never mindful of what they modeled. Back in the day, *mindfulness* wasn't a buzzword like it is now, but the concept of cleaning up your own life so you have something to give is timeless. Our kids deserve better.

If given a choice, no child would choose to grow up in a home ruled by alcoholic madness, or to have parents that lack emotional maturity and stability. Millions of kids flounder because from early childhood they're stuck in unhealthy environments, and they have no say when it comes to their parents' behaviors. Consider that you can't go to a toddler's or small child's birthday party anymore without seeing more bottles, cans, and solo cups than balloons and cupcakes. When did this shift occur? Or consider the grandparents who liberally imbibe and then want to babysit their grandchildren. Their homes are stocked with alcohol; everywhere you look there's booze and more booze. So what do we do? Allow another generation to be brought up thinking that alcohol must always be invited into each and every day?

According to Child Welfare Information Gateway, the National Survey on Drug Use and Health (NSDUH) estimated that between 2002 and 2007, 8.3 million kids were living with at least one parent who abused substances.[11] That was a long time ago. Those numbers have only risen.

An even-sadder note is the fact that because of the mushrooming heroin problem in our country, more and more children are entering foster care because both of their parents have lost custody due to substance-abuse issues or because both parents have died from overdoses. And lest we forget, most heroin addictions begin with alcohol and/or pill use.

We must advocate for the children. On Facebook there are websites that glamorize and joke about moms needing alcohol and pills to raise their children. Hundreds of thousands of women "like" these pages. Why aren't there Facebook pages with titles like "Crazy, Cool Moms Who Can Cope and Kick It with Their Kids"?

I would be ashamed if my sons saw me post to pages titled "Moms Who Need Wine" or "Moms Who Drink and Swear." What sort of message does that send to your child? When did classy, calm, and confident quit being cool? How many more children do we need to hear say, "I get to watch Disney tonight because Mom and Dad will be busy doing beer shots."

Social media touts excessive drinking, and it's shocking to me how many people applaud this behavior. There are apps that are animated so you can post pictures of yourself raising the glass. I saw on Facebook that February 18 was nominated as a day to drink wine. Seriously, do people that drink too much already need another excuse for a tryst with wine?

Why do we glamorize drinking and question the teetotalers like they're doing something wrong? As a society, we need a cataclysmic shift in the way we think about alcohol.

There are too many women whose focus is to get through the workday so they can go home and have a drink. Or they grit their teeth to get through the week so they can drink with their friends over the weekend. Some may justify their drinking by telling themselves they only drink while cooking. Others may stop for a cocktail on their way home from work, and then that one drink turns into three or four.

I talked to one mom, Lindsey, who shook her head in disbelief when she told me about the time she went to pick up a friend of her daughter. The mother of her daughter's friend invited Lindsey into the house and offered her a glass of wine. When she declined, the other mother reassured her that she didn't mind if Lindsey had a few glasses of wine before taking the girls shopping, but again, Lindsey refused to partake.

When I met Lindsey, she'd quit drinking about seven months earlier, but at the time of the incident, she still drank. "There I was, the alcoholic, but what was that woman's excuse? No way did I feel right about drinking and driving those girls around."

Let's not forget that the impressionable twelve-year-olds looked on and witnessed the whole exchange, and of course that doesn't translate well when four years later you instruct your now-driving teenager not to drink and drive. Are we that desensitized to doing the right thing, or are we just selfish?

Lindsey, now a recovering alcoholic, was shaken by the incident. I hated to tell her that not much has changed. In fact, it's getting worse. Mothers camped out in kitchens and on decks drinking and socializing is nothing new, and after four hours of wine coolers they hop in their cars to go pick up the kids from the movies or the junior high school dance. Couples stroll through parks at midday with red Solo cups and toddlers. Women guzzle two glasses of wine minutes before they walk down the aisle to say "I do."

As a whole, I think we have become desensitized to our actions; no one wants to be the cloud of gloom settling over the party and speak up against what goes on, but at some point, doesn't it have to be more about the kids than about the mommy party?

What we model to our children is important; it helps to be mindful of our behavior. My mother used to always say, "You don't have to teach your children a thing; they'll do what you do." She was right about that one! *Gulp, gulp . . .*

I met another young mother who told me that she was sick of the circuitous rat race, and she decided she needed help. Someone had told her to go to the twelve-step meetings. At one meeting, she stated, "I'm a functional alcoholic. I know that. I've been drinking since I was fourteen years old. But my kids never missed a function or a sporting event. I drove them and their friends wherever they needed to go, but I always had a coffee mug full of something besides coffee with me. I'm a soccer mom; that's what we do."

The problem is that for many women, once that first drink is drunk, the rest of the evening becomes about drinking. Even worse, the kids often start doing their own drinking and drugging. Why wouldn't they? The parents are oblivious to what they model every single day. Everyone's parents drink. Right? These kids see it everywhere they go. They hear parents joke and romanticize their drinking and substance abuse, and then later some of these same parents wail in agony if their kids become addicted.

Another young mother confessed that she knew she had a problem because as soon as her kids left the house, she started to drink. "I figured if I was home alone drinking I must be an alcoholic."

Parents exhaust themselves to make sure their kids go to the right schools and have the right friends and play the right sports and go to the right sports camps and achieve, achieve, achieve, yet how many parents stop and look at themselves? Some parents continue to look outside of themselves for the secret to raising good kids, but here's the truth: maladaptive women will likely raise maladaptive children. The secret is *you*. Your kids need you to be a parent and pay attention to what's going on in their lives, which is hard to do if you're always thinking about the next party, the next glass of wine, and your whole life is all about you. Children want and need parents with stable minds and stable emotions who can model good coping skills and healthy habits. And as I can tell you from personal experience, when a child looks up at her mom who has been drinking, she feels a combination of confusion, fear, and disgust.

I have friends who teach in both public and parochial schools. Below are things either they've heard students say or I've heard kids say through the years of working with alcoholic women:

- "She gets home from work and stays on the computer with her wine."
- "No one ever talks to me."
- "She drinks wine and acts weird."
- "Mom is sleeping on the bathroom floor again."

- "Mommy drank wine, and then she fell."
- "She cares more about her boyfriend than she does me."
- "She shouldn't be smoking weed, so I took it."
- "I'm sick of all the boyfriends she lets come over."
- "My mom gets her hair done and goes to the gym. That's all."
- "We never do anything together."
- "She looks stupid when she drinks."
- "She buys wine every day and drinks it all night."
- "She's always too tired to go watch my games. I think wine makes her sleepy."
- "I like her until she starts drinking, and then she's mean and yells at us."

Some of these comments are directly related to alcohol. Others relate to the selfish behavior and poor choices women make when alcohol becomes an integral part of their lives. These are some other things kids have said when things were especially bad at home:

- "I knew she wouldn't come to the parent conference because all day yesterday she was drunk."
- "She told me she wouldn't drink if I wasn't so bad."
- "I got between my mom and dad so he wouldn't hit her, so he hit me instead."
- "My mom smokes dope."
- "We didn't get Christmas presents because she spent all the money on beer."
- "It's embarrassing to see her drunk."
- "She thinks she's cool, but she's not."
- "She says we'll do things, but then she drinks and we never do anything."

- "She doesn't know how to cook because she can only open bottles and cans."

Women are not only harming themselves; their children are stranded in the crossfire of all their drunk drama: divorces, fighting, improper role modeling, and dysfunctional relationships. Women who drink to excess set a bad example all the way around. I can say that with authority because when my mother drank, she was a lousy role model. Passed out in the garden, she couldn't teach us a thing. Pandemonium ruled in our house because my mother was incapable of maintaining any sort of structure. Violence and chaos breeds fear. Children have few coping mechanisms to deal with that fear, so they too often start using substances at a young age in order to cope. Then add emotional neglect and physical abuse—not a good recipe for producing well-balanced adults.

A few years ago I was with my family in Chicago to celebrate my son's engagement. My other son's adorable twenty-something-year-old girlfriend commented about the group of seven or eight women we spotted in the lobby of our hotel. I estimated the women were all in their late thirties to early forties, dolled up in miniskirts or sundresses, stilettos, and painted faces. They had drinks in hand, and like a pack of wild ponies, they tried to arrange themselves for a group picture. My son's girlfriend quipped, "They look like a bunch of washed-up Tinkerbells!"

Here again I think back to my mother. She was a beautiful woman, but what was she thinking, getting all gussied up to prowl the bars—with her daughter, no less?

It's too true that if you're still running the bars in your forties, you look like a barfly, and you look ridiculous trying to act twenty years old again. As women, we need to be mindful and ask ourselves, *Is this who I want to be?*

I've observed one too many mothers hand their daughters' another cocktail when both of them should have stopped drinking three hours ago. I feel deeply sad when I see these mother-daughter duos drinking themselves silly, while often the mother, oblivious to her daughter's saturated liver, thinks nothing of handing over another glass of wine. Does she not recognize her daughter's slurred speech, or is she also too drunk? After all, who else would Mom drink with? It breaks my heart. Alcoholism is blind.

Women who drank while parenting and then sobered up all say that their biggest regret was that they were not the parent that they could've been or would've been had they not drank. I've seen the pain in their eyes. They can never recapture the lost years and make up for the mistakes, the shoddy behavior, or the self-absorption and emotional immaturity that blinded them to anyone but themselves. The fact that they will never get another chance to raise their kids has not been lost on them. Most of them realize they didn't have to pull all of that shit. Seventy percent of it would have been enough; thirty percent of it should've been enough.

Kids deserve to be kids. They don't want to hear about your awful marriage, your lousy boyfriend or girlfriend, your catty friendships, or your job woes. Nor do kids want to deal with your insecurity or the way you use them or their accomplishments to bolster your low self-esteem. Kids most certainly don't want to deal with your substance abuse, the way your mood changes when you're drinking or not drinking, and your hangovers on Saturdays and Sundays. Children don't deserve to be your protector either, all because you can't function as a clear-headed responsible adult because of your drinking or recreational drug use. Codependence is created when kids grow up taking care of the adults in their life. Some believe that codependency absolutely precedes addiction.

Emily, the daughter of Fiona, lent her view on growing up with a mother in active alcoholism:

> *I have a few memories tied to mom's alcohol use. Her leaning against the counter in the kitchen, drink in hand, explaining to me that she knew she drank too much, but she definitely was not an alcoholic.*

My mother was in fact steady. Her emotions never ran high or low. My brother and I used to laugh about the little smile she'd get when she was drunk. We still do the impression of her smiling with her eyes half closed, her head wobbling back and forth.

I think she was there for us to take us where we needed to go. I later learned she drove us to our appointments and functions with wine in a travel cup. I hated that even though she was around, I never felt a connection. Mom was always that wineglass-in-hand figure with one foot in the background of my life.

The biggest crime of my mom's drinking is that it kept her operating at a shallow level. She disassociated from life, from us kids.

Compared to the deep connection I feel with her now, my childhood memories are colorless in comparison. While she more or less supported me during her alcoholic years, she never challenged me.

I cannot imagine my life without her now. Since she's gotten into recovery, she has become the strong, intelligent, beautiful woman that I knew she always was but never did see until she quit drinking. She now pushes and encourages me to live with honesty and integrity. My role model no longer hides behind a bottle or a glass.

Drinking is pervasive in our culture. Drinking has permeated the fabric of everything we do. In the last few years the term *day drinking* emerged—as if sitting around all day drinking should be celebrated. When I sat in a bar all day drinking, I called it *drinking*. Looking back, I see it for what it really was: a colossal waste of time, talent, and energy. I accomplished nothing and wasted scads of time that I'll never get back.

~

My twins played football from second grade all through college. The drinking many parents did during games was excessive, even in peewee football. One game in particular comes to mind. It was a cool morning with a cloudless blue sky. The game was scheduled for 11:00 a.m. We arrived at the school early, and of course parents were unloading chairs, blankets, and whatnot.

What startled me, though, was the number of men and women that announced how their coolers and cups were filled with beer, wine, or spiked cider. It was ten o' clock in the morning.

We have it all wrong, and it's not about swearing off alcohol, unless of course you decide for yourself that that would be the best course of action for you; it is about changing the way we view drinking, recreational drug abuse, and dependence on and abuse of prescription medication. It's about paying attention to what we role model. Our kids are watching.

It is about being mindful of those flippant comments touting alcohol and Ativan that our kids hear and record. Our kids also listen . . . Is that the message you want to impart?

I remember a physician sitting behind me at a football game. I overheard him say to his wife that he couldn't wait to go home, pop a Vicodin, and put his feet up. There is nothing funny about opiate addiction. We need to stop trivializing drugs and alcohol. They destroy people. They destroy families. Ask a child who is now in foster care because of his or her parents' substance-abuse problems whether they think drugs and alcohol are funny.

When my boys were young, I could look at people and families and pretty much predict who would and wouldn't implode. The predictions I made back in 1998 or 1999 all turned out to be true. And now, with the next generation of kids, I can spot it again.

People think they're unique and that it won't happen to them because they have it all under control. I can predict what will happen with such accuracy because I've been immersed in the disease from every angle for over half a century. I don't care if you are wearing Jimmy Choo shoes or Keds from Walmart; the disease and its trajectory are still the same. Women with money die alone with bad livers. Less-affluent women still die alone with bad livers, but they die perhaps a few years sooner because they maybe can't afford good health care. I hate to put it so bluntly, but that is the truth about alcoholism.

Had I not gotten sober, there is no doubt my marriage would've imploded long ago. I can hear women screaming, "Oh, but you weren't happy! You should've left. You deserve to be happy." Yes, and no.

There were unhappy years that turned into happy years. As I healed and changed, so did my husband. The dynamics in our marriage shifted a half a dozen times. By the time our sons were in high school, we were in a totally different place than we were when they were toddlers. All of the crap of the past—and believe me, there was a whole lot of it—was forgiven and forgotten.

I have an amazing husband. We are so proud that our family is intact and that we weathered those turbulent years. The secret to our success was to accept each other for who we were and then give the whole thing to God. I remember telling God, *Either you will make this work or not, but I'm done.* I was not interested in counseling, retreats, or anything of that nature—it was too much work, and I wasn't going to do it.

After I said that prayer, I let it go. Truly, I gave our marriage to God. I trusted he would fix it or he wouldn't, but either way I refused to steer. Instead of trying to control the uncontrollable from a place of fear, I moved on to do the things I wanted to do. I enjoyed my sons. I wrote. I went back to school and got an English degree. I made a life for myself independent of my marriage, and it helped that I could lose myself for chunks of time in my make-believe writing worlds. I guess there was a reason why the first four books I wrote were novels.

I look at the people who used to do what I did but who didn't address their issues, and I look at where they are now and the problems they've had as a result of their alcohol-fueled lives: shattered families, chronic illnesses, angry resentful children. It's a wonderful motivator, and it instills a lot of gratitude in those of us who chose a different path.

Drinking starts out fun, and then it morphs into fun with problems, and then it becomes nothing but problems. A woman takes a drink or a pill and too often the drink or the pill takes them.

I've known mothers who have lost custody of their children because of alcohol and drugs. I've talked to kids who were molested by uncles, stepfathers, and boyfriends of their moms, all because everyone was too busy having fun to keep tabs on their kids. These examples may sound drastic, but I've talked to too many kids who have had these sorts of experiences. Those sorts of things are life-altering events that don't just happen to other people.

I watched horrors unfold during the years I worked in the emergency room. I watched alcoholism destroy my mother and my sister, and it took years for the family to heal. I've listened to women cry about the children they lost because they drove drunk, or how their child fell in the pool and nobody paid attention. I've watched other women end up in the psych wards, devastated by their shitty parenting and poor choices. Their kids never had a chance not to be addicts and alcoholics, because that was the only behavior ever modeled to them. Some women would rather be drunk and cool than sober and sane. We need to flip the script. I can tell you this: I have always felt very cool to be sober and in control of my emotions, my actions, and my choices.

The angst some women feel over what they did to their children, once they get sober and realize the truth, is heartbreaking. I wanted to write this book to help other women avoid having to own that heartache. I know my mother, sober thirty years when she died, on her deathbed still feared that we kids harbored resentments toward her. None of us did, but I don't think she ever totally let go of her guilt. That mom guilt is tough stuff—we were all in our late teens or early twenties by the time my mother got sober.

All of the women I interviewed for this book who drank when their kids were young and then sobered up struggled with self-forgiveness. You don't get a do-over when it comes to your kids.

Marne, Caro, and Fiona all regretted being mothers who were only half alive. In their upcoming stories, they talk about how they were never fully present. I understand their regret because there were still times when I saw that wistfulness hang like a shadow behind my mom's eyes. I think a part of my mother always grieved for the mother she wanted to be but never was.

I've celebrated with women who love to extol the virtues of a sober life. I have yet to hear one woman who used to drink say that alcohol has ever done anything good for her. Sure, at first it feels good to have a cocktail. Who doesn't like that warm-glow feeling? The problem is that, for far too many, that feel-good place never lasts. More and more alcohol is required to hit the sweet spot. Women chase the feel-good place as it moves farther and farther away from their grasp.

Caro's daughter Lucy had deep feelings about her mother's drinking:

> *I know alcoholism happens so slowly that people don't realize where they're headed, and then boom . . . they're in it with no way out. The denial is so great. My mother would stagger all over the kitchen and still deny she had been drinking.*
>
> *Her drinking made me feel second-best. Alcohol always came first. I was a kid. How am I supposed to understand she has a disease? All I could see is that she couldn't go a day without drinking, and she couldn't not drink—for me. She couldn't stop for me—so then I felt worthless. How can people think or say that drinking doesn't affect the whole family?*
>
> *I could see how alcohol affected her. It made her irritable. She would say stupid things to me and my brother. We didn't think any of them were funny. She wasn't enjoyable to be around because she wasn't the same mom. The further she slipped into her addiction, the less and less I wanted to do with her. I even got to the point where I saw her as an example of what I didn't want to be as a mother and a wife.*

Lucy, devastated by her mother's drinking, internalized much of her mother's behavior and thought it somehow reflected back on her. It was only after her mother got sober that they were able to repair their relationship. Women have to be willing to look past their denial and listen to what their children have to say. Women also need to understand that children are helpless. Their fate is whatever environment they are given, and they will either thrive or die.

Here in contrast is an unsolicited letter that one of my sons wrote to me on my birthday a few years back. I decided to share the letter because it was such a pleasant surprise, and it cements what I've tried to impart in this chapter—that kids do pay attention:

Dear Mom,

On your birthday today I just want to remind you how thankful and grateful I truly am to have you in my life. Ever since I moved to Philly and have been on my own, I realize how much you've taught me and the morals you've instilled. I am constantly reminded how selfless you've been while raising AB and me. You've never failed to be there for us at a moment's notice. I remember reading, if you call your mom when you are having a bad day, it will put you in a better mood. I believe this to be true. There is something amazing and unexplainably comforting about hearing your voice. It has been twenty-four years, and I could not be more thankful for the bond we've created. You are the strongest person in this entire world. From helping people in Africa, to taking in the people and kids that you have into your life, from writing your books, getting degrees, or working to sell your pesto and granola, you never cease to amaze me.

You are a real-life constant reminder of how to live. One of the things I admire most about you is how you are fearlessly yourself at all times. You never change who you are for anything or anyone—that is something I still need to work on. You have shown me endless instances where you are authentically just you.

You have taught me to follow God, to do the next right thing, and you have given me the tools to be a real man. Just sitting here writing this I realize I could write a book on you and how badass you are. Today I just want you to know you are the most important woman in my life. I thank you from the bottom of my heart for the sacrifices you have made for me, as well as the unconditional love you have given and will continue to give to me. Grandma is undoubtedly looking down at you with a smile on her face, oozing with pride of the person you have become. Happy birthday, Mom. You are my hero.

That letter had nothing to do with me and everything to do with God's grace. Twenty-eight years ago when I quit drinking, I thought I'd never have fun again. Even though I chose to quit when I did, I was pissed off about all of it: I'd think about the euphoria of parties, drinking at holidays and my birthday; I acted like it was such a sacrifice—but the truth was, I gave up nothing. I lost nothing but a world of hurt and pain. Why hang onto chaos, muddled thinking, and a distorted perception of reality?

Instead, I gained peace of mind, a fabulous relationship with my sons, a stable family, and a relationship with myself, and what I prize the most is that I earned and maintained the love and respect of my children. That right there is priceless.

There is not a drink or drug in the world worth giving all that up. I'd like to see every mother have the respect of her children. I may have been raised in utter dysfunction, but I had a choice to do different. I encourage you to look at the truth in your own home. If alcohol is ubiquitous or is calling the shots in any kind of way, please make a better choice. Your kids will thank you for getting it right the first time.

~ 9 ~
One Step at a Time

As widespread as the twelve steps are, many people still know only a little, if anything, about them. Gamblers Anonymous, Overeaters Anonymous, and Al-Anon are several of the programs that use the steps for healing.

With all the success stories out there extolling the virtues of the twelve steps, people still love to bash them and complain that they don't work. I talked with a friend of mine, a fellow recovering alcoholic and addict, Dr. James. We discussed the reason he thought people dismissed the twelve steps. "People don't like them because they have to do something then," he said.

He's right; it's been my experience that the majority of people who need to get well don't get well because change requires more effort than they're willing to expend. They'd rather go to the doctor and get a pill and continue to dwell in their dysfunction, implode their families, and skip down the aisle of disaster than address the core issue of addiction—feelings.

It is much easier for someone to go to a doctor and get a prescription. More and more we are fed the lies; an example of this is the numerous television commercials flaunting pills to fix every uncomfortable emotion or symptom. The pharmaceutical companies create long-term patrons . . . they offer no cures. The twelve steps are free for the taking and will work for anyone who follows the simple suggestions. Yes, anyone can live a better life.

Whether or not you have a substance-abuse issue, the steps can help you live a more peaceful life. Somehow the author or authors of the twelve steps (no one is certain who first penned them, though some sources credit Bill Wilson) were inspired to understand that alcohol is only a symptom of a deeper personality problem. In addition to having a physical allergy to alcohol, people who drink alcoholically also stuff their feelings. They like to cop a buzz because that buzzed feeling separates them from the emotional pain they cannot handle.

Individuals that don't drink or abuse drugs can still have twisted emotions. They may not have an allergy and react to alcohol like alcoholics do, but they may still have issues dealing with people and troublesome relationships. We all know folks who walk around scowling because they're angry with the world; then there's the person riddled with fear, and the person who hates everyone and everything for no apparent reason.

When worked and applied to a person's life, the steps can assist anyone to resolve feelings of resentment, anger, fear—pick any troubling emotion, feeling, or behavior, and there's a step to help you deal with it.

I believe, as so many do, that Bill Wilson was divinely inspired when he wrote the Big Book. He somehow knew that an alcoholic needed to do a whole lot of inside work; for some mystical reason, that recipe of a higher power, helping others, and abstinence is the recipe for a better life.

A life of take, take, take leaves most people desperate and wanting. Material possessions cannot fill the hole in the soul, and depression often manifests when one is overwhelmingly preoccupied with oneself. If depressed people who drink would stop drinking and make themselves available for service in some way, the size of their world would expand exponentially. Suddenly, all of their waking thoughts would not be spent thinking about themselves. Life is always better when you have something bigger than yourself to focus on.

The twelve steps that are the foundation for numerous programs strip away egos and allow people to gain humility; humility introduces a fresh perspective and allows people to see what they couldn't see before—that they had a hand in most everything that has happened to them because of the decisions they did or didn't make, the people they chose to associate with, and the spouses they chose to marry.

It's important for alcoholics or problem drinkers to take the focus off of what they perceive others have done to them. Most people in recovery aren't the only ones practicing bad behavior, nor are they victims like they once thought themselves to be. There are plenty of people out there doing plenty of hurtful things, but the steps teach us to focus on our behavior. We have no control over what others do. We need to make amends for our wrongs and stay away from people who continue to be hurtful. We can let them go and let them live their lives, and we move on.

In the twelve steps, one can inadvertently find a higher power, have a spiritual experience, or, perhaps, remain a die-hard atheist, but once the steps are worked through with someone who understands them, it's impossible to remain the same person. Change happens.

I saw no point in getting sober to be miserable. I saw no point in getting sober if life wasn't far better sober than it was drunk. I saw no point in white-knuckling anything, because, surely, that was no way to live.

Step one asks that people admit their powerlessness and accept that their life is unmanageable. I got sober because of the second half of that step. I didn't believe I was powerless over alcohol, but there was no doubt my life was unmanageable. I quit drinking more because of the unmanageability in my life than I did because I thought I drank too much.

Women have a lot to manage anyway: careers, kids, spouses, homes—that alone can overwhelm even the most efficient person. Add alcohol or pills to the mix, and you have a brewing storm. The unmanageability results when the woman finds herself unable to deal with her day-to-day responsibilities without frequent meltdowns and more and more wine to cope.

Step two asks that you be willing to come to believe in a power greater than yourself. I had my Christian faith, and believing in God was not an issue. However, I have also successfully worked with or have known people who do not believe in God. Even atheists can recover if they are willing to grasp the program in a way they can accept.

Step three asks that we become willing to turn our will and our lives over to the care of God, or whatever higher power we can grasp. The third step is the crux of the program. In essence the third step says to the alcoholic/addict/troubled person: you cannot seem to manage your life, so give it to a higher power, whatever you deem that to be, and see if you can't find some peace. It further says: you will no longer be allowed to micromanage—not just your life, but anyone else's life either.

Step four is a meat-and-potatoes type of step. You need pen and paper. This step asks a person to go back as far as they remember and write down their wrongs, their resentments, their fears, etc. It asks that a person be thorough and honest in order to clear out all the crap, the affairs, the money issues, or the stealing, lying, cheating, or thieving ways that so many in addiction have come to know intimately well.

Step four stops a lot of people from recovering. Why? Because they've built up their bad deeds in their heads and they think they're worse than everyone else. The truth is, not that many women are all that good at being bad. The guilt and shame they feel tells them that they're awful people. They think they did unforgivable things, or they don't want to face what happened to them through no fault of their own. Another reason women balk at this step is that they refuse to clean up their lives, like the women who refuse to ditch their married boyfriends.

The fourth step says, okay, you screwed up. Lay your shit on the table, be done with the behavior, and move on to step five, where you share what you've done with someone else. It's Biblical: James 5:16 and John 1:9 encourage confession. The thing to remember about confessing to another is that after you confess, the behavior then has to stop. Laying one's sins out to dry brings a dose of humility, but you can't pick them up again and continue to practice them. Pride and secrets allow women to stay sick.

Women can do the fifth step with a pastor or a priest, the homeless guy on the corner, or, hopefully, with a another recovering alcoholic who understands. There are no hard and fast rules. As long as you share it with another human being and are honest and thorough, you're good to go. Again, willingness and action brings about healing.

Through the fourth and fifth steps women come to understand how deep emotions drive behaviors. We start to see the patterns, like women who marry over and over again, thinking each time will be different, though it never is. Until they fix themselves, they will continue to pick unhealthy men and have unhealthy relationships. The steps teach you to look at your behavior instead of focusing on everyone else as the problem.

Steps six and seven are about the character defects that make us tick. They're about ego, fear, resentments . . . the list can be long. The things that make you pulse in a dizzying way are the behaviors or character defects that dictate your behavior. However, once you see the destructive nature of your behavior, you can do something about it—you can begin to let go. We cannot fix what we don't understand or see; the steps help us to see.

For instance, maybe that fibromyalgia you said you had seems to be resolving itself now that you're working a program. Perhaps you don't need to lie on the couch and have others do your bidding. Perhaps sloth or needing attention or any number of less-healthy behaviors rested at the bottom of that fibromyalgia, but you no longer get anything out of a constant state of repose. Instead, you'd rather enjoy life. Character defects come disguised in many outfits.

When you find yourself acting the fool, the steps teach you to pause and ask yourself a few questions: What am I afraid of? Do I feel threatened? Do I feel I might lose something I don't want to lose? What and who am I trying to control? If you're bedeviled by jealousy and have a habit of checking the phone or bank statements of your significant other or spouse, the steps ask you to get to the bottom of that behavior and find the real reason behind your insecurity. The steps provide the courage needed to look at reality and then make decisions based on reality instead of the lies we continue to tell ourselves.

In step eight, you make a list of people you have harmed, and then in nine you make amends to those people. Another blessing of quitting your vice while still in the early stages is that your list of people, places, and institutions will be short. I hadn't done much damage at all other than to myself.

Some say that steps ten through twelve are the maintenance steps. By this point, you've learned how to look at yourself, make amends, pray, meditate, and help others, and you continue to carry the message.

Volumes have been written about the twelve steps, but unless you're in a twelve-step program, it may seem that there's little reason to concern yourself with them. I'd love to see that change. The principles of the twelve steps—such as willingness, service to others, honesty, surrender, faith, and hope—are all concepts that translate well into everyday life. Anyone can live a more peaceful life by adhering to the above-mentioned principles. The twelve steps are not a cult. The purpose of the twelve steps is to bring people to God or a higher power.

I sought out a conversation with a woman I knew named Izzy for two reasons. First, she's a beautiful spirit who also happened to be a dear friend of my mother. Second, after more than three decades of sober living, she's plowed through a lot, and it helps to understand how people apply the principles of the steps to their lives. Izzy shared with me how holding on to the principles of surrender, faith, and hope helped her navigate through a difficult time in her life. This is Izzy's perspective:

Like everyone else, I've had my share of problems related to family, finances, employment—life happens. But my biggest test came when one evening my husband came home and told me that because of his job, we had to relocate. I was terrified to leave the stability of my community and friends. I was taught early on that I had to become God-dependent instead of drug- or alcohol-dependent, but I didn't fully understand what that meant until I had to forge out on my own.

When I first came into recovery I felt incredibly blessed that I had women in my path who were doing this deal. I could tell they were powered by a force, and one of those women was your mother. I wanted what they had. Those women took me under their wings, and for the first twelve years I found the life I'd craved. Through the steps I found peace and built a relationship with God. Then, in that twelfth year when I had to move—the fear was crippling. I couldn't imagine life without all of the stalwarts who loved me back to health.

It wasn't until I had to move that I realized I'd become too dependent on my sponsor and my identity in the program; everyone knew me. I'd been cocooned in a world of security, and soon, that security would be stripped away.

The first time I moved we landed in a small town. I had to pull every bit of principle and courage from the steps. What helped me plug into my new environment was to start over with the basics: I went to meetings. I went to hospitals and talked to women. I depended on God, and not on the fellowship or the people or the meetings. I survived by using the steps.

Early in my sobriety when I felt like I wanted to jump out of my skin because I had no coping skills, I'd call my sponsor, and she'd say, 'Go in your bedroom, get on your knees, then call me in two hours.' In my new town, I felt like I was starting over, so I went back and did what I did in the beginning.

Each time we moved, I had to step out on my own, and each time, all I had to hold on to was God's hand. I had to get my security from God, not people—not a bank account, but God.

I've accumulated so many relationships from multiple moves, and the friendships I've built and the opportunities to help the women I've encountered . . . what a blessing. It took all of those moves for me to understand how strong I'd become. I know I can get through any situation life throws at me by trusting God and the power of the twelve steps.

I can relate to Izzy. I wondered myself how well my sobriety and all this step business would hold up when my mother died. We'd become so close, and even years before she was diagnosed with cancer, I projected how I might not fare so well when she died.

The inevitable day came. I coped, without falling apart. I grieved, I cried, I reminisced and prayed, but I didn't need to drink. I too learned to lean on God and the women in the program. When the steps are worked and applied to real life, there's a knowledge that, no matter what happens, it's going to be okay.

Another woman I know, Mary, used the steps to build a life. She found her true love and married for the first time when she turned forty-seven years old. She said, "Dating can be hard when you're sober, but the funny thing is, the healthier I got, the better men I picked." To further set her apart from the pack, she got sober the day after her twenty-first birthday! Who does that? This is what she told me:

Then one day I had an epiphany. I was listening to a cellist play Bach, and the thought came that I needed to take a composition class. No, not just a class. I should go back to school and get a music education degree, and teach. I didn't see how any of that would work. Both of my parents were dead, and I had to support myself. I had a business degree, and when I checked into getting a music degree . . . it was like starting all over. Plus, the university told me if I wanted to pursue a music degree I needed to commit to being a full-time student. There I was, almost thirty-five years old. Did I really want to go back to living like a college student?

Mary said that she gathered the courage she needed from her sponsor, the women in the program, and the steps: "We don't do this alone. Step eleven, the prayer and meditation step, allowed me to stay open to where God was leading me."

She had hard decisions to make, knowing those decisions would change everything about her life. "After fifteen-plus years in a sales career," Mary said, "I never felt satisfied, but I made great money. I'd have to make a lot of changes in order to go back to school, and at my age, some of those changes were hard." She continued:

I had to sell my two-year-old Volvo, that, by the way, I loved, but I needed the money. I bought a bike. Between the bicycle and public transportation, that's how I got around. Relying on the bus helped me with time-management skills. I had to be more mindful of my daily schedule.

My desire for clothes and cars, and all that material stuff, left. I started waiting tables. Things began to gel. I took a leap of faith and decided to trust God. I also had to be honest with myself about who I was and what I wanted out of life. The steps gave me the courage to make hard choices, and they taught me how to pray and how to listen. The steps gave me the courage to go where I felt God was leading me. It was hard, but worth it.

Of course on the days when it poured rain and the bus was late and the music classes kicked my butt, I started to question whether or not I had made the right decision. Was this God's will or Mary's will? Then, one day as I cruised down the road on my bicycle and the wind was whipping my hair around, clear as day I heard God say, "Mary, I want you here." I knew in the marrow of my bones I was on the right path. I did complete that music degree, and I love teaching. I love the kids, and I feel I am where I was always meant to be.

The principles of recovery help so many cope with the unforeseeable incidents that constitute life. A woman I'll call Patti shared her experience about how she coped when betrayed by a lifelong friend:

I grew up with a girl across the street. I was her maid of honor twice, and this friend was in my wedding. I was the witness in her divorce. I helped her buy a casket for her son when he committed suicide as a result of alcohol. We had a lot of history. I knew her flaws too—she was a thief. She'd take money out of your purse, but not mine because we were friends . . . right?

I owned a boutique, and my friend was out of work, and I needed to fill a slot. I didn't want to go through all the steps I needed to take in order to hire the right person—you have to interview, hire, and train, and then the new person may or may not work out. Hiring people is a process, and I didn't want to go through the process. I took the easy way out and hired my friend.

One day, I was sitting in my office, and it's like I heard God say, "Jenne's stealing from you." I called her up and asked, "Are you putting that money in your bank account or mine?"

She said, "Mine."

I wanted to believe she hadn't done it, but she had; she stole somewhere between ten and twelve thousand dollars. She was in the program too. All I could think was, I hope no one gets drunk here.

Payroll was due, and it was the week before Christmas. I told Jenne she needed to get a cashier's check to my house within the hour so I could make payroll. She had someone deliver the check, and then later that evening she sent me a copy of the movie Beaches. *As if she thought we were the girls in the movie and we were going to take care of each other.*

Was she nuts? I was devastated! I went through all the emotional trauma of it, and I thought, What do I do now? I went back to the steps. I did the fourth step—I looked at my part. By the time I got to the end of writing out that fourth step, I thought maybe I should send her a thank-you note.

Here's how the steps worked in my life: I knew the truth about who Jenne was, but I let my ego run the show. I wanted to believe the lie because it was easier. My ego told me, yes, she's a thief, but she won't steal from you because you're special. Plus I got to be the hero and offer this poor out-of-work girl a job.

I deserved what I got. I knew she was a thief. I should've been mad at myself, not her. There's a part in the Big Book that talks about how we make decisions based on self "which later [place] us in a position to be hurt. So our troubles, we think, are basically of our own making."[12] *Bam! That line smacked of certain truth.*

The steps teach us to look at our part in every situation. When I looked at the truth, Jenne was being who she was. I was the one who was lazy.

The program teaches us to peel it back, peel it back. People don't just walk up to you one day and rip up your heart. You have to let them into your inner circle. When we do the work, we see how we put ourselves in the position to let bad things happen . . . the whole incident caused me to grow.

When you're not used to looking at things from the perspective of the twelve steps, it's easy to assume the victim role, but when you're taught to look at your defects and your motives and your part, usually, the whole landscape looks different. For example, we learn it's unfair of us to trust untrustworthy people and then wail and moan when they betray us. The steps help us shift responsibility back to us. They require honest appraisals and help us to ask ourselves the pertinent questions; they give meaning to the saying "If I'm not the problem, there is no solution."

~ 10 ~
Heroin Heartbreak: One Mother's Perspective

When you think drug or alcohol addiction doesn't affect you, think again. Addiction has become a huge social problem; it affects the people at places where you dine, where you shop, and where you obtain medical services, and it affects all of us as we drive down the road.

Families all over the country are devastated by drug addiction. I knew that I couldn't write this book without addressing heroin, because in this country it has become an epidemic.

There is no such thing as being only an alcoholic or only a drug addict. People may think they're only alcoholic, but if alcohol suddenly became extinct, they'd find some other substance to feed their addiction.

In the late 1930s, when the twelve steps were born, prescription drug abuse was not as prevalent as it is today. There were fewer types of street drugs available, and there was less of them.

I have friends who are recovering heroin addicts, and some admit that they kept relapsing on alcohol because they didn't believe that heroin addiction and alcoholism were the same disease. It was only through relapse and failure that they came to understand the relationship between heroin and alcohol. In any relapse, the drink invariably came first, which led the addict right back to the needle. Addiction is addiction.

Addiction is a family disease. I spoke with Rae, who hopes that by sharing her experience with having a drug-addicted daughter she may spare another family from making the same mistakes she made. It wasn't until she could see that she played a part in her daughter's addiction that she could step out of the fray and hope for a different result. Here is her story:

> *I got sober when my youngest daughter was four years old, but from the way things turned out . . . you'd never know that I wasn't using. Looking back, I can see that although I didn't use for many years, I also hadn't changed. My behavior, and the way I ran my life, impacted my daughter in ways I couldn't predict.*
>
> *I went to meetings, I worked the steps, I thought I'd worked a program, but I missed the most important part. I never found a higher power. My ego wouldn't allow me to accept that a higher power would run my life better than I could, and deep down I believed that needing God was a sort of weakness. All of those character defects that cause alcoholics and addicts so much trouble, those defects propelled my every thought and move: guilt, shame, and control. I got stuck and missed the spiritual piece of the program, and that left me unable to get any relief from my alcoholism. I thought I could control everything—I never let go—I had a type of self-centeredness that didn't allow me to let go. My daughter went through hell, not because I was using, but because I never recovered. There's a difference. I've been married multiple times. We say kids are resilient, but I think that's a lie we tell ourselves to rationalize things we shouldn't do.*
>
> *I met my son's father when I was thirty days sober. Everyone told me not to date—part of the addict's or alcoholic's story is so often troubled relationships. I repeated the same destructive patterns in sobriety that I did when I used. I kept using men for validation and attention.*

Sarah was thirteen when she started drinking. Alcohol turned into pot, which turned into heroin. Over the next three years she would be dragged out of parties, expelled from school, carted home by the police, locked up in juvenile detention, and tossed into rehab—numerous times.

When Sarah was sixteen, her biological father came back into her life. I was unhappy in my marriage to my son's father; his reappearance was the fix I'd been seeking. I left that marriage and was once again off and running. I still wouldn't admit my life was unmanageable even without alcohol. I couldn't see the chaos my untreated alcoholism caused. It would be my guilt over these years of failing my daughter in sobriety that would drive me to be her chief enabler and prolong her addiction.

At eighteen Sarah began using heroin. When I learned of her addiction, my guilt was unbearable. The heartbreak of watching her life unfold was devastating. There was always trouble—lots of it: institutions, jail, and, of course, me, trying to control and manage the whole situation. Deep down, I owned her addiction; I believed it was all my fault.

For the better part of a decade, I spent so much of my time and energy trying to control Sarah and her addiction. I'd show up now and again at meetings looking for relief, but because I couldn't let go and grasp the spiritual aspect of the program, I too continued to suffer. I was as sick or sicker than when I drank.

It took a long time for me to realize that my enabling had more to do with my guilt than it did with helping her. She'd land in jail, and, time and time again, I'd let her move back home. I went to great lengths to second-guess myself when money went missing from my purse. She stole from anyone in her path, yet I kept trying to outsmart her or rearrange things to stay one step ahead of the madness. It was exhausting, but I couldn't bring myself to kick her out. I had this paralyzing fear if she left the house she would overdose alone on the streets behind some dumpster.

The insanity in our home was far worse than it was when I used. My guilt was at the bottom of all that insanity. Her presence in the home took a toll on my other children. My oldest daughter refused to come over anymore. My son showed signs of depression and anxiety.

One night after a particularly hellish argument, I made her leave. I knew she had nowhere to go, and the vision of her standing on the sidewalk with her belongings stuffed into a trash bag . . . that was tough stuff to handle.

We started into a new cycle of I'd throw her out, she'd get clean for a minute, come back home, relapse, and all the while I'm in denial about what a mess I had on my hands. Each time I threw her out and allowed her to come back home, things got worse for both of us.

I got as crazy as my addict daughter. I'd ransack her purse and search for drug paraphernalia. I learned that drug dealers were leaving the heroin in the mailbox when I worked. She hacked into my bank account and drained it. She stole my car and totaled it. There were always fires to douse or the police to contend with. I let cherished friendships slip away because I got sick of talking about my daughter and her messes.

My grandmother recently died; she was ninety-seven. It occurred to me that I missed her last birthday because of Sarah's addiction. I was so busy running interference for the addict who I allowed to consume my life. I had some tough love in me, but it wasn't near enough. I never bailed her out of jail, but I never pressed charges either, even when she hacked into my bank account. I didn't want her to have a felony. I kept trying to control not only her, but also the outcome.

Truth was, I did nothing but set Sarah up. My best efforts only gave her more opportunities to feel bad about herself. I knew when she used she was a liar and a thief, but I'd let her come home. She'd do what addicts do: she'd lie, steal, and cheat, but then I acted all indignant because she betrayed me. I knew better than to invite a drug addict into my home, but I did it anyway.

Everyone kept telling me I had no choice but to let Sarah go. Nothing I did to save her worked.

I acquired a deep realization that my best efforts never changed anything for Sarah. If it were up to me to get my daughter sober, if I had that power, she would've been sober ten years ago. I think now that everything I did for her was to assuage my guilt.

Never again will I let my life go. I want more out of life than to police my daughter. It's no joke when they say that addiction is a family disease. My other two children started to resent my involvement in Sarah's nonstop drama.

Once I finally had had enough and refused to let her come home, my mother stepped in. She allowed Sarah into her house. Once again Sarah had a roof, food, and she did what addicts do—she stole from her grandmother, and my mother was devastated. She knew Sarah stole from other people, but she didn't believe that Sarah would steal from her. People need to understand that addicts will use anyone in their path and they will burn every bridge. I had to quit giving my daughter a bridge.

What I want to impart is that I learned that as long as the addict has one person to enable them, or one more avenue to work, they will use that angle. Their resourcefulness knows no boundaries. It is only when they are completely out of angles that they may attempt sobriety.

When I look back, all of those things I thought I was doing to help Sarah . . . none of it helped her. All it did was act as a balm so I could feel better. My motives and intentions were always about me; how will I live with myself if she dies out there?

Best course of action for a parent who has a child who is an addict, in my experience: I'd say if the child is a minor, do everything you can to get them help. At some point when they become an adult, the approach has to change.

I should've set clear boundaries and stuck to them. I would've let Sarah know I loved her, but I would've kicked her out of the house years before I did. My enabling prolonged her addiction, and it prolonged the agony for us all. She had a decade of me enabling her to be an addict. If I would've let go and took care of myself, she may have hit bottom years sooner. I now understand I can only be a better role model.

What would I suggest a woman do with her heroin or drug-addicted/alcoholic child? It's easy to say you have to let the addict or alcoholic go, but it's so difficult when it's your child. If you're like me, when you look at that child, what you may see is the child that you failed. I saw all the places where I fell short as a parent instead of holding her accountable. When kids are little we feel responsible for their behavior. As my children got older I knew the baggage they all carried because I helped pack those suitcases. With Sarah, I kept saying things like, "I'll forgive myself once I know that she's okay." I felt I couldn't let myself off the hook while she was suffering.

All of that was typical alcoholic thinking to make everything going on with her all about me. I had to resolve my codependence, my guilt, my control. I had to get to the place where I could look at my daughter and see something other than just my mistakes, my shortcomings, my failings. I had to stop making it all about me.

I can finally see that all that guilt and blame I had on myself was my lack of spiritual connection. I never turned my will and my life over to God as I understood him. It's not enough to just not use—I had to change. Really change. In all the years of thinking I was working a program, I wasn't. I ran on self-will. That hurt my children as much as my using did.

Rae's story exemplifies what I've been saying. Maladjusted parents raise maladjusted children. Although Rae said she was sober while raising her children, with further inspection, we can see there was nothing sober about her behavior. She was dry. The difference is startling. Dry people don't use drugs or alcohol, but what about the insane behavior? The men? The inability to be present? The selfishness and self-centeredness? Parents whose lives are focused on their wants and needs cannot be there for their children. Selfishness manifests in a multitude of ways.

When you sit back and look at the damage that is done when parental decisions are based on self rather than what is best for the good of all concerned, it becomes apparent that selfishness can create as much havoc as drugs or alcohol.

It takes work to become a different person. Willingness is required, and as a result of thoroughly working the twelve steps, most people have a spiritual awakening. Just like the Bible wants us to become new in Christ, the steps give new life. It only makes sense that in order to be different, you have to do different. Action is key.

I reached out to another friend of mine, Ken, an MD who practices in the field of maternal/fetal medicine and who deals with a lot of high-risk moms. He sees the drug problem on a daily basis and understands the malady of the disease because he too is a recovering opiate addict. He understands that punishing the addict, as we do now, is not the answer. Our current laws are such that if a baby is born addicted to heroin, the baby is taken from the mother, and she may be in legal trouble herself.

Dr. Ken says that when we look at addiction from the disease perspective and compare it to diabetes, this makes no sense. The pregnant diabetic who doesn't control her blood sugar in the first trimester puts her baby at risk for all sorts of grave birth defects, such as heart, brain, or spinal cord anomalies. Once the baby is born, it can go into insulin shock. These babies are very ill and often need weeks in the Neonatal Intensive Care Unit (NICU) to regulate their blood sugar. So why isn't the mom with uncontrolled diabetes held accountable like the opiate addict is? Why the distorted logic? The reason is that even though addiction is a disease, no one really believes that. "The medical community continues to look at addiction as a moral issue," he said.

We need to change the way we think about the addict. There's a lot about medicine that needs to be changed. Over-prescribing causes far more harm than good, such as when doctors prescribe antidepressants for situational depression. If Mom just died or you lost your great job of twenty-five years, depression is normal, and medication is not the answer.

Dr. Ken told me about a study that showed that when patients are in a doctor's office, they get all of twelve seconds to talk before the doctor interrupts them. Doctors are forced to see too many patients in order to make their numbers. "It's a money machine, not medicine they're practicing. Too many doctors don't even listen to what their patients have to say."

He said some of the nurses he works with know about his past as an addict and alcoholic, and some even ask him what to do about family members they have who are addicts, but for the most part, he doesn't out himself, and most other addicts don't either.

The attitude in the medical community toward addicts has been mostly one of disgust, and when it comes to pregnant women addicted to opiates, in the hierarchy in the opiate community, they are deemed to be the worst of the worst.

These women are overcome with guilt and shame. Their self-esteem is in the gutter. Pregnant addicts are thought to be the bottom-feeders. Everyone who's pregnant knows they need to go to doctor, but often pregnant addicts don't go because they know they'll be judged or they fear that Child Protective Services will get involved and take their babies, which is a legitimate concern. Addicts are judged from the moment they step into a facility, and it starts with the receptionists. Judgmental attitudes are a component of health care, and though everyone working in health care knows this, the general public has little clue. That's a fact.

Pregnancy can end up being a great way to get someone into recovery. They have the added motivation to do something for the developing baby. One solution is to create a safe environment where women can go and not feel judged. The way to handle these addicts when pregnant is to keep them on some sort of opiate during their pregnancy. Going cold turkey puts fetuses at risk for fetal abstinence syndrome. If the mom goes into withdrawal, the fetus can die. Fetuses can't shiver and throw up like moms can. Suboxone is a safe option for pregnant women. After they give birth, they can breast feed, they won't be nodding off, and it'll be safer to wean the baby off of Suboxone than heroin.

Currently, Dr. Ken is part of four state-funded programs for pregnant addicts in Ohio. The pilot project, called Promise to Hope, created a treatment protocol for pregnant addicts. The women are offered:

1) Obstetric care

2) Medically assisted treatment to help with their opiate addiction—Suboxone or Methadone are offered

3) Behavioral counseling

Sadly enough, Dr. Ken guessed from his experience that about 20 percent of pregnant addicts would embrace the Promise to Hope program. That's the heartbreak of addiction.

Suboxone is not an abusable drug because it blocks opiate receptors and has a ceiling effect, but the problem remains that some addicts sell their Suboxone for heroin because they still chase the high, and Suboxone has its own problems too. Doctors need proper credentialing to prescribe it, and there are guidelines that should be followed, including the fact that patients taking it should attend behavioral monitoring and counseling.

Unfortunately, according to Dr. Ken, there are doctors out there who will prescribe Suboxone and then let the patients pay cash and leave. "That is not the standard, but it happens more than people think." The implication is this: another drug to replace heroin can be a risky alternative because people can get a high from it if it's injected.

Alcohol kills more slowly. Heroin kills quickly. "It bears repeating that the highest risk for overdosing on heroin is in someone who's been clean and who then relapses. They have no tolerance. Opiates need to be treated differently than other drugs."

There you have it. We have a national problem: Due to heroin, this country is in crisis. Young people die every day because of overdoses. Another OB/GYN doctor I spoke with, who practices in an affluent suburb, is just as distressed as Dr. Ken by the number of women showing up for appointments in their Range Rovers who are newly addicted to heroin, and many of them are pregnant. The opiate crisis is not only an inner-city problem—it's a problem in every demographic. The solution is to be aware and mindful of addictive behavior and stop the abuse early before it ever escalates from alcohol to heroin. We need to get honest: so often, addiction starts with alcohol, and it's so much easier to never start using then to have to stop.

~ 11 ~
Don't Be a Violet

RELAPSE IS NOT REQUIRED. You don't have to be that girl who has to climb over the glass wall to see what's on the other side. My sister Violet was that girl. Don't be a Violet!

Relapse happens to a woman for one of three reasons: she is not willing to do what it takes, she lies to herself and believes she is fine, or she allows her ego and pride to make all her decisions. Some people in recovery believe that relapse is part of the disease of alcoholism. I tend to believe that relapse is part of the disease but that it doesn't have to be part of every alcoholic's/drug addict's/problem drinker's story. There are people who stopped drinking because it was the right thing for them to do, or they got clean and sober on their first go-around and have stayed clean and sober for many years.

That one-day relapse I had occurred for several reasons, and none was a mystery. First off, I wasn't ready to accept that I was an alcoholic. Second, I had gone to meetings for three months, but going to meetings was all I did. I wasn't willing to work the steps, I didn't get a sponsor, and I was unwilling to make any changes. I was still mostly convinced I wasn't an alcoholic.

I'd sit through the meetings and scoff. I compared what I did to what they did, and, believe me, the things I did seemed fine compared to some of the shenanigans those other people pulled. I made zero effort to relate. I didn't believe I could be an alcoholic because there were so many things I hadn't done—yet. That right there is the whole premise for this book—you can raise your bottom if you so choose.

At the time, I didn't understand how progressive and fatal alcoholism/addiction was. I tried to tell the people at the meetings how I was different. I harped on the fact that I didn't drink every day, but I know that I would've progressed to daily drinking because that's what alcoholism does—when you blink, it sneaks up and grabs you by the throat.

Just because you don't have wrinkles on your forehead today doesn't mean you won't have several creases in that smooth spot down the pike. Same with smoking—stop now or stop later. You can delay the inevitable, but why not stop before you get lung cancer or COPD?

Violet relapsed over and over, all the while lying and saying she was sober. I never believed a word she said. The dead giveaway was her crazy behavior. Her solution was always a handful of settle-down drugs. She'd race to the hospital or one of the many doctors she had dangling on the line who kept her supplied with opiates and benzodiazepines, which leads to my next point about women and alcohol/drug addiction.

Violet pooh-poohed the genetic-link factor. She refused to listen to me or my mom when we told her she needed to get honest, get real, and accept the fact she appeared to have all the same symptoms we did. She was addicted to feeling good. She had a skewed perception of reality. She made a plethora of poor decisions, and there were consequences galore. She had difficulties in all her relationships. Her life was chaotic, but she rationalized that all was well because she managed to hold down a decent job. With Violet, her self-esteem was directly proportional to her jobs, and there were times when she held prominent titles, like VP at a bank. She also had several positions within the federal government. She justified her using because she believed someone with a great job and a title couldn't be an addict.

Her pride and thinking was so twisted that at one point she agreed that maybe she had a drug problem, but she certainly was not an alcoholic "like you and Mom." Apparently, she thought drug addicts were more chic.

Nothing we could say would convince her that the disease of addiction is all the same. It doesn't matter if you're a food addict, sex addict, drug addict, gambling addict, or alcoholic—that empty space, that hole in the soul and the insatiable selfishness are all the same. The disease is the same. That place of addiction has the same roots—it's centered in the brain.

My mother never got to see my sister Violet get sober, but now that she is, I know Mom would be proud. Violet lived most of her adult life in New Mexico, but even from that distance, she stirred the pot and manipulated my parents, and, unbeknownst to them, they helped fund her drug habit. I know my mother harbored guilt about her own using; I believe it was her biggest struggle. Mom used to call me and say, "So how do you think your sister is doing?" Sometimes, during the years when Violet seemed to be holding it together, I'd say, "Okay," but for the most part I'd tell my mother the truth and say, "Not well; she's using."

For decades, my truth-telling put a strain on our sisterly relationship. Actually, we barely had a relationship. I had to detach from her drama. I just couldn't listen to any more of her depressive monologues when she knew where to find help and what to do and yet chose not to do it.

My mother helped other women galore and doled out pearls of wisdom all over the place, but when it came to her own daughter, because she held onto a sliver of guilt, she struggled to do what I know she knew needed to be done. Financially, she wouldn't cut Violet off, and she blamed much of my sister's drama on her single status and lots of bad luck. It was the wrong move, and it kept Violet out there using far longer than she ever would have if my mother had accepted the facts, but, again, it's a family disease.

~

The twelve steps may not be the only way to get sober, but I can tell you, I haven't found a whole lot of happy sober people who have done it other ways. I know many who turned to their church and stayed sober, but many of those people also relapsed after decades of sober living. People in twelve-step programs also can relapse when they quit treating their disease. The reason people keep going to meetings is so they don't forget who they are. People also attend meetings even after years of long-term sobriety to give back what they were so freely given. When people relapse, if they go back into the program, they all say the same thing: I forgot I was an alcoholic. I forgot that I was powerless.

After two stints within two years in psych wards, Violet ended up at the Edna House, a rehab house in Cleveland run by other addicts/alcoholics that has an astonishing success rate. She needed long-term help.

My sister stayed in the Edna House for a year. While living there, women are taught responsibility and accountability, and they don't just get sober—they learn how to live sober. Therein is one of the reasons why people can go to treatment and relapse hours or days after their release: they never learned how to live.

At the Edna House, after ninety days, the women have to find jobs and pay rent. They're required to work, go to meetings, pay their bills, keep the house, make their beds, and do the dishes. They learn how to juggle life and recovery commitments. That was something Violet never managed to do on her own before. She couldn't seem to incorporate recovery into her professional life—her pattern was to immerse herself in work; treating her disease was not a priority. Each time she neglected her recovery, she slid back into addiction.

As one woman at the Edna House pointed out, "It's easy to stay sober lounging around a treatment facility, but there's no lounging at Edna." To be fair, women take advantage of places like the Edna House too. They abuse the revolving-door principle and hop from one treatment place to the next. Nevertheless, addicts and alcoholics do best when they know they're dealing with someone who can see through their manipulation, who will kick their ass when it needs to be kicked, and who can lead by example.

The Edna House understands the selfish nature of the addict or alcoholic. Hence the women are required to do service work in the community. Had my sister gone to another posh treatment facility where they catered to her nonsense, I can tell you—and she agrees—that she'd be dead. The last thing she needed was the ability to con one more person into listening to one more sob story.

I talked to other women who were on the fence about quitting drinking. They'd come into the program for a week or a month or whatever, and then they'd go back out and drink. Some came back with new consequences that they hadn't had a few months before; for others, not much had changed—they were still miserable, but they functioned. However, they all agreed on one thing: they were experts at forgetting the things they should have remembered.

They forgot how they hurt people. They forgot about the outburst that happened the previous night or the previous week. They forgot about the innocent people who got caught in the crosshairs. They forgot about the lost purses, the money spent, and the lost friendships, or how snarky they acted toward the Uber driver when they drank. They forgot that their personality changed and they became ugly and petty and mean and someone who even they themselves wouldn't want to drink with.

Violet kept on using twenty-five years longer than she ever should have. She has paid an astronomical price for her addiction. She used until she hit a low bottom and has suffered consequences related to her finances, health, career, and relationships . . . all because of pride and dishonesty. I'm here to tell you right now that no woman—and I mean no woman—has to go there unless she so chooses.

It can be hard getting and staying sober when you don't have the gift of desperation. The mind plays tricks and will tell you that you're fine. When I got sober I sought out people who had not listened the first time around and who paid dearly for their denial. That helped me to not pick up and play the whole tape forward. People convince themselves they drink because they are miserable. The reality is they are miserable because they drink.

For us women in recovery, after we're done crying, we laugh. And we laugh a lot. One thing we thought hysterical was the ineffective self-help suggestions we'd hear, like the one that proposed an alcoholic only drink after five o'clock and only drink with two or more people; that's like telling a drug addict to take just one pill. Those sorts of suggestions are right up there with the ineffective theories taught in PhD programs. If you want to talk to an expert on alcoholism, talk to a recovering alcoholic. Only an idiot or another alcoholic/addict who doesn't want to quit drinking and drugging would suggest something like take only one pill and only drink after five. If alcoholics or problem drinkers could abide by drinking rules, they wouldn't need to quit drinking.

People sometimes relapse because they think that after a month or two, they have it all figured out and under control. If they had a high bottom like I did, and they felt fine and had no one breathing down their backs, then there can seem like there is no reason to stay stopped. Alcoholics and problem drinkers quit drinking all the time. Look how many Catholics give alcohol up for lent, but they hit the bottle hard once Easter rolls around. Anyone can stop—for a time. But if you are someone who loves your wine or your pills, you won't *stay* stopped for any length of time unless you commit to recovery.

Remember that alcoholism is an allergy to alcohol, but it's also a three-fold disease that affects a person in body, mind, and spirit. Untreated alcoholism manifests as empty souls walking around looking everywhere but to God for something to fill them up. Our egos tell us that we have control and that if we exert a bit more will power, we will be fine. The truth is that fighting addiction with will power is futile and exhausting.

Alcoholics relapse because they have few coping skills and they have dysfunctional emotional responses to life. They can't handle feelings. Alcoholics want to snuff out the bad feelings and only feel the good stuff. Alcoholics and addicts suffer diminished recognition of significant problems, such as their drinking/drugging.

It's worth repeating that people make a conscious decision to indulge recreationally, and then for 10 percent of the population, it bites them in the ass. One argument against the disease concept is that these maladaptive behaviors are a choice. But they're not a choice because alcoholics do not see their behavior as maladaptive. They think everyone else isn't acting right. Addiction is a chronic, deadly disease. Once you cross the imaginary line into alcoholism, there is no turning back. Once you're a pickle, you never get to go back and be a cucumber again.

Some people relapse out of fear of the unknown, or they just can't face and deal with what they need to look at. They refuse to face reality. They refuse to face the truth about themselves. They are addicted to chaos; I can relate to that. I had known only chaos. Not having chaos in my life was, at first, uncomfortable. I felt like something was missing. My solution was to get busy and fill my life with something constructive. I went to nursing school.

Other women want to continue to believe their version of reality. I've known women who live with someone else's husband and wonder why they relapse. They never seem to grasp the idea that getting sober is about cleaning up your life—all areas of your life.

I tell these women if they expect to stay sober, they have to be willing to do the right thing, regardless if they want to or not. We have to clean up the dishonesty in our lives if we want to get sober and stay sober. Women who refute this concept will continue to relapse.

Other women admit they have a problem with alcohol and need to quit but are too scared to take the plunge. They say things like, "At least I know what will happen today." Sure, they'll wake up, send the kids to school, pick up the dry cleaning, throw something in the crock-pot, and then start drinking.

They can't imagine life without all that misery. They'd rather be in control and choose defeat than relinquish control and surrender to God or some other higher power who they can't see or may not even know. At some point, for recovery to happen, you have to leap into the abyss and trust that you'll land on a soft cloud.

Little did I know that my life would start for real the moment I put down the drink. It was at that moment of surrender that I started wading out of the lake of confusion. We alcoholics and drug addicts are the lucky ones. We get to live two lives. Plus, alcoholism is the only disease that allows you to get well and then help heal others. How cool is that?

Another reason women don't make it in sobriety is because they fear losing relationships, some of which need losing anyway: they want to hold on to their husbands, boyfriends, or significant others far more than they want to save themselves. They also have unhealthy attachments to their doctors and therapists. They drink alone in their walk-in closets or take handfuls of pills, but they rationalize doctor shopping and all that drinking and pill popping by saying, "Well, my doctor gave it to me. It's prescribed."

Take Jeannette. I had seen her around recovery rooms, but I couldn't say I knew her well. Then, like so many women, she disappeared. Fiona called one evening and said Jeannette was coming back to meetings after a relapse. Jeannette was bright and sassy, and Fiona thought she needed someone who would cut through the baloney and tell her like it was. My name came up. Fiona wanted to know: would I help Jeannette?

"Sure, have her call me."

And so I met with Jeannette. The first thing I noticed was the faraway look in her eyes and her blunted affect. You can't work in the psych ward and emergency rooms, plus spend years working with alcoholics, and not recognize someone strung out on pills. I don't care if they're prescribed or not. A drug is a drug, and whacked is whacked.

I asked Jeannette what she took: Lamictal, Abilify, and Buspar for mood or bipolar disorder, Celexa for depression, Doxepin for sleep, Naltrexone for cravings, and Antabuse for making her vomit if drinking occurred.

Oh my God. Clearly, she needed to get off the medication or her sobriety would always be precarious. It's one thing to be legitimately bipolar and need medication. It's another thing to be misdiagnosed or, worse, labeled bipolar because, according to one psychiatrist, a bipolar diagnosis allows for heftier reimbursements. Suddenly, anyone who's ever had a bad day or threw a plate at her spouse gets diagnosed bipolar, and women taking that much medication (when they don't have a legitimate need) can't think clearly. Doctors who toss around a bipolar diagnosis delegitimize and marginalize the disease for those who do have it, and, for many, the struggle is real.

I asked Jeannette what she thought of her bipolar diagnosis, and she felt she didn't have the disease. I concurred. This was a bright, educated woman who only came unhinged when she drank. Bipolar people can't turn their symptoms on and off like that. I asked her if she ever remembered staying up for days on end. She didn't. She had no family history of bipolar disease. I asked her why she thought she was diagnosed bipolar. She said she didn't know. She did admit to feeling depressed at times. Of course she did—drugs and alcohol will do that to a person. She confessed to being a shopaholic. A lot of untreated alcoholics are shopaholics, or they overeat or have indiscriminate sex or do anything else compulsively.

"What else?" I asked. "Have you ever felt manic? Severely depressed?"

She shook her head no.

"Give me something."

She had nothing. I suggested she go back to her doctor and tell him that she wanted off all of the medication except the Celexa. The Celexa helped her depression. She agreed. When she laid it out for her doctor and relayed her wishes to be free of so many costly and mind-numbing medications, you know what he did? He shrugged and said, "Okay."

Jeannette is the mother of three children. Those children deserve a mother who can help them navigate life with a clear mind. Jeannette deserves the opportunity to get her life back. All this overprescribing and indiscriminate prescribing by doctors is killing women and robbing them of their lives. Relapse becomes an ongoing issue because these overmedicated women are too foggy to grasp life, or to grasp the twelve steps that can save them.

I asked Jeannette to confront her doctor and have him explain how he could've in good conscience kept her so medicated for so long and then suddenly felt that it was fine for her to come off these medications.

He had no answers. But he did agree to help her taper off of the Doxepin. A lot of women relapse and can't get sober because of doctors who misdiagnose and overprescribe. And I can tell you that as of this writing, Jeannette is still sober. She's uncovering the unhealthy emotions and patterns that had fueled her drinking. She's fully present in her children's lives. She's learning to live, instead of just exist.

Prior to sobriety, doctors had my sister taking trazodone, Seroquel, Effexor, and a few other medications that she can't remember. Now that she's sober, she takes an antidepressant, but that's it. Relapse can be related to the amount and type of prescription medication a woman takes, as well as her desire to live clean.

What counts as a relapse? Well, if you don't drink for a week or a month but you continue to pop three Valiums, Xanaxes, or Ativans every two hours on the hour, that's a relapse, if in fact you had been clean for any length of time. Let's say you have two beers. That isn't sobriety. Having no hard liquor but thirty Bud Lights is not sobriety. Only drinking on holidays is not sobriety. What if you quit drinking, but every day you smoke a joint? The marijuana-maintenance program is not sobriety. Crying about your Valium and opiate deficiency while having a glass of wine is not sobriety. Stealing and taking someone else's pain medication is not sobriety.

Sobriety means total abstinence from all mood-altering drugs/chemicals/alcohol. Sobriety means you get nothing. No, you cannot drink a bottle of NyQuil or pop five Benadryls to help you sleep. No, you cannot take Ambien or any other sleep medications. People do not die from lack of sleep. But remember that in the case of surgery, we are not martyrs. Yes, please take the pain pills, but when the pain is gone, throw out the pills. (No, you cannot save them just in case.)

The main reason people relapse is simple: they want to use more than they want to stay sober. Yes, it is that simple, yet it can be so hard. Women all the time say they want sobriety when they're nudged by the judge, but they say it in order to stay out of jail. Some give sobriety a whirl when they claim they are sick and tired of being sick and tired, but really they just want a break from all the running around. Others attempt sobriety because of the suggestion of a counselor or loved one, or maybe for a minute when they feel physically sick. Others find themselves in the psych ward yet again and say they want to get sober because it sounds like the right thing to say.

I don't know another class of people who can make art out of rationalizations like alcoholics can. People who drink alcoholically act mentally ill. They start thinking they're the president, and the rest of us are Navy SEALs. As crazy as that sounds, it's crazier to hear all the rationalizations of why they don't believe they're headed off the cliff, even when their outlandish behavior screams, "Help me!" and all of their relationships are filled with turmoil and strife.

An alcoholic in denial may not complain of a bad day as much as they would a bad decade. Raising the bottom is about facing and dealing with problems before another day or another year is wasted. I look back at the decade of my twenties. That's the decade when people set up their lives. They pursue their education and figure out their game plan, or at least try. Instead, I drifted through the decade and woke up nine years into it, shaking my head and asking myself, *What the hell happened?*

One reason Violet kept relapsing was because as soon as she could talk, she started lying. She was selfish and self-centered to the core. That's what addiction does—it makes people unable to focus on anyone but themselves. She did frequent geographical cures, always on the run—not from the law, but from herself. She never understood that wherever you go, there you are. If I'd mention that it would be nice if she could have consideration for others, and she'd draw a serious blank and ask, "What's that?"

The difference between who she was and how she shows up now

that she's sober is striking, but living life on life's terms is still a struggle. It can take years to undo decades of wrong thinking and behavior.

She first went to rehab back in the late eighties. She treated it like a month at the spa. She had the staff at the treatment center hauling her around to get her hair and nails done. She hid in the trees to get out of group. She was still calling the shots, and, needless to say, nothing about her thirty-day stint stuck. Therein lies the reason why so many costly treatment centers don't work—the patients never get humbled. The alcoholic/addict has a disease of entitlement. Entitled people don't get sober.

I met Camille, an MD, when she was fresh out of treatment for the first time. She waltzed into the recovery rooms, and anyone with a sliver of insight could recognize she carried a chip. I intuitively knew she wasn't done drinking, and I knew without a doubt that she'd relapse. You can't show up with an air of hubris, a boyfriend you collected in treatment, and an attitude that says, "This is all well and good for you guys, but I'm different, I'm smarter, I'm a doctor, I got this"—and stay sober. I've never seen it work that way.

She was in the process of getting a divorce and had had some consequences, but even the threat of losing her medical license wasn't enough of a deterrent. So what that she crashed her Porsche on the front lawn, or passed out and didn't realize her husband and son had checked her into the Red Roof Inn and left her there until she came to?

Camille relapsed and went to rehab not once, not twice, but three times. She got humbled only when, after the third relapse, she woke up in the ICU and found she was under the care of the residents for whom, only days before, she had been the attending physician. After the last relapse, her medical license was revoked for one year.

The wolf is always at the door. Alcoholism is a smart disease. It will outsmart the brainiest person. It is also the only disease known that has to be self-diagnosed. You have to believe you have a problem.

No matter how much help you receive or how many times you go to rehab, it won't work until you believe you have a problem and that your life will be better if you quit drinking.

Alcoholism and drug addiction allows people to muck up their lives, and they'll muck yours up too. It is the disease of "I'm gonna do it my way." People in the throes of their disease are like balking babies who grab and down the poisonous elixir and then wait for that poison to solve all their problems. Time and time again, they fail to see that it's the elixir that's killing them.

Alcohol loves procrastination. *I'll quit tomorrow, next month, or next year. I'll quit if I start to get bad. I'll quit if I ever drive drunk. I'll quit when the kids notice. I'll quit when I sneak and drink alone.* The problem is that denial is part of the disease, and alcoholics can't see how they kept lowering the bar and have already moved into areas they swore they'd avoid. *I'll quit, but if I relapse over the July fourth weekend, I'll just come back to meetings.* I hear that excuse a lot.

It's true that many have had to try time and again before they could get sober and stay sober. Alcohol entices, and it suggests that it's okay to binge drink just one more time. I've had friends die in car accidents because they just wanted to drink one more time.

A budding alcoholic's brain won't throw up a yield or a stop sign. Instead, an alcoholic's best thinking will tell her to try herbs, diets, self-help books, detox cleanses, and/or antidepressants. Women will try anything but quitting drinking, and they'll blame those tremors on too much caffeine.

Alcohol murders marriages. And some men or significant others like their women sick. Men married to alcoholic or drug-addicted women have total control. They often provide the money, the home, and the stable structure in which a woman can use. Some partners like their women to be dependent. It makes them feel powerful and secure.

A woman's spouse may also have a substance-abuse problem and may selfishly not want to part with the companionship of his or her best using buddy, as in my early sobriety, when my husband balked. Women in relationships such as these often have no motivation to quit drinking. Unless physical consequences or some other catalyst encourages sobriety, these women rarely attempt to get sober, and if they do, they have a high risk of relapse.

For serious sobriety to take hold, a woman has to be willing to lose her husband or significant other, her home, her finances, everything. I am not suggesting that women *will* lose these things—most times they won't—but in order to get sober and stay sober, you have to accept the idea that everything may have to change—or go. It takes that level of willingness.

That concept of deep surrender stops so many. They will not let go of their control. They will not let go of their comfort. It is only when you can get to that place of deep surrender, where you throw up your hands and succumb to a higher power and are at least willing to accept the unknown, that God shows up and the miracle happens.

Relapse is the ultimate battle of wills. We reject what God wants for us because we want what *we* want for us. Alcoholics, and people in general, are not designed to handle the poison we ingest. I know some people who tried to quit drinking over and over because they knew they had a problem and thought they should quit, but they never would surrender.

My drinking wasn't as much the issue, I thought, as was my reaction to life. However, once I ingested alcohol, it caused me and others to pause. The point I want to make is that just like alcoholics show up in a hundred different forms, so too are the excuses and reasons for relapse. It is worth repeating that relapse can be condensed down to one final concept: people relapse because they want to use more than they want to stay sober. Period.

When I was a flight attendant, my coworkers and I did a lot of drinking, and so did the pilots. I can tell you with certainty that I flew with pilots who joked about the bottles on the bar shelf and how those bottles started breathing and talking to them. I can't say that I ever flew with a pilot who drank on the job, but how could they not be hung over? We can't assume that just because someone has a title or huge responsibilities that they're sober or have it all together.

Another woman, Sheryl, works in a large hospital and is a surgical tech on the heart team. People on the heart team are frequently on call and need to be available to work on a moment's notice. She is also a recovering alcoholic, but there were times when her sobriety was precarious or nonexistent. She was in and out of rehab; she went to outpatient treatment; she went to meetings. She lost numerous good jobs due to her poor attendance. She admits, "I kept lowering the bar and crossed every boundary I set for myself. My mentality was more like when someone talked about not drinking, my first thought was *Come on, hang in there. You got this.*"

How did she finally sober up? She got sick and tired of feeling like crap and her life being shit, and she finally got honest about the benzos. (Every time she got out of rehab, she'd start popping benzos.) She justified those lost jobs as being everyone's fault but hers. She was further enabled by her coworkers who covered for her and each other when, time and time again, she or one of the others on the team showed up drunk or hung over.

She continued to go to after-care and twelve-step meetings and would cry the whole time about how none of it worked. It took a lot of degradation and demoralization before she acquiesced and admitted that though there were times she didn't drink, she never quit taking pills.

It pays to remember that alcoholism/drug addiction affects 10 percent of the population. Millions of people have problems, and statistically, only 2 percent of those that need to get sober ever get sober and stay sober.

I hope every woman reading this understands that she doesn't have to wait until that rosebud on her breast turns into a long-stemmed rose before she says, "Enough!" No one has to waste her life, destroy her family, or harm her children. Alcohol, drugs, and pharmaceuticals can rob you of a normal, happy, stable life—they will only destroy you if you allow your fear, ego, pride, and dishonesty to rule. You can save face; you can save your life.

~ 12 ~

Out of the Grave

John C., Licensed Independent Chemical Dependency Counselor. Sobriety date: January 23, 1980

I ASKED JOHN TO SIT DOWN with me because he's one of the few chemical dependency counselors that I know who is also in recovery. There are many counselors out there that have all the necessary degrees and certificates; however, they don't all understand alcoholism. What so many counselors refuse to accept is that an addict or alcoholic will immediately know the difference between a talking head and someone who understands the disease because he or she too has suffered and come out on the other side, recovered.

~

I dug graves, and every three days I wet the bed. That's where my drinking took me. Toward the end, I couldn't even show up to dig graves. There's irony in all of that—little did I know then that because of my drinking, I was digging a grave for myself too.

I bombed out at three different colleges. Drinking had become my primary occupation. It takes time, effort, and discipline to be a student. I had neither of those qualities, but when it came to drinking, I shined. I joined the Army to rein in my drinking. That was a stupid idea.

I knew at an early age that my drinking was out of control. I'd look at my best friend, and sometime around 3:00 a.m. he'd switch to coffee. How did he do that? At the time, my friend could stop drinking. He still ended up dying from alcoholism.

My drinking was a long slow decline. I remember sitting in my dorm room when I was eighteen ruminating about my drinking. When I was in the army I asked the biggest drug dealer at the base if he thought I had a problem. We do that, you know. We take informal surveys when we're concerned about our drinking but don't want to stop yet. It's easy to find someone to tell you what you want to hear.

I went to my first twelve-step meeting in 1977. I'd first read about twelve-step groups in the newspaper when I was six years old. Ann Landers talked about it in her column. Then I heard about the program again when the family used to whisper about an uncle who lived out of state, but he got sober back in the '60s, a minor miracle in itself right there.

During my Army stint, I was stationed in Korea. I worked as a translator and came home with a Korean bride. I drank and pissed the bed; not a recipe for wedded bliss.

I was in and out of the program for three years, and the only sober time I managed to string together was two weeks. My track record looked like this: flunked out of three colleges, couldn't control my compulsive drinking, hated digging graves. It wasn't until I went back to meetings, got serious, got a sponsor, and started working the program that things began to change.

Sober for the first time ever, I visited a monastery, and I realized I wanted to go into chemical dependency counseling. I had all this firsthand knowledge that I felt I needed to share.

Somewhere in all that I went back to school and acquired all the necessary degrees and certifications needed to become a Licensed Independent Chemical Dependency Counselor (LICDC).

Being in recovery has been a wonderful asset. So many counselors counsel alcoholics and addicts, but are they effective? Counselors who aren't in the program or recovering alcoholics or addicts themselves can still be effective if they're willing to educate themselves by going to meetings to do their research.

I've seen counselors who try to strong-arm people into treatment who are nowhere near ready to get sober. It doesn't work. How can you be a counselor and not go to twelve-step meetings to see what it's all about? So many in the mental health field have all the necessary credentials, but none of them understand addiction or alcoholism on a practical level.

Most of my clients find me through the courts or recommendations from early intervention specialists. I use the low-key approach. I try to educate my clients about the disease of alcoholism. I talk to them about their drinking. If you drink a lot when you do drink, that's a problem.

The biggest predictor I have found that a person will get into trouble with alcohol is family history. That has been my experience. If there is alcoholism in the family, watch out. It's a hereditary disease.

Educating a person about their disease is key, but most people still don't want to hear the truth. The most frequent excuse I hear is the pat statement, "I don't have a problem." Regardless of consequences, or the number of people in the alcoholic's life who are distressed over their drinking, the majority of people continue to deny that they have a problem.

The good news is, sometimes years later I'll run into these people at a meeting. The seed was planted, and when things got bad enough, at least they knew where to go.

Today, I stress to clients that it doesn't matter as much what other people think about their drinking—it's what they think that counts. People cannot be coerced into getting sober. There are scores of people out there with drinking problems. Their families all want them to get sober. Their employers want them sober. Their kids want them to get sober. Unless the person affected wants to get sober, it's all wishful thinking.

If you want to get sober, I'd advise you to stay away from psychiatrists. There are some good ones out there, but many of them still don't understand addiction. I know one psychiatrist who'd tell women they weren't alcoholic, especially if they were pretty girls. He'd scold them and tell those women not to call themselves alcoholics. He said that sort of verbiage was "self-defeating." Another psychiatrist was even worse. His treatment for alcoholism consisted of prescriptions for Xanax or Valium.

A lot of medical professionals don't understand the alcoholic or drug addict. Doctors often exacerbate the problem because they're pharmacologically driven. Pills are the only solution they know how to offer. The world is full of addicts and alcoholics. The saddest thing is when a person asks for help and they're pointed in the wrong direction. For many, they still believe their doctor has all the knowledge. The question that needs to be answered is, Why don't doctors understand addiction? Why aren't doctors taught about the twelve steps? All I've seen over the years is doctors leaning toward the only thing they know how to do, and that's prescribe more drugs.

The heroin epidemic is fueled by people who started with pain medication and got addicted. When the pills ran out, they turned to heroin. Heroin especially exemplifies the prescribing problem of physicians: Suboxone, Subutex, and Methadone. A person trying to get off heroin is often prescribed one of these three drugs. The problem is that a person never gets clean. Compounding the problem is that drugs like Suboxone don't address the feelings the person tried to mask in the first place. It's like slapping a Band-Aid on a gaping wound.

All three drugs have ugly withdrawals. In essence, a person is just switching addictions from an illegal drug to a legal substance. The underlying problem has yet to be addressed.

One woman I knew was college-educated, worked, and maintained a life. The use of Methadone allowed her to have a relatively normal existence other than every morning she had to go to Project Cure to get her little cup of Methadone. So for a few, perhaps it does give them a chance, but it usually doesn't work that way. Another woman I knew, similar scenario, ended up dying of an overdose. So often the drug addict starts using again while on Methadone, or they'll sell the

Methadone and go back to street drugs because they want the high. I've heard other heroin addicts say detoxing from Methadone is worse than coming off heroin.

The other problem with prescribing these substitute drugs is that doctors are looking for chemical solutions to a spiritual problem. It rarely works. People that take Methadone don't change their using behavior or their thinking. They don't learn new coping skills. One doctor I know kept his patient on Methadone for ten years! That's not getting clean.

In my experience, the most doomed client and the most difficult addict/alcoholic to treat is the one with a guaranteed income. Whether that income is from a spouse or a disability check, it doesn't matter. Anyone who can drink or use within their income is almost always doomed.

Being in recovery myself has been my biggest asset. I usually mention, just once, to my clients that I'm in recovery. So often, after my admission, there is a noticeable shift in their behavior. All of a sudden I'm not just talking. I have earned credibility. I suppose that counselors that are not alcoholics or addicts can still be effective, but if they aren't willing to educate themselves about how the twelve steps work, what can they really offer? It's impossible to say that the twelve steps don't work when you see hundreds and thousands of people recovering.

Even people with serious mental issues can recover. It's not a black-and-white issue. Some people in recovery may need antidepressants. People taking Lexapro, Zoloft, Cymbalta, their minds stay clear enough to grasp and work the steps. People on antianxiety medication, forget it. Xanax and Ativan are addictive drugs. A recovering person or a person interested in getting sober has to accept that antianxiety medications are not allowed.

The biggest goal of treatment should be to help a person learn that they need to go to meetings for the rest of their lives or chances for long-term recovery are minimal. Anti-twelve-step rhetoric poisons the Internet, but do the people writing all that crap know what they're talking about?

The public still has a skewed perception of the twelve steps. They believe they have to walk into a room and spill their guts. Their perception is that it's a constant revolving door. None of that is the truth.

I continue to refer my clients to twelve-step programs because the bottom line is that the twelve steps absolutely work, if the person is truly interested in working the program. I had the privilege of meeting one doctor associated with an effective recovery center in Louisville, Kentucky. Before prescribing any medication he'd ask the patient to talk about what sort of program they worked. If they didn't have a program, he'd suggest that for thirty days they go to twelve-step meetings, find a sponsor and talk to them every day, and if after thirty days they still felt they needed medication, to come back. He understood that the program works remarkably well when people immerse themselves in recovery.

Most people are surprised to hear how well the twelve steps work. Most people don't realize that it doesn't work when people don't follow the suggestions. Counselors and physicians and treatment centers who are not familiar with the program or how an addicted person thinks all will have you believe that a pill, acupuncture, talk therapy, yoga, Antabuse, massage, any number of alternative therapies will work. The truth is these other therapies don't work. People may stay dry for a time, but there is a huge difference between being dry and being sober. There is also a huge difference between getting sober for a few months and staying sober for the rest of your life—while living a happy, productive life.

There is a saying that if you sober up a horse thief, you still have a horse thief. The steps, when worked and applied to a person's life, brings about a supernatural change as a result of a spiritual awakening. The person will never be the same.

In My Opinion

I concur with John. Why? Because I've seen people struggle and try all sorts of alternative ways to get sober, and, invariably, most times they end up back in recovery rooms, more beat up and discouraged than ever. Or they're depressed and they continue to live isolated lives full of fear. Or those of us who stayed in the rooms of recovery hear about their funerals.

I talked to another chemical dependency counselor who was about to finish his dissertation. As educated as he was, I was disgusted with his response when I asked him how he handled his clients with chemical dependency issues. He said, "I talk to them about moral values, and we set goals along those lines."

What? Seriously, was he kidding me? Was this the crap they were teaching at the PhD level? Or was this his takeaway? I don't know for sure, but to base treatment or therapy on the assumption that alcoholics have a moral-issue disease is unbelievable. No wonder so many people continue to die from this disease. As John C. pointed out, it's terribly sad when someone wants help and doesn't get the help he or she needs.

I asked this guy about his success rate with the moral-issue approach. He shrugged dismissively and answered, "I guess when people want to quit, they'll quit."

Those were the only intelligent words I heard come out of his mouth. He was correct in saying that people have to want to make some changes in their lives before change can occur. However, if you plant the right seeds, perhaps those changes or the willingness to change can come about much sooner than if you berate people for their perceived lack of morals.

The whole system is broken. We need the right people in the right positions to say the right things. The professionals pat themselves on the back because they acquired a stack of credentials, but so many of them still don't understand alcoholism and addiction. Perhaps with some disciplines, degrees mean something, but when it comes to treating alcoholism, the true experts are the people who were alcoholics/addicts themselves, and who have found a way to make friends with their disease and live happy, sober, productive lives.

Any of us who have been through the educational process know that come graduation day, you know only a little. Actual learning takes place when you step out into the real world and have to apply what you learned.

John makes a good case for why people are better off hooking up with a chemical dependency (CD) counselor who is in recovery than one who isn't. At the very least, he recommends that people seek out therapists or CD counselors who are willing to educate themselves about the disease of alcoholism and the twelve steps of recovery.

I had the opportunity to do CD assessments at one of the hospitals where I worked. On occasion, I covered for the CD counselor when he had other commitments. This guy had all the right certificates and degrees, but he didn't understand the addict or alcoholic intimately. You can't talk to addicts about statistical data or topics such as comorbidity and expect them to relate to you. They will immediately view you as someone who knows nothing about their life, their disease, or how they feel.

His idea of success was to coddle the addicts or alcoholics, cajole them into treatment, or talk to them in a didactic way. He congratulated himself when clients entered a thirty-day treatment program. Many of the clients left treatment before the thirty days were up, only to show back up at the hospital. I knew most of them had no real intention of getting sober. They just wanted to regroup.

I watched those same people cycle over and over again through the system. The clients learned that they could go out and use and burn all their bridges, and when they felt bad enough from using and abusing or running from the law, they'd come back to the hospital, see the CD counselor, and he'd put them back in treatment somewhere. These people are savvy enough to know that if there's no room at the treatment facilities, they can threaten suicide and at least get admitted to the hospital for a few days, where they'll get "three hots and a cot."

Addicts and alcoholics can be masterful manipulators. They know how to work the system, and they do it very well. They learn who they can control and which CD counselor will bend to their demands.

I watched this particular counselor enable bad behavior. He bought into their sob stories. In actuality, all that was accomplished was the person on the lam had another thirty days to smooth things over with their families, have a rest, and gear up for the next go-around.

The system is completely broken. The money wasted is astronomical. Most of the patients we saw didn't have insurance. Money was being thrown away over and over again, and people were *not* recovering.

So many people still had no idea about twelve-step programs. When meetings were suggested, the clients rejected the idea. Why? They'd rather not put forth the effort and work for recovery. Plain and simple, they don't want to be inconvenienced, and some don't want to change. It takes work to get sober. It's easier to go to a doctor or rehab and hope that someone will give you a magic pill. People don't want to look at or change their behavior. Unfortunately, some doctors have led them to believe that a pill just might fix them.

Another significant population of patients had heard of the twelve steps, and some had learned about the program when they were nudged by the judge. Others landed, like my mother and sister, in psych wards. If the staff in the psych ward suggested a twelve-step program, you'd hear people whine and complain that they had tried the steps but they didn't work. These were some of their excuses: "I don't want to talk to strangers." "I can't find a meeting." "I need to get a job, so I don't have time for meetings." "I hate going." "I hate everybody at the meeting." "I tried it, but it doesn't work for me." "I don't want to tell all my stuff to strangers."

These same people would launch into soliloquies about how unique they were, how they had mental issues, and how they were certainly not addicts or alcoholics. They felt sure that nobody understood how different they were and that the right medication was all that was needed to put them on the right track. They refused to believe or even look at the fact that they had all these problems because of their drinking and drugging.

We need more medical staff who know to ask these same people a few pointed questions—in particular: "When you tried recovery rooms in the past, did you go to a meeting every day?" They will always say no. If they have time to use drugs or drink every day, they can make time for a meeting every day. "Did you get a sponsor?" "Did you listen to what the people suggested?" "Did you introduce yourself and let people know you were new and needed some support?" "Did you work the steps?" "Did you stop drinking?" "Did you stop using drugs?"

Not one person who claims that the twelve steps don't work has ever really given it a fair shot.

We've already learned that the active alcoholic can appear to be mentally ill. My mother was diagnosed as manic depressive. However, once she got sober she never suffered with depression, and she didn't take any medication. She'd been misdiagnosed. She had substance-abuse issues. Period. Unless professionals know what addiction and alcoholism truly looks like, their misdiagnoses may actually be honest mistakes.

If you find yourself in trouble with alcohol or drugs, seek out family members or friends in recovery. They are the best resource to get you pointed in the right direction. Professionals who are in recovery—and there are plenty of them—can give recommendations on who to see for help. They can direct you to other professionals who understand the disease and will not pump you full of more pills and then send you on your way. There are many physicians in recovery who understand that medications given to a person who is an alcoholic or addict will only exacerbate their problem and make the probability for recovery slim to none. The solution is to not accept a mental health diagnosis without *first* quitting drinking and drugging.

~ 13 ~
Doctors, Nurses, Hospitals, and Health Care

CAMILLE, CARO, AND FIONA are all medical doctors who still practice; all of them admitted they were clueless about the disease of alcoholism and addiction. It was only when they had to deal with their own addiction issues that the internist, the surgeon, and the ER doctor learned something about the nature of their diseases.

What does this say about our health care system? Camille still works with residents, and, to her knowledge, they can opt to spend time with an addictionologist, but the course is an elective. Even with the prevalent heroin epidemic and drug-addicted babies being born, medical schools still don't train doctors to recognize or deal with addiction.

Furthermore, if you don't understand the alcoholic, how can you treat alcoholism? Doctors and professionals who don't understand the disease of alcoholism need to say that and then point their patients in a direction where they can find help.

Emergency room doctor Fiona had this to say before she got into recovery and dealt with her own alcoholism: "It's been my experience after twenty-six years in medicine that I can't think of one person who ever seemed to know or understand anything about alcoholism.

Mostly, we griped or made fun of their messes. I'd recognize the people in end-stage alcoholism, but unless they crashed a car or had red noses and ascites, I didn't get it either."

Fiona was right—doctors and nurses do make fun of the alcoholics and their messes. When I worked in the ER, we all got sick to death of the addicts and alcoholics draining all the resources only to go out and do it all over again. I was in recovery at the time, and I understood the disease, but it still wears you out. No one wants to hear this, but it's the truth.

Where's the compassion? Well, the compassionate thing to do is to quit pretending that all doctors and nurses understand the addict and alcoholic and to instead point people in the right direction. Fiona says:

> *Now that I understand addiction and can spot it in others, I have more patients call me a fucking asshole bitch because I refuse to give them scripts for Percocet. I'm much more apt to counsel patients and talk to them about other ways to relieve their chronic pain. So many patients worry about insomnia; I tell them to get clean and all of that will go away.*
>
> *Most of the physicians I work with are flippant toward the drug seekers and alcoholics. Doctors need to hear speakers or read books such as this one, or do something to educate themselves about the disease of addiction. I know prior to being in recovery I had a patient who told me he didn't want narcotics. I thought, what kind of a freak is he? He confused me. I never understood the correlation between drugs and alcoholism. I thought they were two separate things. I never understood that alcoholism starts long before a person ends up in the ER with end-stage renal or liver disease.*
>
> *Doctors have got to understand the imperativeness of learning something about addiction. Doctors that don't understand the nature of addiction do become part of the problem. I now understand when I see the word* alcoholic *in a person's chart that*

I can't send them out the door with a prescription for Valium and Vicodin. Prior to becoming an alcoholic in recovery myself, I never understood that.

Camille pointed out that she was surprised to learn that addiction/alcoholism came in all shapes and sizes: "People never in a million years realize it can happen to them. I wish I could share my story with other physicians, but I'd feel very uncomfortable doing that. Isn't that a shame that doctors are so judgmental that we can't admit that physicians have problems too?"

Doctors may suggest therapy for addicts/alcoholics, but let's put this into perspective. When you go to a doctor, you pick one that you believe knows something about your condition. If you have AFib, you see a cardiologist. If your knee gives out, you head to an orthopedic surgeon. If you feel like crap and think you have diabetes, you go to an internist. Think about it: how many people do you know that would allow a doctor who'd only read about a surgery to operate on them? It's no different with addiction. We have professionals who have read about addiction, but they've never battled addiction themselves, so their perspective is myopic. They are unable to intimately understand the mind twists of an addicted person and are often too easily manipulated.

Sure, all doctors know something about the human body, but few, if any, feel knowledgeable enough to treat every disease. Doctors need to get their egos out of the way and, when it comes to addiction/alcoholism, have the wherewithal to say, "I don't know," and point their patients in the direction of someone who does know.

Camille admitted that she couldn't see her own alcoholism, and she rarely noticed alcoholism in her patients. That only changed once she accepted she was an alcoholic and got into recovery. "Unless their liver enzymes were off the charts, or unless they had chronic pancreatitis, I never asked about their drinking."

Camille agreed that doctors contribute to the problem because they cave into pressure from their patients. "Most people don't like walking out of a doctor's office empty-handed. A script for antidepressants, antipsychotics, or an anxiety medication such as Xanax or Ativan is all we can offer to the person who insists that the doctor do something."

Our current culture has created customers hungry for more pills. You can't turn on the TV without being barraged with commercials touting one pill after another. People start to believe that a pill can fix every real or perceived malady.

The only times I've ever been aware of doctors asking about their patients' drinking is when they come into the ER already ravaged by alcohol—esophageal varices, bleeding ulcers, damaged livers, weakened hearts—or if the patients admit they have an alcohol problem.

Doctors Fiona and Camille stated that they are much more cautious when prescribing pain medication. Camille agreed that recovery has changed the way she practices medicine, in that she is fully present and no longer tries to rush through her day "so I can use, think about using, and worry about when and where I'll get to use."

Had my mom not crossed paths with the doctor in Toledo who knew what addiction looked like, my mother would've wasted whatever years she had left drunk, in the psych ward, and/or heavily medicated. Doctors would benefit from admitting they have much to learn about addiction.

Violet has metal rods in her back from a surgery. Though she was never in pain all those years after the surgery, she'd say she was and would ask her doctors for help. She said, "After any doctor took one look at my MRI or X-ray of my back with all those rods . . ." They believed her pain was legitimate. None of her doctors ever realized she was an addict. She doctor-shopped and always had a steady supply of drugs. It would be helpful if some doctors would concede that they need help in recognizing the addicts in their practices.

Unless you've jumped in the trench and have been there, you can't understand or recognize the disease. Consider the soldiers: unless you are a fellow soldier who has carried the pack, smelled the smells, heard the grenades, felt the bullets whizzing past your head, and seen your comrades injured, you can't truly know what that experience was like. For some reason, society understands and respects that sort of war; the war of alcoholism and addiction is just as bad, but in a whole different kind of way.

Here's the solution: Long-term, solid recovery continues to point to the twelve steps, but, as previously mentioned, people don't want to hear about the twelve steps because it requires that they do something. The steps are not a quick fix. They require commitment. There's a lot of misinformation out there about the twelve steps, and there's the truth that they are not a foolproof solution either. The twelve steps aren't glamorous, and meetings are cheap; toss a buck or two in the basket at each meeting, if you care to, and that's the end of that.

Alcohol is big business. Perhaps that has something to do with why, even though alcohol kills and maims, the industry continues to glamorize and portray it as something necessary to partake in in order to live a wonderful life.

As I mentioned earlier, Violet found recovery at the Edna House in Cleveland, Ohio. Their program is based on the twelve steps. The Edna House is run by former addicts and alcoholics with long-term recovery. They understand the disease and only allow two medications: Zoloft and Wellbutrin. No melatonin, no herbal products, no Benadryl.

Luxurious treatment facilities and the academic approach aren't the best options for most alcoholics or addicts. Psychology books are of little use, as is any sort of catering to the person who is in the throes of their disease.

Like the surgeon Caro points out in a forthcoming story, she went to the Shepherd Hill treatment center, and, though they treat a lot of physicians, the physicians were thrown in with the rest of the population. Caro was taken aback by the tattooed heroin addicts. She said she was even afraid of some of her peers, but the lesson was not lost on her that being a surgeon didn't mean she deserved special treatment. Addiction and death are the two great equalizers. There's not an alcoholic out there who doesn't need a heaping dose of humility.

One woman I know was diagnosed with congestive heart failure one year into her recovery. Her cardiologist didn't understand addiction either.

He advised this woman to avoid stress. On several occasions he insisted she allow him to write her a prescription for Xanax to help curb any anxiety. She explained that she is an addict. She told him all about her history and how she abused Xanax and other prescription drugs. He said he understood—but he didn't get it at all. Three weeks passed. She had more tests. She had chest pain and felt short of breath. Again, he insisted she allow him to write her a prescription for anti-anxiety medication.

She went through the whole spiel again, reminding him that she was an addict and that if she popped one more pill she'd wake up the beast. She had to drill it into his head that she was not a candidate for benzos. She told him that her medicine was meetings, prayer, and helping another alcoholic. She restated, "If you wake up the beast, I'll eat every single pill you give me, and then I'll be on the streets looking for more." For her, like so many addicts and alcoholics, one Ativan or Xanax is all that stands between life and death. Today, she chooses life.

Therein lies the problem with some medical doctors. Her cardiologist meant well, but he didn't understand addiction. What the doctor saw was a nice middle-aged woman with a job. He didn't see the whole picture and couldn't seem to connect the dots even when those dots were lined up for him. There are too many medical professionals who don't understand what it means when addicts tell them they are addicts. There are too many doctors, like Fiona used to be, who will nod like they get it, and then turn around and write a prescription for

Xanax, Ativan, Vicodin, and Klonopin—anyone who is an addict and wants recovery cannot take those sorts of drugs. Too many people have relapsed on them, never to get back into recovery. Many of them die. I have seen it happen over and over.

I worked on this book in Bimini, where I met a nursing student, Jessica, from the Cape Cod area. Jessica was finishing up a bachelor of science in nursing. We talked about how most nursing students are required to attend a few AA meetings in order to understand something about addiction. Why don't medical schools require the same?

Jessica relayed that her school brought in a registered nurse who had been stripped of his license due to addiction, only to get his license back after he completed a rigorous program that included frequent random drug tests. She said her class was split on their reactions: Half were angry that the nurse was allowed to work. They worried: What if he relapsed again? The other half of the class was supportive.

Like Camille pointed out, it's hard for nurses and doctors to be open about their addiction issues because of the judgments that are made. The people that the public and other medical professionals need to be concerned with are not the recovering addicts and alcoholics who are sober, work a program, and/or receive monitoring, but the people like the nurse anesthetist or the anesthesiologist who use IV Fentanyl every night when they go home, or employees like Sheryl, the surgical tech on the heart team who used to come to work hung over or still drunk. There are countless doctors, nurses, and ancillary staff members working in the medical field who are active in their disease, but no one pays attention because they show up for work, and most people can't sniff them out.

Truth be told, until maybe recently I've yet to work on any unit in any hospital where there haven't been coworkers with addiction issues; either they were already caught and had restricted licenses, or they were active in their disease, but, because they showed up for work, they flew under the radar.

Another aspect of the disease is when people relapse after years of long-term recovery. My friend James, an MD, has a compelling story, because he looked nothing like anyone would suspect an addict to look like; for God's sake, he was the chief of staff at a large hospital. Dr. James's journey is important to include because it proves that once an alcoholic/addict, always an alcoholic/addict, and it begs the medical community to reconsider their uppity stance on addiction and alcoholism.

Dr. James says he relapsed after twenty years of sobriety because "I quit being honest about how fucked-up my life was. My home life was horrible, and I failed to reach out to others, including my sponsor. We quit communicating." He went on:

> *There I was, doing all sorts of noble things. I was the primary caregiver for my wife, I was chief of staff, I taught a course on physician mentoring; we have a medical school in town, and I taught courses there as well. I got involved in Al-Anon, and that kept me sane, but the busier I got, the more my ego grew. I had all sorts of accolades. Everyone thought I made a wonderful chief of staff. I became an egomaniac with an inferiority complex. I thought,* Yes, they're right—I am wonderful, and I'm not an asshole.
>
> *One day I decided to take a break from my sobriety. I stole a few of my wife's Percocets. I relaxed. It felt good. Over the course of several months, I stole more and more of her pills. My wife had no reason to suspect I was stealing. Her illness progressed to where she used Fentanyl patches. I'd read about them on the Internet and thought I'd ingest one. My wife, who normally slept on the couch due to her illness, for some reason thought to come upstairs and check on me. She had to call the squad. I received Narcan, twice. There I was, chief of staff, and they're working on me like they do with every other drug addict that squad rolls in with, all because I put that Fentanyl patch in my mouth. I overdosed, big time.*
>
> *People like me who use after a period of sobriety have the highest risk of a lethal overdose. I had no tolerance. People at the hospital were in shock. A select few weren't surprised.*

The EMS who found the Fentanyl patch in my mouth told the police, and the city pressed charges. I was charged with a felony for diverting a controlled substance. I went to treatment in lieu of conviction.

Back in 1992, before I got sober the first time, the DEA intervened because I wrote illegal prescriptions. My drug of choice was everything: alcohol, pills, whatever. Back then, my license was suspended for six months. I was at the end of my fellowship, and, surprisingly enough, the department chairman at the time knew a thing or two about addiction. He also had some influence with the American Board of Obstetricians, and they still allowed me to sit for my certification.

Even back then I had consequences, but I forgot all about that. I forgot to treat my disease, and, before I knew it, I was back in it. After this last overdose, my license was suspended for seven months. I had to go to a board-approved treatment center. I was the oldest person in the facility. Most all of the other "clients," they called us, were kids trying to get off of the heroin.

Dr. James echoed what Camille said: "The fear of being found out . . . Ohio is still one of the worst states to be found impaired. The state board of medicine continues to view addition as a moral issue. They are rather self-righteous, and their attitude instills fear in doctors and encourages secrecy."

According to Dr. James, "The attitudes of doctors toward addicts has changed marginally. Nothing is taught in medical school. Money pours into treating the symptoms. Instead, we need the money to be put into treating the addiction."

Here again, as a whole, we need to change the way we think. It makes no sense to penalize someone who is working on his or her issue and trying to become a responsible, productive member of society. The surgeon with a scalpel in his hand and two drinks under his belt, which everyone on the heart team knows he's had but, out of fear, no one confronts him—that's who is the real problem. It's like what

Caro, the surgeon, said: "What stunned me the most was the more I learned about alcoholism, the more doctors and surgeons came to mind that I felt needed to be in treatment too."

"A large portion of the medical community still looks at addiction from a moral model instead of the disease model," Dr. James says. "Addiction is a neurological disease. Scientific information says that the addict's brain chemistry is different. The part of our brain that governs moral judgment doesn't function well when alcohol or drugs are in the body. However, the reptilian part functions just fine, and when an addict or alcoholic uses, that is the part of the brain that dictates the behavior."

Dr. James continues: "Doctors, and the medical community, need an attitude adjustment. The days of ignorance need to be put behind us. For years there has been so little training about addiction, and the medical community accepts that it's been that way for so long that no one looks to change it—and that must change."

Dr. James's thoughts support what I believe to be true: People working in medicine are often in need of help themselves, but with all the judgment and misconceptions, who's going to reach out? What hospitals and corporations need to ask themselves is, do we staff our employee-assistance programs with people in recovery who understand the disease, or do we have a bunch of talking heads with degrees who can spout theory but know nothing about the disease and can do little to garner our employees' trust?

~ 14 ~

Spirit in the Rocks and Wind

I CAN'T TALK ABOUT CHANGE or sobriety without talking about spirituality. What is spirituality? It's different things for different people, but the one common denominator is that it's people's connection with the divine, whatever the word *divine* means to them. Women rise above their problems when they come to believe. There is a power in the universe, and if we can turn our lives over to that power, our lives will never be the same.

When I asked some of the women who share their stories in this book what spirituality means to them, their answers all had to do with peace, serenity, and faith. And I believe forgiveness needs to be on that list too. We cannot commune with the divine or even attempt to connect with spirit with a heart hardened by unforgiveness, and that includes self-forgiveness. For so many women that get sober after years of self-destruction, once they understand the damage they've done to their families or to themselves, they have a hard time with self-forgiveness. I gently remind every distraught woman that if she could've done better, she would've done better. Continually beating yourself up for things that cannot be changed is senseless, and God does not want us to do that. (Yet another reason to raise the bottom and stop before the collateral damage piles up!)

It's human nature to want to connect with others, and that includes our craving for a spiritual connection. Don't we all want to know that we aren't alone in the world and that someone or something cares?

My spiritual life increased exponentially when I learned to get myself out of the way and allow God to be God. I was humbled when I realized that God will not clamor for our attention. It is up to us to invite spirit into our lives. It is up to us to be done with self-seeking and self-will, and it is at that juncture that we open the door for God, and he steps in. That is also the place where God (or universal spirit—whichever force you identify with) will make music out of your screams.

My search for God started for real once I got sober. I read books about the afterlife. For a time, I church-hopped. I even visited a holy rolling Pentecostal church where people spoke in tongues and fell into the aisles. I don't know if I witnessed theatrics or if the spirit really did slam all those people to the floor, but I didn't think I'd find my answers there.

For me, once a Catholic, always a Catholic—though I needed to explore, I knew I was on the right path because I began to have beautiful spiritual dreams of the crucifixion and resurrection. I knew God was alive and that I would find my way, but I had to keep searching.

Early in my sobriety I went to crystal readers and tarot readers and spent hours in new age book stores. I started a dream journal, and later, I spent a little time at Linden Baptist Church, where I met Pastor Pam.

Pastor Pam glows. She is beautiful inside and out and is the sort of woman who walks the walk and doesn't just talk the talk. I remember her saying how she couldn't believe God had called her to preach at Linden Baptist Church—at the time, it was a dying church located in a drug- and crime-infested neighborhood whose congregation had been whittled down to all of fifteen people.

"I went to lay pastor school to go deeper with my relationship to God and to be of service to my church," Pam said. "After I finished, I felt God was calling me to get ordained, and I said, 'Father, if you want me to be ordained nationally, you will have to open the door.' One month later an area minister contacted me and said he wanted me to apply to pastor at Linden Baptist; they were down to a few handfuls of parishioners, and he thought I'd be a good fit.

"I told him I never thought of being a pastor—especially not at Linden Baptist! I had zero experience. I had only preached all of four sermons in my whole life. Besides, the church resided in an impoverished area of the city. I kept saying to myself, 'Seriously, God, you want me there?' I sure didn't want to say yes, but I felt God telling me this was where he wanted me, and my job was to obey. That dying, desperate church has grown to almost one hundred and fifty people. We've built relationships in the neighborhood, and the people know we care."

Pastor Pam is authentic, and she exudes love. People are drawn to her spirit, her optimism, and her strength. Her actions speak far louder than any sermon she could preach. I asked her to define what spirituality meant to her: "To me, spirituality is that desire to show that Jesus is real by the way you live your life. Jesus Christ is at the core. He's the foundation. Everything about Jesus is unconditional love. Growing in spirituality requires perseverance; it is not for the faint of heart," she says. "To have a relationship with God, you have to be willing to commit to daily prayer in an effort to communicate with God, and ask him in all things, whatever the day brings, to be able to love the person in front of you. Spirituality is being obedient even when you don't know why God wants you to do whatever it is that he's called you to do. Spirituality is knowing that God is pure love. The God I serve is not an angry God."

I love her description, and I believe that anyone who decides to work toward a relationship with God will be rewarded. I agree with Pastor Pam that obedience is an important aspect of spiritual growth.

~

When my sons were juniors in high school, I had my own experience with obedience. I crossed paths with a then-eighteen-year-old

Ava, who remembered me from a one-time encounter years before at my sons' grade school. I guess I'd gone to the fourth-grade parent luncheon—she was in the fifth grade at the time, and she said I'd worn a furry coat that she liked and never forgot.

Years later, we met again. She approached me and asked if I was the twins' mom. At the time, she was a senior in high school, was a student athlete, and was addicted to opiates and alcohol. Her home life was horrible. She said she wanted and needed to get sober.

I felt God putting it on my heart to invite her to live with me and my family. Truthfully, that was the last thing I wanted to do, but the tug on my heart kept getting stronger. A week after she approached me, I informed my husband that she was coming to live with us. He thought I misspoke.

I was serious. I felt compelled to take Ava in. I told my husband that we had to do it. I didn't know if I was up for the task either, but I felt that was what God wanted me to do, and I wasn't about to say no.

My husband, God bless him, after he caught his breath, just stared at me like I was Medusa.

I moved one of my sons to the spare bedroom and redid his room for Ava, and she moved in and lived with us for almost two years. It wasn't easy—she usurped all of my time and energy. She needed a lot of love, firm boundaries, and infinite patience, and she brought more than her share of chaos. It was a whole different ball game than raising boys. Somehow, we muddled through. I'm so proud of Ava: she went on to finish college, she's employed, and she's been sober for nine years, but the best part is that she's established loving relationships in her life.

Ava said, "Living with Lisa and her family, I learned how to love. I got to see what the inner workings of a functional family looked like. I know that if I hadn't had a safe place to live, I would've never made it."

As I look back on that time, I believe that God tested me to see if I'd obey. It's so easy to say that we trust God and will listen to God until he asks us to do something we'd rather not do. The same went for

Pastor Pam: I'm certain there were plenty of other churches located in better neighborhoods that she'd rather have been assigned to, but she went where God told her to go.

By the time I decided to sober up, my beautiful mother had been sober seven years. She put her life together and made recovery her new vocation. She had a twinkle in her eye and had become the epitome of love and compassion. Although she went to church, she had formed a whole new spin; she too had found a spiritual connection that I don't think she'd ever had prior to her utter demoralization.

I think meetings are what God intended church to be like. People from all walks of life convene together for a common purpose: to live better, God-filled lives. I have witnessed miracle after miracle. In meetings, I'd watch people—some of them hopelessly ill, sick in body, mind, and spirit—begin to recover. Where else can you go in today's world and actually see someone transform his or her life right before your eyes?

I started to think about and question all the man-made rules in religion. I read Thomas Merton's *The Seven Story Mountain* and numerous books by Emmet Fox. I know many women have found strength in the writings of Marianne Williamson and Joan Chittister. I started to pay attention to the miracles all around me in nature. The more you learn about the natural world, the more clearly it points to a divine creator; there's spirit in the rocks and wind.

I reflected on the deep connections that I'd had with the animals in my life: It started with my horse. I always connected with whatever dog we had at the time. And a baby bird I saved one summer came back year after year to roost in our backyard. I started reading the Bible. I fell in love with the idea of becoming a better person, and I found gifts that I didn't know I had, like the gift of knowing.

In February 2014, I had a clear vision of a large shipping port. I knew the vision had to do with my twins. I never mentioned the vision to my sons until well after one of them accepted a job and I later learned he'd be placed in Philadelphia—Philly has one of the largest freshwater ports in the world. A few years after that, my other son landed in Seattle. I know God gave me that vision of a shipping port to prepare me once again to lean in and let go, let go, and let go some more.

Sobriety reveals the true soul inside of a person. Authenticity can't be revealed when it's smothered by drugs, alcohol, fear, selfishness, self-loathing, food, sex, or deceit . . . God needs a clear channel for his spirit to flow. We clog the flow with our selfishness, pettiness, and fear. All of those negative emotions impede the Holy Spirit.

The year was 2006 and I was beginning to feel that my spirit might need a retreat from the world. It'd been some years since I'd gone to regroup in Lourdes, the pilgrimage site located in France that rose to fame in 1858 when an apparition of the Blessed Virgin appeared to a peasant girl there named Bernadette. After Lourdes, I had gone back to school to pursue an English degree, and I was slated to graduate later in the year, but even after writing two novels, I felt like a fraud. I had no recollection of the classics. I needed to know where my alliances stood: Steinbeck (yes) or Joyce (no)?

Over Christmas break, a few quarters away from graduation, I realized I needed a break. My sons were heavily involved in sports. Nursing was a drain—emergency rooms and psych wards can do that to a person. I hadn't written anything creative since I started school a few years earlier. I felt cranky.

I scheduled a retreat to Gethsemani in Bardstown, Kentucky (where the famous monk Thomas Merton once lived), for the week between Christmas and New Year's. The monastery was practically empty. I read in the library, hiked the wooded trails, prayed, and swung into the rhythm of monastic life, even waking for vigils at 3:15 a.m.; the monks' chanting of the psalms was hauntingly beautiful.

There, I learned that I could be with me. The loudest noise was the clacking of silverware and, at night, the wind. Gethsemani is a silent monastery, and you'd be surprised how much noise silverware and wind can make.

Through this gift of retreat I'd given to myself, I reinforced what I'd learned about myself in Lourdes. I was truly okay with me. I could shut off my mind. My heart felt at peace. I knew I could accept where I landed in life and that I didn't have to brace myself for the journey; instead, I could enjoy it. I knew too that I loved my husband and sons and the foursome that we were.

Spirituality, for me, means growth. I've come to understand that I cannot worry about people who don't understand. I look back and realize I wasted too much energy feeling that people needed to approve of and understand me. It's a gift to be free of those sorts of stones that did nothing for me but weigh me down.

I was on my own path. We each have a path, but it's up to us to find that path. The saddest thing to me is when people don't even bother to look. God put each of us here for a reason. Spirituality for me was about finding my reason.

I had to learn and work at letting go. I had to make a concerted effort to live in God's will. I found peace when I accepted that what I wanted might not be what God wanted for me. I struggled for more than a decade to absorb that concept, and then I learned how to truly let go.

I already knew how to talk; now I needed to practice listening. God intended for us all to have rich interior lives, and we cannot hear God when we spend our time engaged in the clatter of the world.

I also had an epiphany at Gethsemani: God gives us families who love us, and when they have our best interests at heart, it pays to consider their viewpoint. Years earlier, when my mother was concerned, by the grace of God, I listened. That one decision to change myself changed the whole trajectory of my life.

Note to Readers

In the following ten stories, you will meet women who came to terms with their drinking and found new lives when they decided to surrender to the fact that they drank too much. Continuing down paths of self-destruction that caused such unhappiness and anxiety was no longer the best option for them. Only when they were willing to surrender, step back, and look at their situations from a clearer perspective were they able to see how their behavior was destroying not only their lives, but, in some cases, their families' lives as well.

There is something to be gleaned from each story (the women in this book have, collectively, over three hundred years' experience living sober), and whether you choose to read their stories all through quickly or savor each one more slowly, cling to the hope that if you have a problem, or if someone in your family or a friend has a problem, there is indeed a solution. Most of the women in these stories at one time felt hopeless and helpless. They never dreamed that alcohol was the problem, nor did they believe that once they stopped drinking, they could know such fulfillment and joy.

Willingness is the one must. Each woman who found recovery decided that her way was not working—she had to be open to something else. They all made the decision to get into the solution rather than stay stuck in anxiety, depression, restlessness, and chaotic relationships.

Each person has his or her own journey. My hope is that these stories will become part of yours.

~ 15 ~
Model Surgeon, Kidnapped!

Caro. Sobriety date: December 8, 2009

IT WAS HARD NOT TO NOTICE Caro when she walked into the recovery rooms. She is tall, blonde, and always beautifully dressed. What I remember more than her beautiful clothes, though, was her crying. She sat in the back of the room, for months, sniveling into a tissue. It took weeks before she raised her head and could look any of us in the eye.

I didn't want to intrude into her private misery, but you can't be in the recovery rooms and not want to reach out to the newcomer still hurting. What I did was offer up a hug and reassure her with a hundred trite but true recovery sayings: "Keep coming back." "It gets better." "One day at a time." "It will all work out." "Just don't drink today."

Caro did all of those things and more. Six months later, she carried herself like a queen. By then, she had shaken off the shroud of shame and embarrassment. She smiled all the time. She made friends.

It was not until many months into her recovery that I learned she was a surgeon. I love that about the program. No one asks or cares what you do for a living. It is a far cry from the monotonous cocktail parties filled with superficial chatter and one-upping that is still part of the social scene. Even today, I have yet to be at a party when someone doesn't ask, shortly after entering the room, what do I do or what my husband does for a living. In the rooms of recovery, we don't care about titles and labels. Everyone is special, but no one gets special treatment.

~

No one in my family had any idea about what made an alcoholic. They didn't know any alcoholics, and I didn't grow up around alcoholics. We lived in a small town. There were bars, and we referred to them as dark, seedy places. No one in my family knew anyone who went into those places of sin.

I didn't start drinking until my late twenties. I never drank in college. When I did start drinking, I drank normally for a long time. My drinking picked up after I had my children. Medical school, for me, came later. I was in my thirties when I went to medical school because first, I got a PhD in neurophysiology.

All this overachieving perhaps had something to do with my mother. I felt I had to compete with her for a relationship with my dad, like we were in direct competition for his affection. When I told Mom I wanted to go to medical school, she reacted nothing like I expected. Instead of being proud, she said, you'll get divorced and throw your whole life away. She didn't speak to me for a month. I wanted her approval, but I never got it—not the way Dad approved of me.

I started drinking to fit in with my peers. I was sick of being the nun in the group. I remember drinking amaretto sours and zinfandel wine, just to fit in. My natural disposition leans toward serious, but I always felt like the *most* serious person. I wanted to fit in, and alcohol loosened me up.

As with so many women, my drinking was only occurring in social settings. Toward the end of my surgical residency, I was going through a divorce. I discerned that wine helped quell some of my inner turmoil. I had all these feelings jutting out all over the place: hurt, anger, fear, rage. I couldn't deal with them.

The divorce threw me completely off-balance. My husband, out of the blue, said he wanted out of the marriage. I had had inclinations that something was amiss. He started taking trips. He locked his phone, and if I was anywhere near he'd let his calls go to voice mail. I could see he was not in the marriage anymore. He didn't like my medical friends. He didn't want to be a part of anything that I did. I felt more and more lonely. Again, I felt I didn't fit in.

I had no awareness of the disease of alcoholism. In my mind, there was a moral and social prejudice to being an alcoholic. If someone is stupid enough to lose control of their drinking, then they deserve what they get. They shouldn't have let themselves go.

Even before I got to the point where I needed to drink, I wanted to drink more than most people. That's when I got an inkling that maybe I had a problem. I tried to label my issues. Could it be immaturity? Do I have a coping problem? Social insecurities? I realized early on that I liked alcohol a lot. When someone came to dinner with a bottle of wine for four people, my first thought was, *No way, this will not be enough.* My tolerance was higher than most people's.

I'm a people pleaser. The one thing a people pleaser never wants to do is be a disgrace. Toward the end of my drinking, when I thought I needed help, I was paralyzed with fear. *How do I come out with this? How do I get help and still keep my secret? I'm terrified of how to tell my partners—what to tell them. If I come out with this, will I still get referrals from other doctors? What about my social network? Are they going to avoid me now if they know I am an alcoholic? Will the community and the hospital where I practice reject me?* I had all this fear.

I didn't even think about what I had been doing to my children. The last few years of my drinking, I started to remember things. I was in the grocery store with my son, who at that time was around five years old. It never occurred to me he noticed how much wine I purchased. Right there in the grocery checkout line, he piped up and in a loud voice asked, "Why do you buy so much wine?" My daughter's face fell flat when she'd see me pour a glass of wine. As my kids got older, they noticed that a wine glass became like another appendage. I drank a lot of wine. I felt a lot of guilt.

Work was a complicated mind game. I felt like a performer who needed to deliver an A-1 performance, each and every day. How could I juggle alcoholism and work as a surgeon?

I know I drank more than a normal person, and the only way to stay in denial was to divide my personality between who I wanted to be and who I was. As a physician, as a mother, I became a master at separating my nighttime drinking from my daytime profession.

Daily, I saw patients who reminded me of me. There was the forty-five-year-old woman with pancreatitis. I told her to quit drinking so much. I was stricken by these women, patients in their fifties, who would come into the hospital with cirrhosis, and a voice in my head would say, *Well, that could be you.*

I felt like a fraud. I wanted to shut down. I divorced the notion that I could be anything like my patients. I didn't drink at work. I didn't drink when I was on call, but thoughts of drinking, and the anxiety of not being able to drink, was always present. I wanted to believe there was a world between me and those patients, but the lines blurred. Come morning, I'd already be thinking about drinking.

Here I was, chief of surgery. I did consulting work, taught med students, and published articles. I had patients all over the place lying there hopeless. I felt I was far, far away from that.

They never talked about alcoholism in medical school, and they still don't in surgery rotations. Some medical schools give some appreciation for twelve-step programs, but they also look at them as a cult.

I knew I had a problem for two or three years before I addressed the problem. Alcohol kidnapped me. I ruminated about drinking, constantly. My parents kept telling me I drank too much. I took drinking tests and answered yes to all ten questions. I dismissed my parents' concerns and accused them of jumping to conclusions.

I didn't have a last drunk. As I mentioned, I worked as chief of surgery. My colleagues often talked about the hospital-sponsored wellness program for employees. I started to pay attention. Perhaps the wellness program was an option for me.

The final day came. I had several surgeries that day. I came home, had a glass of wine, made dinner, and went back to hospital. I was done living the lie. I wanted to come clean. I talked to the VP of staff and told him I had a drinking problem. He and another physician first asked if I was overreacting. Then they asked if I thought I was an alcoholic. I said, "I know I am." They looked incredulous, like it couldn't be true!

The next day, I went to treatment. I called my parents and told them where I was going to rehab. I asked for their support. I sat my kids down and explained that I'd be gone for seven weeks.

My kids were totally supportive and even relieved. Terrified as I was, I was more terrified that if I didn't do something about my drinking, I'd end up in an embarrassing situation that I might not be able to get out of so easily. I didn't want to humiliate my kids. I no longer wanted to be the person disconnected from their responsibilities. As a physician on numerous committees, the dichotomy of knowing but not knowing was killing me. I lived in that hypocrisy. That was my bottom.

I couldn't take the guilt anymore. Near the end, the disappointment on my daughter's face when I'd pour wine stabbed me in the heart, but that didn't stop me. It got to the point that I drank more often out of a Solo cup. The wine glass was just too small.

No one at the hospital suspected a thing. I pre-drank before I went anywhere so when I got to a function, I could have a few and no one would balk. I never had headaches. I didn't shake. I went to work every day. I drank to stop the voices in my head and take the edge off. I never blacked out. I was a maintenance drinker. I realized, working in medicine, that pills were not an option. Those scripts are traceable.

In treatment, I learned about the twelve steps. I didn't know there were programs available or that they were anonymous. After settling into treatment, I started to dwell on some of my colleagues. What stunned me the most was the more I learned about alcoholism, the more doctors and surgeons that came to mind that I felt needed to be in treatment too. Then I was pissed. These doctors, these surgeons, so many of them were drinking uncontrollably. *Why am I in treatment and they're not?* It wasn't fair.

When I got to a twelve-step program, I sat in the back of the room. I felt nothing but disgrace. I thought I was a disgrace to myself, my family, and my profession, and, most of all, I feared for my reputation. How could I know this was where I was headed? I didn't start drinking more regularly until I was thirty years old. How did this happen to me?

The whole process disturbed me. The people told me to get a sponsor, work the steps, give time, time. I was in panic mode. What if those steps stripped off my layers, then what? *I will be left cold, shivering, and everyone will see down to my core.* That is the sort of stuff that went through my mind.

I didn't like not knowing what would happen next. During years of working as a surgeon, you learn to prepare, and I was in control, but I couldn't prepare or control this process. You learn to be in control, and I couldn't control the recovery process either. I knew nothing about the program or the twelve steps, and I didn't understand how they could help me. Alcoholism is a scarlet letter in the medical field. I continued to fear that having alcoholism or addiction issues would destroy my career.

I was even less proud of myself during treatment. It became clear to me that I had to stay in treatment, but it felt like jail. I couldn't make phone calls. The people around me scared me. I thought I was going to treatment with other physicians, but they threw us doctors in with the regular lot: heroin addicts, alcoholics, and meth heads with ear gauges and tattoos. I guess I wasn't so special after all.

For whatever reason, once I was released from treatment, I felt like that girl Susan Smart. Once released from the kidnapper, she was free. When I left treatment, I felt free.

I am still terrified I may want to escape disgrace by hiding in the bottle. Yet, the truth is, I have nothing to hide anymore. I am no longer living behind a veil of secrecy. Alcohol allowed me to hide a lot of things. It all started in my head and came out in my behavior.

When I got out of treatment, I went to meetings. They told us that meeting-makers make it. I'm good at following directions. I didn't want to go backward. I am the kind of person who doesn't have to learn the same lesson twice.

My most vulnerable moment after treatment was asking someone to sponsor me. God sent me a woman who I allowed to wrap herself around me. I felt protected. The obsession to drink lifted. I'd be remiss if I didn't say that deep down, there was still a part of me that wished I could drink like a lady, or even to excess without repercussions, but I've accepted that I can't.

I am stronger sober than drunk. I feel solid now. I don't want to go back to feeling insecure.

Before I went to treatment, I tried other avenues to fix me. I went to counselors for depression and coping skills. I lied about everything, including my drinking.

Once I had a sponsor and continued to attend meetings, the counselor told me I could stop seeing her. She reminded me that the program works quite well if you stay willing and allow yourself to keep unfolding and unfolding. I had to lay it all out to someone (not everyone in the room, but a trusted sponsor). Listen, absorb, and let go. I had to commit, and I had to give it time. The program gave me the forum to keep playing the game. I will never lose the game if I stay in the game.

Admitting powerlessness was a huge hurdle for me to catapult over, but if I wanted recovery, I had to accept that I was powerless over alcohol. That was a difficult concept. I didn't believe in powerlessness. I always thought, *Just work harder.*

I learned that the third glass of wine was not my problem. It was the first glass of wine that got me every time. For me, the obsession was huge. I thought about alcohol constantly. I thought about shopping for it, pouring it, and how I couldn't wait to get home so I could drink. That insane obsession was like an identity crisis. I didn't realize that obsession was addiction. I thought the obsession was my weakness.

So I'd go to these meetings, and I'd be terrified that patients might see me there. My fear was that they'd start wailing, "Oh my God, she operated on us when she was drunk!" It was a big deal to go to my chief of staff. I still don't appreciate his incredulous response. Unforgiving disgust heaped upon medical doctors and nurses who admit they have addiction issues is hard to believe.

As I worked through the steps, I began to understand me. Step five in particular helped me tremendously. I had never had anyone's perspective about me other than my critical mother. Step five helped me see how I was laced-up. It wasn't so much about the holes. I've learned to meander around them. My disease is my strength; it's not my weakness.

It's not my biggest sin, being an alcoholic. Yes, drinking was a horribly destructive habit, but at the time alcohol was my only solution. Being an alcoholic has enabled me to be more compassionate. I now understand other peoples' struggles, such as obesity.

My first husband, the father of my three children, though I loved him, I think we work better as friends. We got married while I worked on my PhD. I kept a picture from our wedding. I went to kiss him, and he turned away. Why do I memorialize that photo? Why do I even still have it? The things we do to ourselves when we don't have self-love.

Sometimes I still wish I could figure out how I ended up alcoholic. My grandparents were married sixty years. In love the whole time. Nothing ever fell apart for them.

My inability to cope started long before I became alcoholic. In college I lived in a coed dorm. On the wall by the elevators we painted a blue sky and clouds. In each cloud we painted our names and the names of our roommates. I remember I came home from class one day, and someone had erased my name right out of the cloud. I was crushed! The resident assistant (RA) told me sometimes people just don't like you. I was emotionally devastated. I remember thinking, *My God, Caro, you can't handle anything.* How did I get this far through life and not have any coping skills? Had my life been too easy?

I was three years sober when I met my third and, God willing, last husband. We were at a big dinner meeting with a health care company. Pre-dinner, everyone gathered in the bar. I sat in a chair, and I had a vision of the actual me and the ghost me. Ghost me had a glass of chardonnay, was loud, with a crazy laugh, like the person I used to be. The actual me, the sober me, sat there like a lady, with a glass of club soda in my hand. I remember thinking, *I'm so grateful I am who I am. I am strong, in control, no longer riddled with fear. I'm not that drunk—that girl who fell apart so easily. I am finally my best me.* I will never forget that moment.

~ 16 ~
All-American

Valerie. Sobriety date: August 22, 2005

VALERIE LOOKS LIKE ONE EDGY CHICK. *She has spiked black hair, tattoos and piercings, and mocha skin. I like her style. She's authentic. I love her big beautiful smile that doesn't quit. I love the way she struts with confidence. She always seems to be in perpetual motion, like she has somewhere to go and something to do, and that's because she does. She got sober and jumped back into the mainstream of life. She works full-time and goes to school full-time. She's doing all the things she meant to do but couldn't get around to doing while using. Sobriety gave her back her life. She sobered up at the age of twenty-four. According to Valerie, that's when life began.*

My first drink occurred when I was eight or nine. I sneaked sips from the boxed wine that my mom kept in the refrigerator. By the age of thirteen, I drank alcoholically. I had been warned that alcoholism ran in the family, but when you're a kid, you think you're invincible.

I have a white mother, and my dad is black. One of my earliest memories of him was when the police came to the house and restrained him while we packed our things. I was six years old at the time. Alcohol was the reason he was violent.

Mom remarried a white guy, and he had two sons. Now everyone in the family was white. I didn't fit in—literally. I lived with all these people who were white as marshmallows, and I felt like the black mascara smear on a white pillowcase.

I had a natural ability to play sports. I loved baseball. In high school I played shortstop. One night after a game, the coach, who happened to be gay, and two other players, we all went to a gay bar. Did I mention that I'm gay? We all got hammered, and I spent the night at the coach's house. Someone found out about the all-night festivities, and, just like that, my future unraveled.

There was a massive rumpus over the whole thing. Once the media got a hold of the story, I knew it was over. The end result: I got kicked off the baseball team.

I lost my varsity letter; the scholarship offers that had been rolling in, one by one they left the table. It was heartbreaking. Our team had Olympic potential. We had played for the national championship in Oklahoma. My whole future changed because of that one night—that one alcohol-fueled decision changed everything.

I graduated high school and was offered a full academic scholarship to Bowling Green State University. I turned down that scholarship because I didn't want to fail. Already, I knew that my drinking was out of control. I figured I'd drink myself out of the scholarship anyway, so why go? Instead, I stayed at home and went to a local university, but when I got tired of school, I quit.

I had a fake ID, and weekend drinking was my thing. Eventually that weekend drinking turned into Wednesday and Thursday drinking. I told myself that because I wasn't a daily drinker, that meant I wasn't an alcoholic.

I ended up much like my dad. When I drank, I became a violent aggressive drunk. I'd smack my significant other around. I continued to rationalize my behavior and told myself things like, *She shouldn't have pissed me off. If she hadn't said the shit she said, I wouldn't have hit her.*

In 2001, I got busted for driving under the influence. That's also the time when my drinking took a hard left turn. My best friend, she was a year younger than me: beautiful, smart, loved sports, she was my hero. Her brother was in the police academy. She said she wanted to see how fast he could draw, and when he drew, the gun misfired. The bullet hit her in the chest, and just like that—she was gone.

She was the all-American girl I wanted to be. After her death, I just gave up. I gave up on me. I gave up on life. I just didn't care. I was furious with God. Seriously, I wanted no part of a God who would take someone so beautiful.

Her death initiated my downward spiral. I got another DUI. I was juggling and manipulating women like a clown juggles rings. I always had three or four relationships going at any given time.

As a result of my drinking, my kidneys started to fail. I ended up in the hospital for eight days, but I didn't think I had a problem. Look. I had dogs, and they were cared for. I had a job. Maybe I would show up a little late here and there, but those tardies were forgiven because once I showed up, I worked hard. I never got hangovers.

I surrounded myself with people who drank like me. If you mentioned my drinking, you were cut out of my life. Every girlfriend I had told me I drank too much. I didn't listen to any of them. Instead I'd do things to prove them wrong. I'd quit drinking for thirty days just to shut people up, but deep inside I always knew that alcohol was out there at the end of the rainbow. I'd train and then run a half marathon to prove I wasn't alcoholic. My competitive nature and willpower allowed me to muscle my way through pretty much anything, except this disease. No matter how long I quit drinking, I always went back to alcohol.

On the outside, everything looked fine. I still had my car, and maybe even insurance. I paid my bills. I worked. Everyone thought I was fine. My mother had no idea I was living in hell. Most every day, I wished I'd die. I felt rotten inside.

Loneliness was my archenemy. I never felt connected. I always felt so alone and misunderstood. I felt less than . . . never equal to you. I was the gal who was the life of the party. I surrounded myself with people. I couldn't stand being alone. The only time I had ever felt a part of anything was when I played sports.

The last six months of my drinking, I had progressed to a daily drinker. I even drank at work on my lunch break. And then I met a girl. There was something different about her. One weekend, she went out of town, and I went to the bar. There happened to be a dart tournament going on that weekend. I had my pro card for darts. Sweet. I joined the tournament. There was a spread of food, and on the table a basket of money. Everyone tossed in a few bucks to cover the food.

The next morning, when I came to—I didn't wake up, I came to—I found all this money in my pockets. *Damn. Did I win?* That night I went back to the tournament, and when I walked into the bar, the owner picked up the intercom and announced to the crowd, "A thief is in the house."

I fessed up. I guess I took the money. People at the bar saw me take it, but I had no memory of stealing. My girlfriend came home, found out what happened, and she said she was done. She said she had had enough of watching me destroy myself. She left.

That was my bottom. I had done a lot of sick stuff, but I never stole anything from anyone. I decided I wanted to get sober. I stayed sober for thirty days on my own, and I was bat-shit crazy. I bought a bottle and was about to drink it when a friend came over and poured it out.

Since I had experience with those DUIs, I had heard of the twelve steps. That day I called to inquire about meetings. The person who answered the phone pointed me in the right direction. That night, I went to a meeting, and I continued to go to meetings, but only one a week. That's all I did. I didn't do a damn thing that was suggested. None of it. I didn't get a sponsor. I didn't go to ninety meetings in ninety days. I didn't work any steps. Six nights a week, I hung out in bars and threw darts.

Fate intervened. At one of those weekly meetings I met a woman. She came up to me and said, "I'm going to be your sponsor. I can make the noise and the voices in your head stop." Remarkable deal! How did she know I had been obsessing like crazy about alcohol?

I was miserable and riddled with fear. Fear of the unknown. Fear of what my life would look like without alcohol. Fear of not having any fun anymore (although drinking had ceased to be fun, but I still believed it was fun). I mean, I was twenty-four years old. *Never drink again? Are you kidding me?* That's what I thought.

I started to allow that woman to teach me. We worked steps. I began to see me for who I was. All that promiscuity I engaged in was nothing more than a way to feed my ego. I had to admit, I had a huge ego. All those women and relationships, it was a competitive game for me: look who I can get; look how many women I can tamper with at one time. I thought I wouldn't feel so lonely, but you know what? No matter how many women I had, the loneliness never left.

I had to get honest. I believe that lack of honesty is one of the biggest obstacles to sobriety. I had to start to look at me, and it wasn't pretty. I had to humble myself. I had to ask for help, and that was hard. As I reviewed my drinking career, I realized that for a long time, I couldn't have just one or two drinks. Many times I had said I was going to have a couple drinks and go home, but come 2:00 a.m., I'm stumbling out of another bar. I did that over and over again. I was powerless. Deep down, I knew I was powerless. I just didn't want to admit it, because if I admitted it, I would have to do something about it.

Smacking all those women around . . . the guilt and remorse was horrible. I shattered a car window with my fist. I think a lot of the violence was to prove to myself that I wasn't weak like my mom. I could see and connect the dots, but I couldn't not drink.

The twelve steps leans toward finding some sort of God or higher power. I had a problem with that concept. I blamed my friend's death on God. My sponsor told me I could make up my own higher power. I choose my best friend, the one who died. She became my higher power.

Spiritual growth has been an ongoing process. I didn't box God into a religion. I was open to all sorts of beliefs. Eventually, I formed my own opinion that went something like this: I had come to believe there is a power in the universe, and that power is God. I came to believe that God was kind and forgiving. I learned to hit my knees every day. I asked this God to help me stay sober, and at night I thanked him. I believed, and still do believe, that my higher power wants me to stay sober. I was a menace to others when I was drunk. I know that God's will for me is not to lash out and hurt others.

I went back to school for biomedical engineering. I can go anywhere and do anything. I still go to NFL games and support my Steelers. I am surrounded with a loving family. I've had periods of time when I didn't have a girlfriend. I learned to befriend myself. I learned to date myself. I learned to take a trip—alone. Spending time alone was new.

I discovered that sobriety didn't restrict me in any way. If I wanted to go to a sports bar and watch a game, I went. If I wanted to go to a concert, I went. People in the program used to tell me I could go anywhere, even a bar, if I had a good reason to be there. The Big Book talks about that too. Sobriety gave me choices. Sobriety set me free.

~ 17 ~
Hurry, Drunk Dial Now!

Jennifer. Sobriety date: July 19, 2004

I ONLY HAD THE PLEASURE *of working with Jennifer for a short time before she moved back to Texas. If you could see how put together this southern belle is . . . well, it's just hard to picture her any other way. I didn't know how powerful her story could be, but for any woman who's lost a baby, and to the woman who always wondered about her first love, this one is for you.*

No surprise here, I grew up in an alcoholic home. My father was the alcoholic. He was physically and verbally abusive to me and my sister. My mother stood silently by, a horrible codependent. My father was in the military, and of course we moved constantly. I spent most of my childhood in the great state of Texas, and some in Germany.

My first taste of alcohol was when I was a toddler. My father thought it was funny to give me sips. I just read an article that says if parents allow their small children to take those sips, the children have a 33 percent higher chance of becoming alcoholic. (Don't quote me, but I think I read that stat.)

We had this big scary liquor cabinet in our house with a wooden roll-down door. One day I decided to take an empty Coke bottle and fill it with all sorts of liquors. I just poured whatever looked good into the Coke bottle. I drank the whole bottle. I went off to a basketball game, falling-down drunk. None of the adults called me out. I got home and I puked all over the bathroom.

The next morning my dad asked if I wanted to talk about last night. I told him, "No, sir." He offered up a half-smile, and that was the end of that. I had no consequences. I felt like I'd been admitted into some secret club.

I don't know why I started drinking. I can't say for sure if it was because we moved a lot, but I always felt isolated, like I didn't fit in.

I was in the National Honor Society in high school, yet I picked a boyfriend with a fake ID and a tattoo. Already, my life was incongruent. Come my senior year, I had few plans, and since neither one of my parents had gone to college, they discouraged education. My dad refused to sign any of the admission or loan forms. Around this time too, my sister had run away from home. My parents were all caught up in her drama.

I didn't know what to do with myself, so I got involved with men. I'd get engaged, break up, get engaged, and break up. I eventually met the man who would become my first husband. He passed out on our first date. I didn't see a problem with that. We moved to California and got married.

He turned into a real sonofabitch. He beat me up to where I had to get stitches and whatnot. I didn't know what to do most days, because I was too drunk to help myself. So I slit my wrists. I was twenty years old. That suicidal gesture was the impetus that precipitated my first admission to the psych ward. I stayed in that ward three weeks. During those three weeks, I had one awareness: I learned that my dad was a real alcoholic. No one ever asked me about my drinking. I saw no connection between my drinking and how it affected my behavior and/or decisions.

I stayed married to Mr. Violent for a year and a half. The grand finale to that holy mess came the day he ripped off my clothes. Fearing for my life, I barricaded my naked self in the closet while he tried to beat the door down with a hammer.

Since I was young and already having problems living life, someone suggested I see a therapist. I went to therapy, and my drinking never came up.

By then I was working as a sales rep for a temp service. I ended up getting married to a guy who worked in the human resource department. He too was an alcoholic, but we stayed married for ten years and had three children. My first child was stillborn. My baby's death was a turning point in my alcoholism. I realized I couldn't cry, couldn't mourn without a drink in hand. I was numb.

I went on to have two daughters. My husband drank a lot, but he started hiding my booze because he thought I drank too much. My one daughter was a preemie. A lot of challenges come with a preemie. I didn't handle any of it well. I woke up wishing for nighttime so I could go to bed and drink.

I was a stay-at-home mom. I passed too many days plunked on the couch, especially during the O. J. Simpson trial. I spent all day watching TV, completely enmeshed in the trial like it was someone I knew or something. When they read the not-guilty verdict, I was devastated! I got super drunk over that one.

Sometime during the O. J. Simpson trial, a commercial came on about domestic violence. The 911 number on the screen caught my eye, so I called, and then I promptly forgot all about my drunk dialing. A few minutes later I heard a knock, I skipped over to answer the door, and boy was I surprised to see the police. I tried my best to make excuses and blow the whole thing off. They insisted on coming inside, because by then, they realized I was drunk. They saw the baby articles all over the house and asked about my kids. Thank God, they were in bed. The police checked on them, and then those same police came back later that night and told my husband what happened.

In my early thirties I made my first foray into recovery. I decided I needed to do something. I'm not sure how I knew to find a twelve-step meeting, but I picked one that was as far away from my house as possible. I couldn't relate to anyone there. They were street people. I was a nice lady from the suburbs. I refused to buy a book or do any of the steps. I was bitching and moaning that I wasn't going to do all that crap. There were people there who tried to talk to me, but I was enveloped in denial.

Then someone said, "Maybe this isn't for you." I agreed. No, meetings weren't for me. I bought a bottle on the way home and drank for another ten years.

I divorced my second husband. Before that divorce was final, I had already scoped out husband number three in a chat room on the Internet. I had always wanted to be a nurse. He was a psychiatrist. We had medical interests. Surely, he was my true love. For a while we had a long-distance relationship, and then after a short time I moved to be close to him. I started nursing school, and we got married.

The psychiatrist needed a psychiatrist. Seriously, he was a total alcoholic! Here he was in private practice and a hospitalist at one of the major hospitals, yet he was a complete mess. He needed to quit drinking for sure. His addiction was crystal clear to me, but I still denied my disease.

I was already powerless over alcohol, though I didn't see how I was also powerless over the insanity that permeated my life. I remember going to Weight Watchers. The first thing I calculated into my points was how much wine I could drink. Without fail, I used all my points on alcohol. But I was so hungry! I had to make a choice. If I ate, I had no points left for wine. If I drank, I had no points left for food. The whole thing pissed me off. I decided that Weight Watchers was a bunch of shit and it didn't work anyway. Then pills entered the mix. More powerlessness.

My husband, who I discovered had been unfaithful our whole marriage, started writing prescriptions for me. (He probably liked me knocked out.) I had a little dental work done; I needed pain medication. When he quit writing scripts for me, I "developed" fibromyalgia and chronic pain. I got adept at manipulating doctors. I knew I'd die taking all those pills and drinking like I was, but I didn't care.

I'd always been particular about my hair and my makeup. Toward the end of my using, I didn't care how I looked. I'd take a handful of pills and knew enough to understand that my respirations were shallow, but I didn't care. I truly didn't care if I lived or died. I couldn't look at myself in the mirror. I felt trapped.

My husband had a bad car accident. Along with the accident, he was cited for driving under the influence. He quit drinking. He started going to meetings. He wasn't going to meetings to get well, though; he went to find women. I didn't see him get any better, so when I tried to quit drinking, I just did it on my own. The problem was, I could stop drinking . . . I just couldn't *stay* stopped.

The day before the anniversary of my baby's death rolled around. His birthday was always a good reason to get drunk. I felt entitled to drink. That year, though, I felt entitled to start drinking a day earlier. I was grieving, okay? Requisite wine glass in hand, I had a whole ritual that went something like this: Set up an altar with white roses and candles, cry, clutch wine glass, and keep refilling wine glass. Write wretched poetry and sob. Every year, that was how I honored my son on his birthday.

However, that one particular day, I took it too far. I ate up all the pills I had and drank whatever booze I could find. I left to go get more wine, and that was something I hadn't done before—drive drunk. When I got to the store, I fell out of my car. I staggered into the store, bought the wine, and drank the whole bottle in the parking lot. On the way home, I blacked out and drove through the closed garage door.

The next day, the actual day of my deceased baby's birth, I woke up, and I felt his spirit around me. In my thoughts I heard him say, *Mom, you don't have to do this for me anymore.* I knew then and there that the gig was up. My wretched behavior wasn't honoring him at all.

My husband had a Big Book. I picked it up and started reading it. I didn't understand most of what I read. I was confused by the steps, but I did understand step one. I knew I was powerless and that my life was unmanageable. I started going to meetings online. I stayed sober fourteen months with that regimen of online meetings, white-knuckling it, acting crazy, and reading the Big Book.

Near the end of that fourteen months, I suffered a transient ischemic attack (TIA). I had no history of smoking or obesity. I sensed maybe God was trying to get my attention. My husband and I were both dry drunks. Still insane, just not drinking. Our collective kids were a mess. I finally had to look in the mirror. I wanted to drink, but I kept picturing myself passed out on the floor. Someone at the online meeting convinced me to go to an actual twelve-step meeting, and I went.

People at that meeting talked about all sorts of disasters, but everyone was laughing, happy, and they all had found a way to enjoy life without alcohol. Also at that meeting, I heard someone tell a story about getting divorced and going to nursing school. I asked that woman to be my sponsor.

I commenced the process of getting my life together. I started back to nursing school in a real way. I had always been ashamed that I hadn't gone to college and always lied that I had. I looked at my husband and realized it was going to be him or me. I asked him to leave.

I kept hearing at meetings, "If you're having trouble with relationships, go back and make amends." I didn't realize the significance of that message until I had a dream about a man who kissed me three times. Shortly after the dream, I was going through some old pictures, and I realized the man in the dream was my high school sweetheart. We'd gone to the prom, and the night of prom I broke up with him. At seventeen, I was awesome like that. I didn't care who I hurt. I broke up with him because he had plans to go to the Air Force Academy, and I had none.

I sent him a light email, and the first sentence of his email read, "I have been wanting to ask you for thirty-one years . . . why did you break up with me at prom?" I knew then that I needed to make amends. I sent him a long email and told him everything. He admitted that he had trouble with his drinking too and didn't know what to do. I directed him to the recovery rooms. He quit drinking, and our relationship progressed.

On the thirty-third anniversary of our senior prom, we got married at the Air Force Academy in Colorado Springs. In August of that same year, my sister died of a drug overdose.

I have a great life. I love being married to the love of my life. I realized by working the steps that I was not a horrible person. Instead I was driven by selfishness, self-centeredness, and fear; those defects in my character caused so many of my problems.

I put my daughters through so much, and none of it was their fault. I regret that my children remember some of my drinking but more of my screaming. That's what this disease does: it makes us into people we'd rather not be. My drinking consumed me. I am blessed beyond belief to have found recovery, and to have stayed in recovery. I no longer waste precious time being miserable, hung over, and remorseful. Life is good.

~ 18 ~

Who, Me? Self-Supporting?

Grace. Sobriety date: November 30, 1987

GRACE: PETITE, BLONDE, SOFT-SPOKEN. I knew she was serious about sobriety, and when she spoke, I listened. I have watched her over the years, and she walks the walk and doesn't just talk the talk.

I also happen to know her husband, a man she met in recovery. When I heard they had coupled up—well, if you knew them, you'd know that they look like they were meant to be together. They have built a life, something Grace was unable to do before she quit drinking.

I grew up in Kansas City, raised in a big Catholic family of nine children. Out of nine children, four of us found recovery. I believe my dad was alcoholic. My grandpa was alcoholic, and Mother had one brother who was an alcoholic.

I can say with certainty that the event that sent me careening off onto a new trajectory was when, after twenty-five years of marriage, my parents divorced. I was eleven years old. All nine of us attended parochial school. Back in 1964, divorce was still a big deal. I felt the community rejected our family. We were all stigmatized because of my parents' decision, and I felt overpowered by the feeling that I didn't fit in anymore.

I started drinking and smoking pot at fourteen years old. I was a weekend warrior. I kept my virginity intact until I turned eighteen, and then it was on.

Promiscuity was a part of my story; I could make you a list of men in ten-point font as long as your leg. That's how it was for me. I wanted validation, and I wanted someone to take care of me. When my parents were still together, Dad modeled inappropriate behavior. He did things like grab Mom's boob in front of us kids or slap her ass—you get the picture. I equated sex with love.

College wasn't pushed. Just like that, I didn't go. Instead, I partied like I was living in some sorority and was about to be kicked off campus for out-of-control drinking. I crossed the imaginary line into alcoholism. At eighteen years old, I was a blackout drinker. I continued to black out until I found speed. Amphetamines kept the momentum going, and I didn't black out as soon as I normally would.

At twenty-three I married an alcoholic who both my mom and my aunt despised. They were correct—he was a womanizer. Of course my family members were spot-on, but I was in love. He'd change. Did I mention I met him at a bar?

Domestic violence played a role in that marriage. He was a control freak. He wanted me to do what he wanted me to do. He thought I should stay home—all the time. He'd hop from one happy hour to the next, but I was supposed to stay home and wait for him. I flitted off to happy hour anyway.

One night he found out that I had been out drinking without him. He pulled a gun. Looking back, I knew the day after we married that I had made a mistake. He was an insanely jealous, sick man.

A few years after the divorce, I sought a geographical cure. My brother lived in Colorado Springs, so I decided to head west, and, lucky me, I found the perfect job for an alcoholic: I got a job driving the liquor cart around a real swanky course. Someone had to serve drinks to all those thirsty golfers.

While in Colorado, I met a wealthy man. He put me up in an apartment because he lived with his other girlfriend at the time. He paid my bills, and I didn't have to work. My new love was a drunk too, and I was getting drunker. He had condos in San Francisco and Palm Springs. Now I was surrounded by all those rich people, and, again, I felt like the misfit. I guess I hoped that running around with all those drunk, moneyed people would make me feel okay, but it didn't. Instead, my self-esteem circled the drain. I felt lower than a snake's belly. Money couldn't fix what was broken in me.

This old sap was twenty-seven years my senior. I got to be the bimbo that all the other women whispered about behind my back. Somewhere along the way, my conscience caved. I no longer felt comfortable being a leech, so he sent me to beauty school and bought me a condo.

I graduated beauty school and found a job. I drank every day, but I still maintained. I rationalized my drinking because I didn't get drunk every day, but I also couldn't predict the next blackout.

A woman from the beauty shop fixed me up with a man, who later became husband number two. This woman had a brother who was an alcoholic, and she asked me if I wanted to go with her to an Adult Children of Alcoholics (ACOA) meeting.

I went to those meetings with her for six months, and boy did they make me itch. My discomfort was palpable. I couldn't believe how those people talked about me! They hashed out all the gory details of how it was to live with a drunk. It was all too much. I couldn't take them talking about me all the time, so I went back to Kansas.

I failed every drinking test I took. I had constant turmoil in my life, yet I was the main player. Those ACOA meetings were my first introduction to the twelve steps.

Now that I had all this twelve-step knowledge from those ACOA meetings, when I returned to Kansas, I had a mission. I recruited the whole family to recovery groups. I told them they must go to meetings.

I wanted to save them. They needed my help. I convinced my mom to go to Al-Anon. My sisters frequented the ACOA meetings. They were all reading the books. This was our ticket to stellar mental health. I directed them all to the right path, and then I split.

Again, I ran from me. I called Lewis, the guy I had previously been with in Colorado Springs. He agreed to come get me. I needed to get out of Kansas. All the people around me were getting recovery. Alcoholism was eating me up, but I was not ready to let go of it yet.

Back again in Colorado Springs, I married Lewis. He was a nice man, and he wasn't an alcoholic. He became my anchor. He smoked a lot of dope, but as soon as his job started drug testing, he quit. I couldn't understand how he could quit.

On the day of our wedding, I was high on coke and drunk. (That marriage lasted one year.) It was 1987. I went to my first meeting. I stopped drinking for eleven days. I was a raging bitch. Lewis suggested I have one drink. *Sure, good idea. I think I will.*

For Thanksgiving that same year, we went on a ski trip. I drank, did coke, and couldn't get high. That weekend hit me hard, and I started to admit I must be an alcoholic.

I was scared to death. In the marrow of my bones, I knew if I wanted to live, I had to quit drinking. I was appalled at the thought of having to go to those meetings. I knew nothing about treatment, but I knew the twelve steps could help me.

In addition to the drinking problem, from the age of eighteen, I struggled with depression. The worst kind of depression. Everything looked black, all the time. I didn't understand why I felt so depressed, but I noticed that the depression got worse after a weekend or week of heavy drinking.

Lewis was so good to me. I had to sabotage the marriage. The people in recovery rooms told me to wait. They said to not make any major decisions during that first year. I didn't listen. I left him because he was just too good. I feared that once he figured out what kind of a girl I was, he'd leave anyway.

It was tough trying to accept this alcoholic business. I didn't have the consequences that people could see. The marriages? Well, it takes two, so none of it was all my fault. I never got a DUI. I never had trouble with the law. I thought an alcoholic was the man under the bridge. Not someone like me. Never mind that I was filled with self-loathing and had used men instead of my own resources.

It's interesting to note too that during my first year of sobriety, a guy came up to me in the meeting. He wanted to know why I kept smiling. I still wore the facade. I wanted everyone to think all was well, and, from the outside, things looked great. Inside, I was dying and falling apart. His remark stuck with me for a long, long time.

I eventually realized that my self-destructive behavior was tied to my low self-esteem. Forever, I kept looking outside of myself to make me feel better. If I had a better man . . . if I had a better car . . . if I had a better job . . .

Two weeks after I separated from Lewis, I met a player. This guy was screwing every woman he could get his hands on, and I wanted him to be mine! He turned out to be husband number three. Here again, everyone in my family said no, no, no. This man was emotionally unavailable. He showed no affection unless we were screwing.

Shortly before he proposed, he moved to Turkey for a government job. Once he got over there, he couldn't find a woman. I was still in Colorado Springs, and I couldn't find another man. He called from Turkey and asked me to marry him. My inner self was screaming, *Don't do it!* I told that inner-self girl to shut up.

I quit my job, sold everything, and moved to Turkey. The whole experience was a living hell. He stole my passport and hid it. He did something with my visa. He started pushing me around, dragged me by the hair across the floor. There were limited meetings there. I didn't have a sponsor. I was crazier sober than I was drunk, but I didn't drink. After two years, we left Turkey.

I promised myself I would give this marriage another year. We ended up in Ohio, but instead of jumping back into the program, I plotted my relapse. I'd had enough of this man. We tried counseling. He went once and stopped, but I kept going. That whole relapse plan scared me enough that I came home one night and told my husband we were done. I moved out.

I stayed single for ten years, which was unusual for someone like me. I finally listened to that first sponsor. I quit relying on men. She told me to rely on God. She told me I could take care of myself.

The common thread in all the marriages was me. I wanted someone to take responsibility for me. Fear told me I couldn't do it on my own. After the third disastrous marriage, I finally understood that I must learn to take care of myself. I needed to learn to be self-sufficient.

At three years sober, I joined the Navy reserve. I needed discipline in my life, and the Navy was the only branch that would take me at thirty-seven years old.

I found a job at the VA hospital in the admitting department. I bought my first house! I didn't need a man. I could do this. Somewhere along the way the obsession to cling onto a man left. That feeling of not being good enough left. I was comfortable in my own skin.

Adult children of alcoholics are approval seekers. I never felt my dad approved of me. I spent most of my life living in some relationship, looking for and wanting approval. All those toxic relationships ever did for me was further lower my already-low self-worth and self-esteem.

I spent years blaming my parents for all my relationship troubles, because they spent twenty-five years drinking and fighting and were lousy role models.

I'm grateful that I didn't have children. I couldn't imagine the damage I would've caused, dragging a child from marriage to marriage, place to place, all of it, riddled with so much insanity. I sponsor women, and many have children. Their biggest regret is always tied to being a terrible parent. I am grateful I don't have to live with that heartache.

What kept me coming back to meetings after all these years was the camaraderie, the laughter, the acceptance. I was welcomed into the rooms of recovery with open arms. These people understood me.

The obsession to drink didn't lift for six months. After I got sober, I worked the steps, and all the while I was eating like a horse. I got down on my knees and asked God to please not let me have to deal with food issues too. It worked, because my weight hasn't changed in many years.

After ten years of sobriety, I still struggled with depression, especially when I went through menopause. I went to the doctor and started on antidepressants. I know now that I don't have to suffer, and I have choices.

The hardest step for me was the fifth step. I didn't want to tell anyone anything about me. I thought I had done horrible things that no one else had done. I feared I would be judged. Turns out that was unfounded. Most alcoholics have had bad behavior. That's just the way it is. People in the room call it "drunk stuff." *Oh, that's just drunk stuff. Let it go. It's over. You're on a new path now.*

Working through the steps enabled me to change my thinking. I started to live life. I love to dance and bike. I got active. I sponsor other women, and I still find it so rewarding to guide them on their journeys. It's always a thrill to see people grow and change into the person God intended them to be.

The spiritual principles of the program have helped me to make sense out of nonsense. Here's an example: When I initially moved to Colorado Springs, within two weeks, my brother's wife left him. She ran off with the minister from their church and left behind two children. I moved in with my brother and helped with those kids.

He got through what he thought was the worst thing that could ever happen, and then he got sober. Sometimes we don't see the bigger picture, nor do we understand why things happen the way they do. Clarity always comes in hindsight.

I was sixteen years sober when at a twelve-step meeting I met a man we'll call Ray. I'd known him and his wife, before they divorced. A year or so after their divorce, Ray called and asked me out. I told him no. Six months later he called again and asked me out. That time, I said yes.

He was the first man that I dated and didn't have sex with in the first week. We waited three months. That was God showing me that I didn't have to sell out. God wanted me to see that it was better to base a relationship on friendship and love than sex.

I am happily married, but my sobriety still comes first. All of the blessings in my life are the result of being sober. I never want to go back to that drunk lady with low self-esteem. I love the shape of my life. I thank God I became willing to quit drinking. It's wonderful to have serenity.

~ 19 ~
Saucy Socialite

Marne. Sobriety date: September 4, 2009

MARNE WAS IN HER SIXTIES by the time she entered the rooms, and it wasn't hard to pick her out of the crowd. In addition to her requisite look of disdain, her silver hair was perfectly coiffed. She always looked regal, like she might have to zip off in the middle of the meeting for a lunch date at The Inn at Little Washington.

If you looked closer, beneath her classy exterior was someone distraught to find herself at a meeting. She later divulged that the meetings felt beneath her. It took months for her heavy sighs and eye-rolling to cease.

It took time for her to concede that maybe she had made a hasty judgment. She is not the same woman who walked into the rooms back in 2009. She is her best self, living, as she will tell you, in peaceful contentment. She pointed out that her life isn't perfect, but at least she can accept life on life's terms, something she'd never before been able to do.

~

Alcohol had a constant presence in our family. Growing up, drinking was a huge part of my parents' life. Both of them were functional alcoholics. Every evening before dinner, they had cocktails. All the relatives drank. It was party all the time. That's just what my family did, and everyone thought it was normal.

I never drank normally, but I never had consequences. I drank in college, but so did everyone else. At that age, no one questioned whether or not they were alcoholic. My capacity was quite high, so I never got sick.

I met my husband through a friend. He went to Notre Dame Law School. We dated for eight years and were on and off the whole time. We drank a lot together. We married and landed in Great Falls, Virginia.

I was from the era when women were still somewhat subservient to their husbands. I loved him, and my goal was to create a home. I hung on his every word. He used to tell me that without him, I'd be nothing. For the next thirty years I believed that lie.

At one point in our early marriage he told me I was an alcoholic. As I said, I listened to everything he said, so when he insisted I find a twelve-step meeting, I obliged. He bought me a Big Book. I didn't get a sponsor or work any steps, but I stayed sober for one year. During that year of not drinking, I continued to host big parties and served lots of alcohol, but I didn't drink. I was now convinced that I didn't have an alcohol problem. I believed I had everything under control.

That stop-and-start pattern of drinking became my norm. I began to have children. My first child was born in 1976. I drank through each pregnancy, though not heavily. Back then, no one cautioned me about drinking while pregnant. Everyone drank and smoked, pregnant or not. My husband stopped drinking, and for fourteen years, while raising my children, I did too.

I lived an entitled, luxurious life. We lived in a multimillion-dollar neighborhood, and I had the mini mansion and the right zip code to prove it. Our house had all the bling bling: a wide circular drive, tennis courts, and a sparkling swimming pool. It was glorious. The terraced gardens were to die for. My house had niceties galore; all the bells and whistles had bells and whistles.

But behind the facade of all that glamour, it felt like hell. My husband was verbally and, on occasion, physically abusive. After my two oldest children left for college, I started drinking again. I just couldn't keep the lie going. I remember cooking and sipping sherry. Perhaps I used my husband's bad behavior to rationalize and justify my drinking. More and more though, I needed alcohol as a crutch to cope with my husband. I started going to the liquor store. I'd buy a few mini bottles, not unlike the sort they serve on airplanes. I'd drink two of those just to have enough courage to open the garage door and go in the house. I suspected he knew I was drinking again, but he never said a word. My alcoholism progressed.

I had a huge walk-in closet, and, literally, I became a closet drinker. I'd sit in that closet, drink, and then try and figure out how to disguise the empty bottles. I packaged them up and took them to a big dumpster in some office parking lot. I wasn't all that concerned about my drinking, even though it felt sneaky. I soothed any misgivings with the rationale that I didn't obsess over or crave alcohol.

When my oldest daughter graduated from college, she entered the Peace Corps. She ended up in Africa, so the whole family went to see her. I remember thinking, *This is my vacation*, and I wanted a glass of wine. One night at dinner I announced to the whole table that I was going to have that glass of wine. No one said a word.

By the time we got back to the states, my husband and I were off and running. We drank and traveled the world: Paris, Argentina, Ireland, and Antarctica. By the time we got to Antarctica, I was drunk almost all of the time. But we had fun! I felt we had rekindled the romance in our marriage. Back in DC, we went to dinner and the theatre, and life was good.

And then, my disease caught me. I drank to excess every day. I was careful not to start drinking until the acceptable cocktail hour. I drank in the kitchen while I cooked dinner. It got to where I'd push the dinner hour back later and later, because I didn't want to ruin my buzz. One night my husband said he thought we needed to cut back, and we both agreed. Not long after he uttered that statement, we were right back at it.

The drinking caused a mammoth rift in our marriage. I sensed him pulling away, but I didn't care. He started an affair. If you would've asked me prior to finding out about his mistress if he'd ever have an affair, as sure as taxes, I would have told you, no way.

Perhaps my denial started there. I continued to take care of the house, and we had sex like nothing was wrong. Then he began to lose those good jobs that had kept us in the lap of luxury. He raged and raged. I think he was angry at himself, and I believe he kept getting fired because of his arrogance and his inability to work with others. In spite of his job losses, I never worried about money. I preferred to stay oblivious to the brewing storm.

For our thirtieth anniversary, our children spent a year planning an anniversary party on Block Island. They had invited all these people. I felt so torn because by this time, I knew my husband had a mistress. I continued to live in denial. I showed up at the party like the loving wife everyone thought I was. I had a blast. I drank and drank. I enjoyed all the guests. I was adept at creating my own reality. In my reality, I had a loving husband and plenty of money.

That frame of mind only lasted so long. I was fed up with all the lies he told in order to continue on with his mistress. I found out he spent copious amounts of money on his other life and created alibis that took a tremendous amount of plotting and planning. I believed his lies because that was easier than facing the truth.

With puppy-dog eyes, he told me he and some friends were supporting a non-profit called So Others May Eat. He said the organization helped men in the DC area acquire job skills and whatnot. The group met, religiously, every Tuesday. I don't recall what tipped me off—maybe it was instinct—but I became suspicious about his Tuesday-night commitment and inquired. I found out the organization he claimed to support never even existed! Then he said he had enrolled in a class. I checked up on that too, and the instructor said that yes, he had enrolled, but he'd never shown up—not even once.

The final lie was that he was going to Chicago for business. I packed a picnic for him to enjoy on the way. I found out later that while driving to the Outer Banks, he and the mistress enjoyed the lunch that I made.

I'd had enough. I packed my things and headed to the city, where my son and daughter lived. I went to them under the guise of wanting to spend time with the grandchildren. I stayed six weeks and then decided to go back to DC. I figured my husband would be thrilled to see me.

Boy, was I wrong. He wasn't happy to see me at all. He was still with the girlfriend, and I was still drinking. I ran back to my kids. This time, my husband came to me. He said he wanted to reconcile our differences, but he refused to give up the mistress.

I was drinking with my niece, like, all the time, until my sister intervened. She demanded I seek treatment, but, like any good alcoholic, I begged for a week to think about it. *Take my wine? Oh, my God, no!* I drank the whole week. My sister took me back to her house, where I stayed for ten days to dry out. I went back to my daughter's, and she took me to my first meeting.

The biggest hurdle for me was that I thought I was better than everyone else. Was that my ego? I felt that "my" type of person wasn't represented at the meetings. I thought the steps and getting a sponsor were hokey ideas. Didn't they know who I was? Plus, I wanted to be in charge. I was used to committees where someone *had* to be in charge, and it was usually me. I thought it was weird that none of the twelve-step groups had a governing body. How did this organization keep itself together?

It took a while for me to take to the program, and I was certain the women would sympathize with me and realize I had been the victim. None of them did. My sponsor pointed out that I had a huge part in all of it: I chose to stay in the marriage. I chose to keep drinking. If I'd been healthy, I could have learned other ways to deal with my husband. I didn't expect to hear those sorts of answers.

Recovery became academic for me. I just put my head down and plowed through. I knew if I didn't stick with it, the rest of my days would be awful. I had originally thought that if I put down the wine, all would be well, but I learned drinking is only a symptom of my thinking.

I had no idea how to live life. I had no coping skills. Working through the steps was like school for me. My kids started to notice the changes. I didn't so much see the subtle changes, but physically, I felt so much better. My head was clear. I didn't wake up with hangovers. Steps four and five, the inventory steps, taught me to look at my part. I am no longer allowed to scream *victim*. I learned that I was filled with false pride.

I had regrets, and, of course, the most painful regrets had to do with my children. Although I didn't drink all that much during the years I raised them, I wasn't fully present. I was so mired in my own misery, licking my own wounds, that I wasn't present emotionally for them.

My life looks nothing like it used to. I live in a modest apartment. I have wonderful relationships with my children and grandchildren. For the first time in thirty-plus years, I'm single. Sometimes I feel lonely, but I have a lot of great friends and a full life. The biggest reward is that I can say I love myself. I am worth something. I will never allow another man to define who I am, or who I can become.

~ 20 ~
Naughty in Nebraska

Morgan. Sobriety date: June 13, 1982

IT'S HARD TO BELIEVE that the motherly woman Morgan is today could be anything but loving and stable. She has a solid long-term marriage, three grown children, and grandchildren. She's the kind of woman who gets involved in everything! She tutors, she volunteers, and she makes glass beads that she sells at craft shows. I have never met anyone who possesses more empathy. She cries unabashedly when she hears of your struggles. She feels and relates to others' brokenness with such depth. I believe that that sort of recognition of others' brokenness only can happen because at one time, she, too, was so broken.

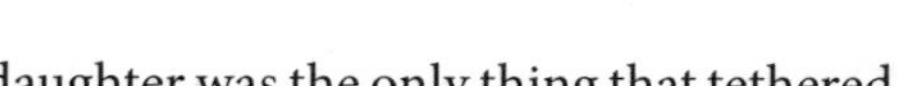

My daughter was the only thing that tethered me to this earth. I believe she was part of God's plan to keep me here. I got pregnant before my sixteenth birthday. At the time, I thought it was the worst thing in the world that could have happened.

My father was an alcoholic who found sobriety through the twelve steps. When I was two years old, my mother joined Al-Anon. My dad was in the military, and we moved eight times before I entered the fourth grade. We ended up in a small town in Nebraska, and Mom enrolled me in the country school. I became the volleyball princess and the class president, but with only twelve kids in the class. Eventually, that school closed and merged with another school. Now I was tossed in with sixty other kids, and I was no longer the big deal I was when there were only twelve of us.

I started drinking at fourteen. I drank as fast and hard as I could, would vomit, function in a blackout, pass out, and do it all over again. Every single time. From the very beginning, that's how I drank.

At sixteen I delivered my daughter. The doctor told me she needed a blood transfusion, and he said something about brain damage. I couldn't get a hold of anyone, so I started bargaining with God. I told God that if he let her be okay, I'd quit drinking. I didn't drink another drop until I went to college. Instead, I survived on the marijuana-maintenance route.

My mom was upset by the whole pregnancy. She set firm boundaries and pretty much said, "You will pay the hospital bills, buy diapers—you will do it all." I was allowed to live at home, which was a saving grace.

I supported my child by working at a feedlot. Cows dropped their calves in that feedlot, and I made a deal with the guy who ran the lot that I'd take the calves he planned to toss. My brother bottle-fed the calves until they started eating corn. Once the cows were raised, I sold them. People in town knew I was trying to sell the cows to take care of my baby, and, God bless them, they upped the sale price to help me get more money.

I stayed in Nebraska for college, but I selected the school I'd attend based on *Playboy*'s list of party schools. As I sashayed off to college, my parents threatened to take my daughter, for good, if they ever found out I was drinking. That threat didn't deter me in the least.

I knew from the first drink at fourteen that I had little control over alcohol, but I was fine with that assessment. My problem was the unmanageability. I always had all sorts of crap going on, but from the outside, I looked great. I'd run away from home but do my algebra homework first. I was on the dean's list, and I joined the orchestra in college. I struggled with unmanageability, but I never felt powerless. I'd twist things in my head to suit me, and life went on. *Powerless. Who, me? Never!*

I was outrageously promiscuous. I had thirty lovers by the time I was eighteen. So many men that I quit counting. I traipsed around in a bra and miniskirt. I'd jump in any stranger's car . . . and sometimes it didn't go well. Was that rape or drunk stuff? I wanted to quit sleeping around, but once I put alcohol in me, all bets were off.

There was this thirty-year-old guy who kept coming on to me. I was not the least bit interested. He kept telling me he had a vasectomy. I finally asked him, "What do you want me to do, get stoned and let you do what you want?" He said yes. So that's what I did.

I felt I'd been raped, and I decided to kill him. I got a knife, got drunk, and hid in the bushes outside of his house. I planned to jump him. Instead, I passed out. I woke up the next day, in the bushes with the blade by my side. I felt total shame, but I still didn't think I was powerless.

College was another turning point in my drinking. I couldn't get pot, so I went back to my first love—alcohol. My daughter, who ended up healthy, stayed with my parents when I went to college. I'd come home on weekends. I kept drinking in front of her, and it dawned on me that I shouldn't be drinking. I realized then that I drank in front of her because I had no choice in the matter. I couldn't stop.

I got pregnant a second time and lost that baby. My parents were all but done with me. Friends were done with me. I felt suicidal all the time. Seriously, I just wanted to die. I was nineteen years old and done with life.

Like I said, my daughter was the only thing that kept me tethered to this earth. I'd thought about quitting drinking, but that seemed so drastic. Like any good alcoholic, I tried to skirt every which way around the problem and tried any number of ways to make things better without doing the one thing I needed to do, and that was quit drinking.

I thought maybe a good man would cure my alcoholism. I dated my neighbor while pregnant with my second child, even though he was not the father. He left Nebraska and went to Hawaii to be a missionary, but he'd come back. I thought being around someone with godly aspirations would make me a better person. It was not to be—the missionary started drinking again too.

One weekend as I drove across the prairie, I was headed home to see my daughter and the missionary, and for some reason I prayed the whole way. I felt the presence of God in my car. I prayed to be happy. I wanted peace in my life, and then I noticed the missionary's car in my friend's driveway. I went inside, and there he was in bed with my best friend.

My plan to use him to make me a better person blew up in my face. That same afternoon, from across the lawn, my dad came up to me. Under his arm, he carried the Big Book. He said, "I hear you're not doing well."

He opened the book and read me the promises. I couldn't imagine even one of those promises coming true for me. He told me if I quit drinking, got sober, and worked the program, he guaranteed that every one of those promises would come true for me. That same day, Dad took me to a meeting.

My compulsion to drink lifted; any desire to drink was simply gone. That was proof enough for me that God was real. He answered my prayers to be happy in a far better way than I could have dreamed. He answered that prayer for my life, not just for a moment in time. Prior to that experience, I was certain there was no God. In just a few days, I had come to believe.

Those last few weeks of my drinking were so hard, but they were necessary. That struggle was what brought me to God. The whole of my experiences and struggles allowed me to be compassionate and empathetic to others' struggles.

I was a nineteen-year-old kid living in a rugged farm community, and I hated going to meetings. I was fed up with people hugging me and sick of them telling me they spilled more than I drank. This one man accused me of lying about how much I drank. I drove fifty-two miles in the opposite direction just to avoid him. Through that experience, I learned that we need to be careful of what we say. Someone is listening to your words, so make it the truth, and make it real.

The only reason I kept going to meetings was because I was terrified that if I didn't go, the obsession to drink would return. I found a group of old drunks in my hometown who supported and loved me until I could love myself. They were serious about sobriety, and with their help, I started to learn how to live.

I ran into that jackass who almost ran me out of the program by his unkind words. I spit a zinger his way. I told him that I had a right to be in these rooms, and I said, "By the way, I don't think you're a real alcoholic either. You couldn't have drank as long as you did and still be alive."

Looking back, I don't know why I became alcoholic. Was it the genetic link? I just know that I had a feeling of emptiness and fear that I couldn't shake. I became alone in a room full of people. That loneliness, fear, and feeling separated from others was at the core of my drinking. I just couldn't feel their love. I could see that my parents loved me, but I didn't feel loved.

I graduated college with a degree in education. I thought I'd stay in Nebraska and teach, but God had other plans. Back then, no one wanted to hire a single mother. I ended up joining the Army. I stayed in the Army for nine years, and that's where I met my one and only husband.

I am grateful for the sober decades I've stacked up behind me. I'm grateful for my husband, our children, and our grandchildren. I no longer hide behind my ego. I no longer do things to get other people's approval. I do things because I choose to do them. I feel that when that obsession to drink was lifted, I'd been given the gift of faith. That wasn't a self-help thing; it was a spiritual solution. God just lifted the obsession to drink right off my shoulders. The only solution to the disease of alcoholism is a spiritual solution. I had to be sad, scared, sick, and alone to become willing. Once I was willing, God showed up, and he'll show up in your life too.

~ 21 ~
Babies and Booze

Fiona. Sobriety date: October 16, 2005

I FIRST MET FIONA some time in 1996 or 1997, when during her residency she rotated through the ER where I worked. I immediately liked her and remember chitchatting with her in a congested area behind the nurse's station.

I couldn't have guessed that nine or ten years later, we'd meet again—only this time at a meeting. She stomped into the room like a bitch on fire. She had just gotten out of treatment and was told to find a sponsor. Everything about everything pissed her off. She asked me to sponsor her. I took her through the steps, and, slowly but surely, over the course of a few years, she waded through the anger, and the miracle of recovery happened for her too.

I was such a bitch, my third husband made me go for an alcohol assessment. I was honest with the counselor about my drinking, and he gave me an ultimatum. "Go to treatment right now, or we will notify the medical board. If you want, you can let them decide what to do with you." I was so, so angry! I felt tricked. I said I would go for an assessment, not rehab! Were they fucking kidding? No, they weren't.

What could I do? I had four children. I needed to hang on to my job in the ER, not to mention my medical license. I was the primary breadwinner of the family. The man I married was also an alcoholic and was marginally employed. But we drank so well together! He also happened to be a good handyman, and he fixed my computer, cooked gourmet food, and made great cocktails. Wasn't that why everyone got married? It was right after 9/11. I was pregnant with his child. The whole world seemed insecure, including me, and I wanted to feel secure, so we married.

My motives for my first two marriages weren't much better—similar absurd reasons—though at the time, I was blind to my motives. I married my first husband because I needed medical insurance. I married my second husband, the father of three of my children, because I was pregnant. The baby was kicking inside me, and my thinking was, *I can't raise this baby alone.* I was a medical student. I had no money, and the logistics of raising a child alone . . . I knew there was no way I could do it and complete medical school. My motives were all sad: I needed help. I was fearful. I was insecure. I didn't want to be alone. But he had a bad temper and was verbally abusive.

So when I met my third husband, he fit into all of us surviving. He helped with the kids. He was an excellent stepparent. I liked coming home to fine dining and cocktails. All those things about him looked good on paper, but the reality was that there was zero intimacy. Someone described intimacy like this: "Into me you see." I was not capable of intimacy. He wanted intimacy. Superficially, we got along. Once I found sobriety, not so much.

As a physician, you would think I'd know a little something about alcoholism, but the truth is, I knew nothing about the disease. I was oblivious to alcoholism, so much so that when the time came to pick a specialty, I jumped on emergency medicine. Not because I wanted to save all these lives, but because I felt that working in the ER would allow me the most freedom to drink. Yet, at this point, I wasn't a daily drinker, but already alcohol was calling the shots. My thinking went something like this: *I can't ever be on call. What if I I'm drunk and the hospital calls?* I saw nothing wrong with my logic. I didn't want a job that would interfere with my precious drinking. Didn't most people protect their drinking time? Emergency medicine was the way to go. You do your shift, and that's the end of that.

I drank all though medical school and my residency, without any consequences. I thought I was normal, like the other students who all drank too. My drinking picked up when I finished medical school. I no longer had all that studying and reading. For me, the road to alcoholism started at the end of my shift. Regardless of what time my shift ended, whether it was 7:00 a.m. or 11:00 p.m., I rewarded myself with a cocktail or a glass of wine. I worked hard; I deserved that drink to relax.

I was on top of it though. Every six months, I checked on my liver enzymes. Normal people do that, right? I guess I started to realize that the three bottles of wine a night that I drank could do some harm. My enzymes were always normal. I figured that meant I was a superior drinker! I was meant to drink all that wine.

I had people come into the ER, their livers were failing, and they drank less than I did. *Well, okay, I truly do have a superior liver.* I never saw myself in those patients. I took it all in stride. I would think, *That poor sap, she really needs to quit drinking.* I never once thought that about myself. When someone came through the doors with an outrageously high blood alcohol level (BAL) of 570, instead of feeling concerned, I'd hoot and holler. If the patient could still walk and talk, a celebration was in order. High fives all around. *This person is a serious badass!*

One time a kid landed in my ER after a car accident. He killed two people in that accident. It was his fault. He was drunk. That was the only time I ever felt a twinge—that feeling like *Oh, shit, I hope that never happens to me.*

But car mishaps did happen to me. I drove drunk with my kids in the car all the time. Not falling-down drunk, just drunk enough to swipe off a car-door mirror, or something small like that. When I was drunk, I never felt impaired. But does anyone? I always said, "I'm fine, I'm awake. Aren't we talking?" Then in the morning I would wake up saying, "Oh, shit. How did I get home? How did I drive my kids home?"

I always carried wine to soccer games and sporting events. I simply would not do without. When we went on vacation that meant drinking started at noon.

I remember one vacation we stayed at my sister's. My youngest was a baby. We had put him in a bassinet on the floor next to the bed. His father and I were both blacked out. Apparently, my son screamed and screamed. Neither one of us heard him crying. My sister finally came into our room and took the baby. The next morning, I found out what I had done. How irresponsible I was. She couldn't rouse either one of us. Did that make me want to quit drinking? Heck no. I was on vacation. Remember? Things like that can happen. I shrugged that one off too.

For a while I worked the night shift. I'd wake up late in the afternoon and start drinking. It dawned on me that I wanted to drink closer and closer to my shift. I started to juggle my cut-off time. For instance, if I had to be at work at 11:00 p.m., I felt I needed to stop drinking at least by 7:00 p.m. It was totally not okay. I justified that drink by telling myself I needed to grab a little nap before work. How else was I going to relax? The unmanageability was starting to set in—big time.

My home life was a mess. I didn't see my selfishness. I failed to get to know my children. I fed them, dressed them, and took them to the dentist. I did all the things I was supposed to do. We lived in a beautiful home. Our lives on the outside looked exemplary. *You should all aspire to be us.* Forget the fact that I was nothing more than a mechanical mother. Drinking was always in the back of my mind. Me. Me. Me. When could I get home and have my wine?

One of my daughters was balled up on the couch crying over some boy who dumped her. She was fifteen. I had no idea she was even dating. She told me all this stuff that was going on in her life. I was clueless about it all. I was stumped about how to react to her. It was like a stranger was sitting on my couch.

I had been too busy working, drinking, and then trying to manage my life around my drinking. I wasn't emotionally available or present, for any of them.

I spent my free time hobnobbing with other drinkers. My husband and I attended wine tastings, dinners out, and more wine-tasting dinners. I had no friendships. The only "friends" I had were people at these drinking events. It was all a fantasy . . . I thought they were my friends, but they weren't friends. Once I got sober, I never heard a word from any of those people. If I ran into them, they were like, "Hey, where have you been?"

I rarely drank when pregnant with my first three children. But by the time my fourth pregnancy rolled around, my disease had progressed. I was in my first trimester, and I drank a whole fifth of scotch over the course of one night. The next morning my oldest daughter tried to wake me to take them to school. She couldn't rouse me. I was passed out. She called a woman we knew to come over. I'd scared her that bad. The whole next day, I vomited. The thought came: *I hope I didn't hurt the baby.*

I still didn't think I was an alcoholic. I justified all of it, but the internal dialogue started. I kept thinking I wasn't alcoholic, but then I remembered drawing stop lines on my bottles. I never honored those lines though. I'd just dilute it and drink fifty spritzers or whatever it took to make up for the dilution.

I read my kids bedtime stories with one eye closed. They'd laugh at me as I swayed in their bedroom doorways. They'd make fun of my sappy drunk voice. I can't imagine how I must have sounded to them going on about how much I loved them, yet I knew and they knew that I didn't know them as people. I had a hard time staying on my feet, but, hey, wasn't that why we had doorframes?

I justified that it was okay to drink wine while nursing. I still hear some people say that it helps with the letdown, you know, if you're relaxed. So I drank some wine. Well, enough wine that I blacked out.

The thought came: *What if something did happen to my son?* Anything could have gone wrong, and I would've been too drunk to know. The headline would read: "Baby injured! Mother passed out while breastfeeding."

My husband didn't insist I get an evaluation because I passed out breastfeeding or that we left our son screaming on the floor of a bedroom. No, he insisted I go because after a few drinks, I lost my filter. A lot of the time, I was a bitch, and when I was home, we drank. In the morning we'd wake up, and he'd be pissed. I'd have no idea why he was ticked. Then he'd say something like, "I can't believe what you said last night."

I'd sit there dumbfounded. I'd have no clue what he meant. That right there was evidence of the family disease. Sometimes the family surrounding the alcoholic is just as sick as the alcoholic. In my case, we were both alcoholics. His neediness and selfishness made everything about him. My selfishness made everything about me.

As I mentioned, I had no choice but to go to rehab—for two months. The whole time in rehab, I seethed. Raw-gut anger. Here I was, having to go to treatment because I was honest about my drinking, and now I was being punished. I felt it was so unfair. I didn't believe for one minute that I had a problem.

By the time I got out of treatment and resumed our life, I realized I had nothing in common with my husband. When we both were drinking, our superficial booze-addled relationship had worked. Once the alcohol was removed, I wasn't sure I respected him at all. I also realized that fear and insecurity were flimsy reasons to stay married.

Early sobriety was difficult. I had no spiritual beliefs. I was full of fear and anger. I wasn't allowed to take Xanax for the panic attacks I had. I also was mandated by the medical board to go to twelve-step meetings. As proof of my attendance, someone at the meetings had to sign my paper—for five years. In addition I was subjected to random urine tests.

Those five years turned out to be a blessing. I stayed angry for the first two years, maybe longer. I wasn't convinced at all that I was an alcoholic. The only thing I did right was allow Lisa to take me through the steps. I listened to how other women in the program stayed sober. By working the steps, little by little, the denial got stripped away. I came to see that I didn't know my kids, I drank a lot more than I believed I drank, and my motives were almost always selfish.

Whatever normal happy people learned in life, I never got. I was always discontent and restless. The concepts and teachings I've absorbed in the program have allowed me to cope with things that used to baffle me. After ten years of sobriety, I have come to understand how to live life instead of just react to situations that are thrown in front of me.

I learned I was powerless. I was powerless not only over alcohol, but also over people, places, and things. I learned I was a control freak. Controlling made me feel more secure. The steps all work together. Step three mandated that I let go of my hold on everything and turn it over to whomever, whatever "it" was. Step four forced me to look at my part in every situation that caused me grief. I had always assumed I was the victim. I had to look at my part. My motives. Talk about painful, yet enlightening! I asked whoever was "up" there to soften and lighten my heart. I needed to make amends to the people I hurt or neglected.

Today, I go to meetings. I work with other women. We alcoholics are quick forgetters. My old thinking will come back if I'm not vigilant. I need to hear recovery, over and over. By helping others, I've learned about me.

When I got out of treatment, my thinking told me to hurry up and get a divorce. The women in the program cautioned me to wait. They said I shouldn't make any major changes during the first year of sobriety. They assured me I would know my course in due time. I ended up staying in that marriage another six years. I was growing and working a program; my husband was just dry. He quit going to meetings. He quit working steps. We were on two different paths. I chose to leave.

Today, life keeps getting better and better. I am still learning who I am. I have real relationships with my children. I've developed hobbies, something I never had while drinking. I have friends who are real friends, not just drinking buddies. And those patients who come to the ER . . . well, I no longer hoot and holler when I see a high BAL. I see alcoholism for what it is: a destructive disease that tears up and destroys whatever is in its path.

~ 22 ~
I Said I Do (Until I Don't Anymore)

Lee. Sobriety date: January 2, 1986

I ASKED LEE TO SHARE *her story because she is relatable to any woman who has ever looked for validation through relationships with men. That feeling of not belonging is a common thread and is often the core issue. Today, she leads a peaceful life, she makes beautiful silver jewelry with all sorts of stones, and, most importantly, she knows her own worth.*

It didn't start out well. My father was from Kentucky, and my mom from Japan. Back in the day, Japanese women had the mistaken impression that all Americans were rich. She was sorely disappointed when she ended up with an alcoholic hillbilly. Mother taught me—and my sister, who happened to be the love child between Mom and Dad—that our role as women was to serve the man.

I had my first drink sometime between the ages of ten and twelve. I drank with my uncles. They made homemade grape wine, and I *always* volunteered to fill their glasses. A glass for them, and one for me. When I was fourteen, someone handed me a bottle of Colt 45 malt liquor. I drank it down.

What a rush! That one beer changed my life. All my fears of not feeling like I belonged washed away like chalk on a sidewalk after a hard rain. That one beer changed everything. Suddenly, I did fit in. Give me a beer, a cigarette, and a man, and life was good.

Part of the reason I felt left out was because I couldn't relate to my mother or my sister. I settled for male attention, since the females in my family weren't responsive. I believe I suffered from touch deprivation. The back of my head is still flat. I asked my mom why, and she said, "You didn't stay on your side, so I just let you be."

That feeling of not belonging, coupled with low self-esteem, was a perfect storm for this alcoholic. For years I didn't understand what low self-esteem meant. It was a term as foreign to me as the Japanese language. All I knew was that once I drank, I felt better. Drinking helped alleviate the fear. I also had no idea who I was. After I downed a few drinks, I could be whoever you wanted me to be. Usually, there was a man involved; I'd start out feeling strong, and then I'd drink too much. The man drew closer, and like a cowboy roping a calf, he caught me. I believe that defect of character, low self-esteem, accounted for all four of my marriages.

Husband number one gave me my daughter. I was a senior in high school, and pregnant. I married my daughter's father right after the senior prom. That marriage lasted two and a half years. I liked drinking, a lot; my husband, not so much. I thought he was a lightweight. He'd get drunk just smelling the bottle cap. He was also a jealous man, and a control freak. He inspected my clothes before I could leave the house. He thought my role was to take care of him, the house, and the baby. Needless to say, that marriage ended.

My second husband was best friends with my first husband. I fell in lust. I had two requirements for this marriage to work for me: he had to like to drink, and he must love sex. I got everything I bargained for in that marriage. He married me to slow down his drinking. I married him so I could drink freely.

Not long after we married, pot and speed were added to the mix. Then, the fighting and insanity began. Our house was the party house. Anyone running around with a six-pack, twelve-pack, joints, pills, hell yes, come on over!

I imagine the only reason we lasted eleven years was because he worked construction and was gone a lot. During those eleven years, I learned to be independent. I still had a safety net, the marriage, but I was free to run the bars.

I worked as a cosmetologist. Hubby's jealousy kicked up a couple notches. He became more and more controlling. He wanted a puppet instead of a wife. He couldn't stand it that I was employed.

We lived in a small town. All the wives stayed home. I didn't; I cruised the bars. Word got out that I liked sex. The men were like flies on birthday cake, all looking to gain a little sweet. And bless these men; they were all so sympathetic. They said they felt bad about my crumbling marriage. Of course I ended up in bed with one of them. Once I ingested alcohol, I couldn't say no—to anyone.

I was terrified of being alone. My drinking was out of control, but I worried about dying alone. I knew drinking made everything worse, but quit drinking? I thought the problem was that I didn't know how to pick the right man.

I separated from my second husband, only to reconcile with him. Nothing changed. We were both still insane. Somewhere along the way I had a moment of clarity. A tiny voice inside whispered, *It's your drinking. Stop drinking.* The problem was, I had no idea how to quit, and I had little, if any, *desire* to stop.

What I did want to stop, though, was the insanity. I wanted all the running around with all those different men to stop, yet I had conditions. I only wanted things to stop if I could still hang on to the booze.

December 29 through January 2, 1986—those last days of my drinking were one continuous drunk. It all came to a head when I hit my husband in the head with a beer can and gave him a concussion. I thought maybe I really did it this time. I hightailed it out of there. I took my daughter and left.

My sister-in-law had a black belt in Al-Anon. The next day, she rounded us up and took us both to a meeting. He stayed sober six days. On day six, he told me I was the problem. He said I had thirty days to find an apartment. I kept going to meetings and Al-Anon too.

I went to these meetings, and I compared myself to the men. I thought they were one screwed-up bunch. I didn't do half the things those men did. So many of them spoke about DUIs, stints in jail, bar fights . . . I didn't do any of that. I did all my fighting at home!

I kept going to the meetings, but I struggled. *Am I an alcoholic? Maybe I'm not.* The fog started to lift. If I wanted to get well, I needed to look at me. I needed to get honest. I had done so much damage, but on the outside, all looked swell.

As I worked the steps, I learned that I was riddled with fear and self-pity. The only time I didn't feel sorry for myself was when I drank. I am a master manipulator. As long as it's someone else's fault, I don't have to take responsibility for all my bad choices. I blamed others for everything bad that happened. It took time for me to see that I was not a victim. I loved playing the victim. Perhaps I wore the victim hat well, because as a child I was a victim when my grandfather molested me that day I sat on his lap.

Through the recovery process, I learned some unpleasant truths about myself. I blamed my innocent daughter for everything bad that happened. My rationale was that if I hadn't had her, my life would've been completely different. The reason I ended up married so many times was because of her. If it weren't for her, I would've picked different men. If it weren't for her, I would've made different and better decisions. I wanted to be someone else and not feel afraid.

My daughter hated my drinking. I left her alone so much while I ran the bars. She hated all the men I brought home, and here I thought I was slick—I'd make them leave before she woke up. She knew.

Thank God for the women in the family who stepped in and picked up the slack when I couldn't be a parent. Maybe I'd come home, maybe not. My daughter fended for herself. I am ashamed to admit it, but I didn't even know that she ran track. She told me she did. I had to go to the library and get the yearbooks to see if it was true.

I sobered up when my daughter was sixteen. At eighteen, we had a terrible fight. She moved out. I realized then that I had to deal with my rage and anger toward her. It took time, but the relationship started to heal.

I shower my grandkids, her children, with attention. I know she wonders why they get the good me and she got stuck with the lousy parent. What she may not understand, or what maybe I need to better explain, is that devoting myself to my grandchildren is my way of making living amends. I wish I could erase the bad mother part and start over, but I can't. It's still my biggest regret.

Despite the overwhelming evidence, I continued to struggle with the question, Am I an alcoholic? Even though I wasn't convinced I had a problem, I kept going to the meetings. For the longest time, I thought all the problems in my marriages had to do with my husbands. They drank too much. Not me—them.

Between the women in recovery and the women in Al-Anon, I received validation. I started to realize that if I hadn't been drinking, most of what happened wouldn't have happened. Those men controlled me with guilt and shame. I wasn't a good mom, but I knew that. All that sick stuff I had done to my daughter. I had to own up to the correlation between alcohol and the chaos in my life.

When I decided to leave my second husband that January of 1986, I was cruel. I tricked myself into thinking I was just being honest, but that was a lie. I wanted to crush him. One night in a drunken rage, I viciously unloaded every minuscule detail of all my extramarital affairs. I tried to hurt him as bad as I could. When I didn't think the words I hurled at him hurt bad enough, I attacked him with the beer can. I never once looked at our relationship from his perspective. Here he was, betrayed by his best friend, betrayed by his wife, and I thought I was the victim. That man never stayed sober. Last I heard, he drinks a gallon of vodka a week.

As we say in recovery rooms, sometimes quickly, sometimes slowly. When it came to men, I had a few more rounds to go before I got it right. I was sober two years when I met another man. He was a counselor.

I was drawn to the counselor because of his openness about feelings. I realized later that he knew nothing about anything when it came to relationships. He said all the right things, and I decided this man could be my teacher.

Turned out, he didn't teach me anything. What he wanted was for me to save him from the mundane chores he didn't want to do. He couldn't keep a house, or a job. He spewed all this feeling gibberish, but all he did was talk.

We dated five years, though the entire time we were on again, off again. It was an abusive relationship, and, just like that, I was right back in that cycle of dysfunction.

I was millimeters from bailing on the whole mess when he proposed. The moment we married, I realized I'd made a mistake. He had volumes of unresolved issues with his ex-wife. He wanted a caretaker. As far as I could see, he wanted a mother, not a wife.

The sordid marriage forced me to grow. It put the focus right back on me. Why did I feel I needed a man? I learned to quit focusing on his issues and started to deal with my own. He'd throw a hurtful zinger, and I got strong enough to put my hand up and say, "Stop."

We stayed married for four years. During those four years I continued to work on me and attend meetings. I began to realize that clearly, this relationship was not healthy. I was not angry. I was just done. I understood that we could part ways without destroying each other. I could be honest yet have compassion. I didn't need to be brutal like I was to my second husband. I felt no need to hurt him. That was huge growth for someone like me.

Maybe people don't realize that it takes time to get well. A whole lifetime of booze and men didn't just stop when I put down the drink. The first three years of sobriety I spent in a group with alcoholics and codependents. I opened up about the incident with my grandfather. I came to understand that when I was drunk, I'd let men get close. That had set up the pattern with men for my whole life. I couldn't say no. I'd take men home, not even wanting to most times, but I didn't know how to say no.

I started to learn things in recovery. I began to learn about the disease of alcoholism, that it's progressive and fatal. I was terrified of drinking again. I didn't want to die anymore.

Step one was the hardest. I had to admit powerlessness. I had to let go of all the excuses and blame. Every time I drank a beer, I wanted the magic to happen. That's why I kept drinking. I forever chased that perfect buzz. I had to accept that there was no more magic at the bottom of the glass.

The other steps helped me deal with the guilt, shame, and remorse. I no longer had to try to numb the pain with alcohol. In sobriety, I learned how to value myself. I learned that NO is a complete sentence. When you invite God in, he allows you to be aware of things. I realized I had had choices. Even after I got divorced, I found myself flirting back and forth with husbands two and three. However, that old behavior started to feel dirty. Recovery was working. Something had shifted; using sex and men to feel better felt wrong.

Just like that, I snapped. I told God I was done with men. I told him, "If you want me to have another husband, you'll have to pick him." I had to plow through the fear of being alone. I had to accept that if I drank again, I really might die. I also knew I had to be done with the bars. I understood that drinking was a symptom of me not wanting to feel. It's not how much you drink, but what happens to you when you do drink. I thought back to that first can of Colt 45 malt liquor. All my fears evaporated.

Step three, where we turn our will and our lives over to the care of God, helped me change my thinking the most. That step became my focus. I needed to be willing to trust God and not drink. God wasn't punishing me. I had to change that perception.

Another hard concept for me to grasp was that if I wasn't the problem, there was no solution. Taking responsibility and realizing I had a part in everything that happened was huge. I had to own up to the part I played in every lousy thing that ever happened to me.

At meetings, I met a man named John. I liked that he talked about God. He asked me out for ice cream. He'd been married three times too. Like me, he too was done with relationships.

We got married in 2002. Everything about this marriage is different. For one, we are both sober. We got to know each other first. We invited God into our marriage. Four years later, in 2006, I was diagnosed with breast cancer, and, using the principles of the program, I made it through. Shortly after, I discovered I have a talent for making jewelry. I am a survivor.

With John, I have a peaceful, happy life. He's my rock, and for the first time in my life, I feel safe in my own home. I'm comfortable in my own skin. I am loved for who I am and not what I do.

~ 23 ~

Just Beer

Kathy. Sobriety date: July 23, 1978

KATHY WAS IN THE ROOMS of recovery long before I had even thought to quit drinking. She smiles all the time. She can admit that life still isn't perfect, but whatever comes her way, she deals with it in a healthy manner. I always admired that she entered the rooms when she was only twenty-three and never looked back. It is baffling that some women refuse to look at the truth and get well, while others like Kathy rally even when they're young and say, "That's it, I'm at the end of the drinking line."

Even today, women dunk their toes into recovery but flee soon after because they believe they are not like everyone else. Have a seat. Take a deep breath. Try to keep an open mind. Listen for the similarities.

For starters, beer kills too; alcohol is alcohol. Period. Beer drinkers can be just as alcoholic as the woman who downs a fifth a day. With almost four decades of continuous sobriety, I think Kathy has learned a few things about alcohol, about life, and about living sober!

I came from a family of alcoholics. Everyone except one sister qualified. Three of my four alcoholic family members died from alcoholism, and my father died of cancer. You can be an alcoholic on beer. Some people don't believe that. I remember looking at my sister in her last days of cirrhosis. All she ever drank was Miller Lite. She died, at fifty-six years old.

Everyone in my family drank beer. My parents both thought it was fine. I started with sips when I was two years old. I graduated to a juice glass full of beer. My parents and sisters thought it was funny to watch me stumbling around as a toddler, drunk on beer.

I remember that when I was five, I spent the night at a friend's house. My friend's mom said she would get us a snack. I pulled a beer can out of my overnight bag. I told my friend's mom I needed the beer so I could sleep. Aghast, she called my mom, and my mother said, "Yes, she can have it. It's the only way she can fall asleep."

From the time I was twelve years old until I quit drinking at twenty-three, I was a daily drinker. It didn't seem to affect my schoolwork. I went to college at an all-girls Catholic college. I was "campused" a lot because we weren't supposed to drink. I drank anyway, and got caught—a lot.

The first person to ever say anything about my drinking was a guy I dated in college. As we sped down I-75, I tried to jump out of his car. I was drunk. He asked me if I thought I might be a teenage alcoholic. I was already a blackout drinker, and that was the first time I ever heard the word *alcoholic*. However, that day he planted a seed for me.

I wrecked my car on I-75. The only thing I remembered was some guy pounding on my window. He took me back to college. The next day, someone took me to get my car. I couldn't believe the vehicle's twisted condition. How did I even survive? I called the police. They wanted to know why I hadn't called when it happened. I told them I didn't think they were open that late.

Perhaps my alcoholism resulted from my mother allowing me to drink at such an early age, or perhaps it was the death of my father when I was twelve that sent me over the edge—I was devastated. Completely devastated. I started to look to males for attention. Promiscuity was so much a part of my story. I wanted a man in my life, and I wanted to drink. It made all the pain just go away. My mother couldn't handle her grief either. Her idea of grieving was to drink, and she didn't want to drink alone. I became her drinking buddy.

I graduated college and started working retail. I still thought I was fine. I had a job and a car, but I looked like hell. I was drinking close to a case of beer a day. My tolerance was high until that turned, and then it wasn't anymore. I was skin and bones except for my stomach, which was so bloated that I looked pregnant.

Here I was, still in my early twenties and completely disgusted with myself and with my life. I started to hate myself, yet I pedaled on in spite of how bad I felt. I rationalized that I was fine . . .

Until the day I had terrible pains on the right side of my stomach. I was at work. My boss was so kind to me; maybe someone in his family was alcoholic. He suggested I leave for the day and go see a doctor. The doctor took one look at me and asked me how much I drank. Of course I said two beers. Alcoholics always say they have two beers.

That doctor told me right then and there that I had alcoholic cirrhosis, the pain was probably pancreatitis, and, later, that my liver was 80 percent gone. He told me if I didn't stop drinking I was going to die. I was so young. I couldn't imagine my life without drinking beer. I was gut sick and heartsick.

I left his office with a prescription for Librium to help calm me down. I was afraid to take the pills because of my liver. For two weeks, I didn't drink. Those were the worst two weeks of my life. I shook like crazy. Every single day I wanted to drink. Talk about living in hell.

I lasted two weeks off the beer and said the hell with it! I went to a bar and got so drunk. I came home and saw the bottle of Librium on the kitchen counter. I decided life was too hard. I wanted to go be with my dad. I downed the whole bottle of pills. My next thought was, *My God, what have I done?*

I woke up my sister, who had come to stay with me for a few days. I confessed that I downed all the pills. She called the ambulance. I made it to the ER—alive. Clear as can be I heard the doctor say to the nurse,

"We're going to lose this one." As drunk and incoherent as I was, I heard and remembered those words. I can still hear them today like it was only yesterday.

I started to pray, *God, please help me. I don't want to die.*

I woke up on a medical floor. My doctor stood there shaking his head. He said, "It's a miracle you are here." I thought back to uttering that prayer. I knew it was a miracle that I survived, and that God heard and answered my prayer. I spent five weeks on the psychiatric floor. I was terrified. They had me mixed in with all these people who were seriously mentally ill. I kept thinking, *I'm not crazy; I just like to drink beer. Why am I here?*

After a week in the psych ward, someone asked me if I would talk to someone from the program. I agreed. Oddly enough, they sent a man. Perhaps those people knew I needed a father figure. The man who came had been sober four years. He left me the Big Book of *Alcoholic Anonymous* and a list of meetings.

Back then they gave passes so you could leave the psych ward and attend meetings. Someone from a twelve-step program came to the hospital and picked me up. I was the youngest person in the room, but I felt a sense of belonging immediately. People were kind. I just knew I was in the right place. I felt surrounded by love.

People went around the room introducing themselves as alcoholics. When it came my turn, I only said I was an alcoholic to fit in, but the minute the words came out of my mouth, I knew they were true. I was an alcoholic.

Once released from the psych ward, I kept going to meetings, and they became my lifeline. I knew if I drank again I'd die. After thirty-plus years, people can't believe that I still go to meetings. Like a diabetic needs insulin, I need meetings.

Some people label the twelve-step meetings as a crutch. They're not a crutch. It's a fellowship. I go to meetings now to share my experience. I have a responsibility to pass the message of recovery on to others as it was passed on to me. I also go to meetings because I need to be reminded of where I came from, and where I could surely return.

This disease is progressive and fatal. If I decided to pick up a drink tomorrow, my disease would take up right where it left off. There is no doubt in my mind I'd be worse off than when I quit.

It was hard being so young when I quit drinking. I still wanted to hang out with my friends. I'd go to a meeting and then hit the bars with my friends and order a Coke. After a year of playing pretend, I gave that up too. I realized I was people-pleasing.

Sobriety does not guarantee a pain-free life. In 2002 my mom died from alcoholism, and in 2003, my sister suffered the same alcoholic death. I lost my job. My daughter chose to go live with her dad. Life happens, but I didn't have to drink over it. I went to lots of meetings. I cried. I surrounded myself with women who allowed me to talk until I had no words left. I knew in my gut, no matter what else happened, I could deal with whatever life threw at me as long as I didn't pick up a beer. That coping mechanism—the drink—was no longer an option for me. God gave me a second chance to get things right.

I tried to find happiness with a relationship, but it wasn't meant to be. I was engaged three times. None worked out. The last engagement gone awry was particularly devastating. We'd been together three years when one of his friends turned me on to his mug shot. The guy was a pedophile when he lived in Alabama. The first thing I did was ask my daughter if anything ever happened. Thank God, she said no.

It took ten years for my liver to regenerate. It was that far gone when I quit. It took just as long for me to grow up. Emotional growth stops when we pick up that drink. Chronologically you may be twenty-five or forty-five, but if you started in addiction young like I did, emotionally, that's how old you act.

Getting the right sponsor was crucial. That woman helped me change my thinking. She was kind, yet she could be blunt. When I'd protest about some person or situation, she would pat my hand and say, "Now, honey, now, honey, you really have to look at this."

Alcoholism is a disease of perception. We alcoholics distort reality. Our perceptions are mostly inaccurate. I couldn't see that, nor did I believe that I couldn't get right with myself and the world around me until I stopped drinking.

I had to learn to make amends. That's the ninth step. I had mouthed off to my ex-husband's new wife. I felt insecure. I was worried she would try to steal my daughter from me. I feared being replaced. I had to learn to keep my mouth shut. I had to apologize to that woman. I was wrong. I had to let go of the buckets of fear that I still carried around sometimes.

Back in 1978, it was hard being a young woman in recovery. Looking back, I realize I was dealt the best hand of cards. I thank God that I didn't have to die an alcoholic death like my mom and my sister. We all have the same choices. Life comes down to choices.

~ 24 ~

The Gin Stole the Gems

Marilyn. Sobriety date: August 15, 1989

I MET MARILYN TWO MONTHS into her sobriety. She was a godsend. She was fun and fabulous, and, despite our age difference, we've been sharing laughter, tears, and fond memories for over twenty-seven years. She sports an infectious laugh, and she too dispels all of the stereotypes about what an alcoholic looks like.

So many of us scraped off the rough edges of our disease at Marilyn's farm, where there's a cabin that sits all alone in the middle of a meadow. Marilyn invited packs of women in various stages of sobriety to come on down. On those weekends we'd stuff ourselves silly, then hash out and expose all of our wacky quirks—those outrageous twists of mind we all shared and dissected. It was always a riotous group of fabulous women; there was so much laughter. Suffice it to say, the farm provided a place of refuge for many troubled souls.

My drinking had an effect on my entire family. I remember it well. My husband called both of my sons and told them he was divorcing me because I was an alcoholic. My one son called my mother to ask what could be done. I don't know what my mother said, but my stepfather was right about one thing: he said there was nothing they could do.

My biggest regret is that my three children were all grown by the time I found recovery. I can't help but wonder how different things could've been if they had been raised in a sober home. My husband and I both drank. I know now, it was too much.

My mother was an alcoholic, in recovery, or so she claimed. She only went to one meeting a week and never made any amends. She never worked a good program. I think she only used the recovery rooms as some sort of therapy couch.

I always drank, but not alcoholically until later in life. When my kids were young I drank at parties. I didn't drink while I cooked, and I certainly didn't drink during the day. I was busy raising a family, and for thirty years I modeled for a department store. I earned a degree in home economics. Yes, I can make a mean pork tenderloin and throw together a dinner party on a moment's notice.

I believe I drank socially until I bought the family jewelry store. Once I started a habit of martini lunches, my drinking escalated, rapidly. In five short years I was a hot mess. Everything I said I would *never* do, I did.

I had watched my mother decline with alcoholism and swore, like so many do, that I would not end up like her. I said this while chugging a bottle of vodka. I started to not only have martini lunches, but I'd also stop and have a drink before going home in the evening. Once I got home, I had more drinks with my husband, because he too drank quite a bit. The pattern was set.

I loved the feeling I got from drinking. Along the way I lost every moral and every value I ever had. It got to where as my drinking progressed, my morals and values ceased to exist. Alcoholism will do that to a person.

There I was, a business owner of a sparkly jewelry store, dressed in a white designer suit, and a customer found me curled up in a ball under the desk, sleeping. Okay, maybe I passed out!

No surprise: I lost that jewelry store. I failed to keep abreast of the trends and failed to innovate. We kept losing money trying to run it the same old way. I was too busy drinking to pay attention to the bottom line.

Once the store was gone, my drinking took off. Our house got robbed by someone who knew that I had brought home all the leftover jewelry inventory. I sat in the basement for three days, drinking and crying. *Poor me. Pour me another drink.*

My son found me in that dark basement wallowing in a sea of self-pity. Instead of telling me to pull myself together, he ran out and bought the record with the song by Bobby McFerrin, "Don't Worry, Be Happy." The song failed to lift my spirits, but I thought perhaps a new house might do the trick. My skin looked ashy; I was smoking and drinking and drinking and smoking, and I couldn't do anything to help myself.

My mother had wanted me to see a psychiatrist. I had pent-up rage over my brother's death. He died of brain tumor while still quite young. Then in 1976, my dad died. Grief was a huge trigger and an excuse to obliterate my feelings.

I hated my marriage. I hated my stepfather. I hated everything, and, most painful of all: I had no control. I couldn't fix any of it. When my husband announced he was divorcing me, I said, "Okay, that's fine."

I got arrested for a DUI. I watched in horror as a tow truck carted off my brand-new car. There I was in jail. And people had the nerve to start calling me an alcoholic! For God's sakes, I felt certain I couldn't be an alcoholic . . . alcoholics don't go to jail dressed in Anne Klein, do they?

I was mandated to go to the Whip Program for an alcohol assessment. I was happy to report to those people that my mother was the alcoholic, and, yes, I was quite familiar with the twelve steps, and I went to meetings, but I hadn't quit drinking. I found no harm in putting a little something in my coffee. I went to meetings for four years before I actually quit drinking.

At the meetings, I whined and lied to those people like it was my new occupation. No one ever called me out. All they said was, "Keep coming back." They knew, but I thought I was the smart one. I thought I had everyone fooled.

On August 6, 1989, I went to visit a friend in Florida. She took me to some arm-waving Pentecostal church. As expected, the hoopla began; people moved up and down the aisles, talking in tongues, waving their arms, and over to the right, they had what they called a miracle wall. I had no idea what they meant, but I had my own version of a miracle. I felt the presence of my dad and brother standing over there next to the miracle wall. I felt them saying to me, “Marilyn, it’s time. We will be there for you.”

A torrent of tears started to fall. My friend leaned over and said, “The Holy Spirit entered you, precious.” I looked down at the brochure in my hand and realized it was my brother’s birthday.

When I returned to Ohio, something had changed. I still drank, but I couldn’t get drunk. The buzz was gone. It wasn’t fun anymore.

The following Tuesday, I went back to the recovery rooms, and after the meeting, a woman invited me to lunch. I thought my mother had paid her to ask me. That woman looked me in the eye. She said, “When are you going to shit or get off the pot?”

I was appalled that she had me figured out. She asked if I drank that day. I lied and told her no. She suggested I try not to drink the rest of the day. She told me to ask God for help.

I listened. I said a prayer, and the desire to drink left. The obsession was lifted. I didn’t crave a drink that night. I slept fitfully. The next day, I went to another meeting. I sat in the back of the room and met Lisa. We formed a bond. We went to meetings. We went to the farm. We started to heal.

I never imagined I’d find so many great friends. Friends that I could be honest with. Friends who I could tell my outrageous stories to and without being judged. We howled at our insanity.

I took up golf. I’ll never forget the day when Barbara’s gorgeous new Cadillac sank down in the mud after a hard rain. We were at some golf course in some hill town near the farm. We couldn’t ask for help because we’d mooned all of the golfers on the course that day. One lady chirped up that she had a rope, and she proceeded to pull a clothesline out of her purse! We had a blast. I was so scared to quit drinking because I thought I wouldn’t have any fun anymore. I was so wrong. The good times had just begun.

The camaraderie carried me through when nothing else could. We did this together. I discovered my brokenness by listening to their stories. I still can't explain how it works. We were all tortured souls, but, together, the hole in my soul started to fill.

In early sobriety, I wrote my husband a seven-page letter (bad move). I told him to look at his own damn drinking. I told him he needed to do that for the sake of our children. He was furious, and, today, he still drinks.

Living with an alcoholic as a sober alcoholic isn't easy, but it can be done. Why did I stay in that marriage all these years? I fell in love with my husband when we were in the seventh grade. I knew I'd marry him. Though he can't love me the way I want him to, I know he loves me still. I learned to accept things. I learned I have choices, and I chose to stay.

My three children honored the family tradition. All three have been to jail and have had DUIs, and they continue to have consequences because of their choices. None have quit drinking. It's a family disease. My children have seen me sober, and they've seen me drunk. I believe they prefer the sober mom. I hate watching them suffer, but I'm powerless over them and their choices.

Of all the gifts in my life, and they have been numerous, the gift of sobriety is the most precious. I need to nurture and water this gift like you would a delicate flower. Sobriety is that precious.

Raising the Bottom
L.B. Speaks

Twelve Steps

1. We admitted we were powerless over alcohol—that our lives had become unmanageable.
2. Came to believe that a Power greater than ourselves could restore us to sanity.
3. Made a decision to turn our will and our lives over to the care of God *as we understood Him.*
4. Made a searching and fearless moral inventory of ourselves.
5. Admitted to God, to ourselves, and to another human being the exact nature of our wrongs.
6. Were entirely ready to have God remove all these defects of character.
7. Humbly asked Him to remove our shortcomings.
8. Made a list of all persons we had harmed, and became willing to make amends to them all.
9. Made direct amends to such people wherever possible, except when to do so would injure them or others.
10. Continued to take personal inventory, and when we were wrong, promptly admitted it.

11. Sought through prayer and meditation to improve our conscious contact with God *as we understood Him*, praying only for knowledge of His will for us and the power to carry that out.
12. Having had a spiritual awakening as the result of these steps, we tried to carry this message to alcoholics, and to practice these principles in all our affairs.[13]

Acknowledgments

I want to thank all of the contributors, including my late mother, for sharing their heartaches and their triumphs. I am proud to call this vibrant collection of talented, bright, and sometimes-wacky people my friends.

A special thank-you to three special people who have shown unconditional support for my writing endeavors:

Wendy Nikolai, in so many ways, you are angelic. Thank you for everything you've done, but especially for your love and support.

Mike Dougherty, you have always supported my literary endeavors. Your encouragement means a lot.

Diane DeWall, God bless you, and thank you for fearlessly tearing through my first draft: you were blunt, honest, and mostly right.

My editor, Barrett Briske, thank you! In every way you were a joy to work with. I know all of the contributors will appreciate that you did your utmost to uphold the integrity of their stories.

A big shout-out and thank-you to the team at She Writes Press, particularly Brooke Warner: she's honest and frank, and she never failed to deliver.

And always, a thank-you to my husband, sons, and sister Violet, who have been my biggest cheerleaders. My husband and sons have had a front-row seat to this twenty-three-year writing journey. My sons tell me they still remember playing on the floor in my office with their wooden blocks and Legos during the years when I felt compelled to write yet had no idea why, or where I was headed. Truly, it has been God's grace that has sustained me and sent me back to the keyboard time and again even when the journey looked so dark, but now I'd like to think that this is the book my mother had always hoped I'd write. Sometimes God's time takes a long time, but, like Mom used to say, when he's ready, he works real fast, and his timing is always perfect!

By the way, Violet has come a long way and continues to get better and better.

Dr. Ken continues to advocate for the pregnant women who fall under his tutelage.

John has his own counseling business and continues to help his clients to find solutions, sobriety, and a new way of life.

The women in the stories and vignettes that you read all continue to help other women find their way out of the lake of despair. When you look at the impact one sober person can have and the lives that are touched, truly, it's easy to see that the grace of God is the force behind it all, and for that, I think I can speak for all of us when I say, we are grateful.

Rae is working to establish what she hopes will become a recovery house for women in Dayton, Ohio. A percentage of the proceeds from the sale of this book and the sale of bags, T-shirts, and other memorabilia decorated with the adorable mascot, L., that you saw on page 248, standing on the upside-down wine glass, will be donated to various charities that support women and/or children in addiction. I plan to select a different cause or charity each year. Please contact me at my website, www.RaisingtheBottom.com, if you think your organization is a good fit. Please, buy more books and tees!

Notes

1. *Alcoholics Anonymous* (New York: Alcoholics Anonymous World Services, Inc., 1976), 33.

2. *Alcoholics Anonymous*, 33.

3. *Alcoholics Anonymous*, 33.

4. *Alcoholics Anonymous*, 58.

5. "What Is Moderation Management?" http://www.moderation.org/whatisMM.shtml.

6. Regina Walker, "Remembering Audrey Kishline, the Founder of Moderation Management," *The Fix*, January 7, 2015, https://www.thefix.com/content/remembering-audrey-kishline.

7. Susan G. Komen, "Table 3: Alcohol and Breast Cancer Risk," May 7, 2015, http://ww5.komen.org/BreastCancer/Table3Alcoholconsumptionandbreastcancerrisk.html.

8. Centers for Disease Control and Prevention, "Excessive Alcohol Use and Risks to Women's Health," March 7, 2016, http://www.cdc.gov/alcohol/fact-sheets/womens-health.htm.

9. Kelly Wallace, "Study has more disturbing findings about campus rape of freshmen women," *CNN.com*, May 20, 2015, http://www.cnn.com/2015/05/20/living/feat-rape-freshmen-women-new-study/index.html.

10. "Twelve-step program," https://en.wikipedia.org/wiki/Twelve-step_program.

11. Child Welfare Information Gateway, "Parental Substance Use and the Child Welfare System," October 2014, https://www.childwelfare.gov/pubPDFs/parentalsubabuse.pdf.

12. *Alcoholics Anonymous*, 62.

13. "Twelve-step program."

About the Author

© Ashley Lynn Photography

Lisa holds a BA in English and is the mother of twin sons. After short stints where she trained polo horses and worked as a flight attendant, hairdresser, and bartender, she revamped her life and settled in as a registered nurse. For the past twenty-eight years she has worked with hundreds of women to overcome alcoholism, live better lives, and become better parents. *Raising the Bottom* is her fifth book, though her first nonfiction. She was prompted to write *Raising the Bottom* when she realized, after twenty-four years of working in hospitals, that doctors and traditional health care offer few solutions to women with addiction issues. She lives in Ohio with her husband.

SELECTED TITLES FROM SHE WRITES PRESS

She Writes Press is an independent publishing company founded to serve women writers everywhere. Visit us at www.shewritespress.com.

All the Ghosts Dance Free: A Memoir by Terry Cameron Baldwin
$16.95, 978-1-63152-822-4
A poetic memoir that explores the legacy of alcoholism and teen suicide in one woman's life—and her efforts to create an authentic existence in the face of that legacy.

Scattering Ashes: A Memoir of Letting Go by Joan Rough
$16.95, 978-1-63152-095-2
A daughter's chronicle of what happens when she invites her alcoholic and emotionally abusive mother to move in with her in hopes of helping her through the final stages of life—and her dream of mending their tattered relationship fails miserably.

Insatiable: A Memoir of Love Addiction by Shary Hauer
$16.95, 978-1-63152-982-5
An intimate and illuminating account of corporate executive—and secret love addict—Shary Hauer's migration from destructive to healthy love.

Blinded by Hope: One Mother's Journey Through Her Son's Bipolar Illness and Addiction by Meg McGuire $16.95, 978-1-63152-125-6
A fiercely candid memoir about one mother's roller coaster ride through doubt and denial as she attempts to save her son from substance abuse and bipolar illness.

Catching Homelessness: A Nurse's Story of Falling Through the Safety Net by Josephine Ensign $16.95, 978-1-63152-117-1
The compelling true story of a nurse's work with—and young adult passage through—homelessness.

Fire Season: A Memoir by Hollye Dexter
$16.95, 978-1-63152-974-0
After she loses everything in a fire, Hollye Dexter's life spirals downward and she begins to unravel—but when she finds herself at the brink of losing her husband, she is forced to dig within herself for the strength to keep her family together.